STEVE PIDD

HEALING AND FREEDOM

THROUGH 'TRUTH ENCOUNTERS'

*Receiving Gods provision for
Spiritual, Mental, Emotional, Physical,
Relational, Sexual and Addictive problems*

ABOUT THE AUTHOR

Steve and his wife Em have spent the majority of their Christian life serving as Senior Pastors in a local Church environment. They have been involved internationally in training and ministering in the areas of healing and freedom for over 20 years. They have developed and conducted their 'School of Healing and Freedom' in various locations in Australia and across the World during that time. In more recent years their ministry abroad has mainly involved teaching and mentoring Pastors and leaders, as well as churches, to be equipped in the areas of healing and freedom ministries. Steve is the founder and International Director of Agape Orphanage Network Australia inc. For information on how to help children in need go to our website. www.aon.org.au

For information regarding locations for Schools in the U.S.A. contact us through our website: www.418centre.org

Copyright
Written and compiled by Steve Pidd
April 2019

All enquiries can be directed in writing to:
Steve Pidd
Email: contact@418centre.org

All rights reserved. This book is copyright. Apart from any fair dealing for the purposes of private study, research, criticism or review, as permitted under the Copyright Act, no part may be reproduced in any form (including electronically) without written permission.

THE HOLY BIBLE, NEW INTERNATIONAL VERSION®, NIV®
Copyright © 1973, 1978, 1984 by Biblica, Inc, ™
Used by permission. All rights reserved worldwide

THE NEW KING JAMES VERSION (NKJV)
Copyright © 1975, 1982 Thomas Nelson Publishers
Used by permission. All rights reserved

HOLY BIBLE, NEW LIVING TRANSLATION®, NLT®
Scripture quotations marked (NLT) are taken from the Holy Bible, New Living Translation, copyright ©1996, 2004, 2015 by Tyndale House Foundation. Used by permission of Tyndale House Publishers, Inc., Carol Stream, Illinois 60188. All rights reserved.

ACKNOWLEDGEMENTS

I want to thank my amazing wife Em who has been my ministry partner throughout the journey that we are on. She is a powerhouse in my life, and has been, and is all of the support that I could ever hope for. I also want to acknowledge our resilient and incredible children Kassie and Daniel. They have patiently endured a seemingly endless stream of people invading their home who were seeking healing and freedom. They have flourished in spite of some of the strange paths that we have taken, I can proudly say, growing into the wonderful adults that they now are.

I would also like to express my gratitude to Professor David Giles and his wife Pauline for all of the hours that have been put into editing this publication.

I would also like to note the generosity of Nigel and Tracey Walters for being instrumental in producing this first edition. They are truly Kingdom minded people.

PREFACE

When Jesus walked the Earth, He noted that the people searched the Old Testament scriptures in the belief that if they learnt the right verses, that they would have a better future. However, without His work on the Cross that which they sought would remain out of reach.

John 5:39-40, "*[39] You search the Scriptures because you think they give you eternal life. But the Scriptures point to me! [40] Yet you refuse to come to me to receive this life*". (NLT)

In much the same way, I have observed that modern believers search the New Testament in the hope of finding a verse that will set them free from their problems or bring healing. Yet these verses point to the work of the Holy Spirit. His ministry coming initially through Jesus, then the Apostles, and finally in our time through the gifts and ministries that He has placed in the Church.

CONTENTS

FOREWORD   8
INTRODUCTION   10

SECTION 1 - TRUTH ENCOUNTERS: A BIBLICAL PERSPECTIVE
Chapter 1: Truth Encounters and 'The Fall of man'   17
Chapter 2: Why grace?   21
Chapter 3: Understanding the biblical meaning of the 'Heart'   27
Chapter 4: The role of memory   33
Chapter 5: Grasshoppers and faith   39
Chapter 6: 'Strongholds' and spiritual warfare   40
Chapter 7: Beliefs produce feelings or what we term emotions   45
Chapter 8: The example of the Apostle Paul's dilemma   49
Chapter 9: Sanctification, healing & freedom come through truth   53
Chapter 10: What is a Broken Heart & who is broken-hearted?   55
Chapter 11: Physical healing through healing the broken heart   59
Chapter 12: Gods own perspective for those suffering in this area   65

SECTION 2 - MINISTERING TRUTH ENCOUNTERS
Chapter 13: Accessing the Heart via the mind and emotions   71
Chapter 14: Sources of & Influences on Heart beliefs   79
Chapter 15: Memory   99
Chapter 16: Types of Beliefs   109
Chapter 17: Problem areas that you may periodically encounter   135

SECTION 3 - DISCERNMENT
Chapter 18: Rejection   147
Chapter 19: Results of rejection or non-acceptance   157
Chapter 20: Pride   171

SECTION 3 cont.
Chapter 21: Rebellion — 181
Chapter 22: Control — 193
Chapter 23: Principles of Anger — 213
Chapter 24: Unforgiveness, resentment and bitterness — 217
Chapter 25: Dealing with Fear — 223
Chapter 26: Guilt and shame — 243
Chapter 27: Grief — 245

SECTION 4 - DEALING WITH THE DEMONIC ELEMENT
Chapter 28: Spiritual dynamics and setting the captives free — 249
Chapter 29: Unholy spirits, are they inside or outside? — 255
Chapter 30: The Strong man's goods — 267
Chapter 31: Names of demons and touching the spirit realm — 277
Chapter 32: Breaches — 281
Chapter 33: Final thoughts — 297

SECTION 5 - DISCIPLES AND THE WORKS OF JESUS
Chapter 34: The Church and the Holy Spirit — 307
Chapter 35: The 'tools or equipment' of the Holy Spirit? — 315
Chapter 36: Healing Streams and the river of God — 323
Epilogue — 355
Finally — 359

Appendix 1 - Redemption and atonement Scriptures — 360
Appendix 2 - Sample testimonies — 363
       - Sample testimonies from leaders
Appendix 3 - Centre details and faith statement — 370

FOREWORD

Having attended a great many conferences over the years, my observations are that the modern church is largely concerned with matters such as leadership, growing the numbers in congregations, or church planting. There is no doubt at all that these are wonderful and necessary topics to facilitate the building of the Kingdom of God.

There is, however, very little focus on healing ministries and as a consequence, doctors are the first port of call for physical problems. For many churches, even large city congregations, if there are mental or emotional issues, the people are sent to psychiatrists or Christian counsellors trained in secular techniques.

In contrast if we look at Jesus as the model, His focus was on healing the sick, freeing those with demonic bondages and healing the broken hearted. His disciples freely received this ministry from Christ themselves before they were commissioned to take the World.

*"Heal the sick, raise the dead, cleanse those who have leprosy, drive out demons. Freely **you have received**, freely give"* (NIV, Matthew 10:8, emphasis mine).

Perhaps we could look at it this way. Imagine if you were putting together a football team and selecting your players. "Alright, I choose that man over there with one leg, the blind guy, that deaf fellow, the man with one eye, those chaps with the back braces on, and those cripples." Then you launched them out onto the field, yelling with great enthusiasm and encouragement; "Go get them guys!"

It doesn't make much sense to me but many of us have been around churches where the focus is on trying to motivate broken people to live a victorious life of faith. We have all seen the fallout and problems from people with unresolved issues active in a church environment.

Remember the 'Vasa'
There is an old Swedish warship housed in a museum in Stockholm called by the name of 'Vasa.' She was commissioned to be built by the King of Sweden, Gustavus Adolphus, for use in the war with Poland-Lithuania. The boat was constructed between 1626-27. Upon completion she was considered to be one of the most powerful warships in the world at the time.

A tremendous amount of resources were put into her construction, and she presented with rich and ornate decorations. She was loaded with large and powerful guns. Unfortunately, all of the expense and efforts went into her appearance and equipment for war. Not enough time was spent on the design and what was done below the waterline out of sight. The result was that she appeared to be a splendid, dangerous and formidable enemy, when in fact she was unstable in her foundation and not well ballasted. The guns had just been fired as a grand salute to onlookers as the vessel left Stockholm. Sadly only 1400 meters into her maiden voyage she encountered a gust of wind which caused the ship to capsize and sink.

The lesson seems to be that if we spend all of our time on presentation, and how things look, and neglect dealing with the sub-surface problems of the church, we may not even get into battle. If we train people in leadership and develop or release gifts but don't deal with the unresolved issues in their lives, are we building on sand?

We have found that if we focus on people being set free, the gifts and leadership come with a motivation that God is pleased to bless. At times I have ministered to leadership teams of larger churches and have been amazed at what is going on in the background. I thoroughly believe that healing the broken-hearted and setting the captives free was the main ministry of Jesus for a very good reason. If we want to be the church that God is pleased to anoint, we may need to consider spending a little more time on working below the water line and sorting out the areas that are not always visible.

INTRODUCTION

How we began ministering 'Truth Encounters'
In the early 1990s we had an elderly man in our Church who used to tell me how he had been wonderfully set free of the problems he carried. The vehicle of his freedom was a process he termed the 'healing of the memories.' He was in his 80s at the time and reported that these miraculous changes had occurred in the early 1960s. He would periodically reminisce about the amazing changes that God had brought into his life through that ministry. He was a delightful old man of God who went on to live until he was 94 years old.

In those days I did not fully understand the concept, and to be honest, at the time for me it was all about setting people free from demonic influences and teaching them to come into line with Biblical principles in order to stay free. That is still good advice, but we have come to understand that there is usually much more to the picture of being completely free than this.

Around that time, I read a book by an Australian man by the name of Thomas Foster. His publication was titled 'Miracles of Inner Healing.' This was first available in 1975 and had a subheading on the front cover stating, 'How Jesus Heals Your Memory.' Although I found the topic interesting, I was fairly convinced that what we were doing was all that was needed.

A few years later I met one of his daughters and her husband. They remain good friends to this day. They have been in ministry themselves for many years and report that they first heard Thomas Foster speak on the subject in the early 1970s. There was a later edition of the publication which I believe is still reprinted from time to time today. Later I went on to find two books on the priority of inner healing, written by David Seamands entitled; 'Healing for Damaged Emotions.' (First printing 1981), and the second entitled 'Healing of Memories' (First printing 1985).

Our first experiences of God healing in this way
In 1998, we had a lady booked in for a ministry session with a fear problem. At that time, 'healing of the memories' as it was called, did not fit into my World. It was still not a part of what we understood as to how to help people get the freedom that God has promised

for us. We had however come to realize from the scriptures that *beginnings* were important. When the man in Mark chapter nine brought his mute son to Jesus for freedom, Jesus asked him this question,

"How long has this been happening to him?" And he said, "From childhood" (NKJV, Mark 9:21).

Another example noting beginning points would be the woman who was bent over with the Spirit of Infirmity in Luke chapter 13.

"And behold, there was a woman who had a spirit of infirmity eighteen years, and was bent over and could in no way raise herself up" (NKJV, Luke 13:11).

Something happened eighteen years ago that was an entry point for the spirit, and apparently nineteen years ago she did not have the problem.

It became clear to us that Jesus was looking for the beginning of the problem; the source of the issue. This indicated that there was some event or experience which was the starting place for what was going on now. In other words, the *beginning point* for ministry is an individual being asked to re-member and *describe* what had happened at a particular time in their lives? We knew enough from the scriptures to know that whatever problem a person came to us with, *something had happened somewhere* to produce the issue. This 'cause and effect' could be an event of some kind or possibly a generational influence behind the presenting situation.

In the case of this lady with the fear issue, we began asking questions regarding what she feared and where it had come from. It didn't take long and we accessed a memory that held the fear feeling and the belief producing the anxiety. As was my custom I prayed for her, asking God to set her free and addressing the spiritual dynamics that I believed to be behind the fear. She was sitting with her eyes closed remembering the event and focusing on the feeling of fear. Instead of simply feeling freer, we could see that she was having some changing facial expressions. After a few moments she opened her eyes and reported being peaceful in the memory and the fear being gone.

My wife and I had been watching her and looking at each other and wondering what was going on. We proceeded to ask her what had happened. She explained to us that once we had identified what she was afraid of, and prayed for her, God had given her a picture. What the picture meant to her had resolved the belief that she held about the situation in her memory. She remains a friend today. At the time of writing, it was around 20 years ago that she was set free. She has remained free of the belief that produced the fear. As an aside, pictures are 'one way' that God communicates with people. Indeed, some people 'think in pictures.'

As I thought through what happened in this time of ministry, I came to understand that she could not deal with her feelings with her conscious mind. The beliefs producing the emotions were learnt in a past event. It was a conscious event at the time that it happened, but what she decided at the time of the event went from being head knowledge and thoughts in her mind, to being beliefs that she held in her heart. I will explain this conclusion in detail in another chapter.

In any case, this ministry experience had me searching out my few books on 'Healing of the Memories' to take another look. It was also the beginning of seeing a great many people predictably and regularly being set free through this type of ministry. Since then, in Australia and across the World, we have taught and ministered this model of ministry, as being a part of what God offers, along with other streams that bring healing and freedom.

Others in ministry who were having similar experiences
Around 5 years later we began to hear of others who were having the same kind of freeing moments when trying to help people afflicted with emotional and mental issues. I began collecting their writings and video materials to glean whatever I could in order to be as effective as possible helping others.

I found that there were people doing this ministry from all kinds of Christian backgrounds. There were some using a lot of psychology terminology who did not believe in the gifts of the Spirit or that healing is for today, ranging through to people who pursue extra biblical manifestations as a component of their faith. The common denominator is that they were all good genuine people, regardless of their theological backgrounds and beliefs, who desired to serve

God in helping the broken hearted and setting the captives free. All of them were reporting some positive results, with God working through them to change people's lives.

Most of the models that I looked at had done some great work in putting together teaching and training manuals to help the body of Christ to be fully equipped in this area of ministry. I encouraged people in our church at the time to look at a variety of manuals and teachings for a balanced approach.

Some ministries experienced something in a simple prayer event as we did and then developed what had happened into extensive training courses. These studies can greatly help those who learn from books. We have, however, trained people, and seen others who would never complete a training manual, who have proven to be brilliant at setting people free once they receive some mentoring and understand some simple principles.

We progressively developed our own teaching materials, drawing directly from what I found the scriptures to say on the subject. So, although our ministry practices may be very similar to what others are doing, our basis and doctrine on the subject might be considerably different. This book is our offering and contribution to add to what others are bringing to light on this important and much needed ministry.

'Truth Encounters'

Truth Encounters, and other Biblically endorsed areas of ministry, need to be underpinned by a Statement of Faith (see appendices). We respectfully make some distinctions in our statement of faith that may perhaps be different in terms of the beliefs of other ministries doing this work. This is not pertaining to who is right, it is how we understand and experience the truths revealed in the Bible. We first heard the expression 'Truth Encounter' quite a number of years ago used by Pastor Mike Connell from New Zealand. During his address, he made a comment that sometimes we have 'Power Encounters' and at other times we have 'Truth Encounters.' It was such a good way of describing what we were experiencing in this area of ministry that we adopted the term, 'Truth Encounters.'

SECTION 1

TRUTH ENCOUNTERS: A BIBLICAL PERSPECTIVE

Section 1: Truth Encounters: A Biblical Perspective

CHAPTER 1
Truth Encounters and 'The Fall of man'

Why does the truth make us free? We begin by considering how man came into bondage. Every activity, good or bad, that occurs in the Earth is a result of what people believe. It is the result or consequence of their choices and what they decide that they want to do. This begins at the individual level and outworks itself on the World stage with the instigation of events such as war. For everything to work in harmony, beginning with the internal workings of our bodies and extending to our relationships with God, others and even ourselves, we require TRUTH AT EVERY LEVEL OF OUR BEINGS.

Satan continues to work very hard to prevent this from happening, opposing God's perfect ways for mankind. The Bible gives us a very instructive picture of the working of Satan to bring about the fall of man, stating that,

"Now the serpent was the shrewdest of all the creatures the LORD God had made." "Really?" he asked the woman. "Did God really say you must not eat any of the fruit in the garden?" (NLT, Gen. 3:1).

What just happened? The devil just brought Adam and Eve under his counsel by deception. The deception came about by creating a perception about God's love, goodness and provision for them. 'Really,' implied that God was not caring and was in fact keeping something good from them. Clearly this was *not the truth*.

"Love does not delight in evil but rejoices with the truth" (NIV, 1 Corinthians 13:6).

We can say that what we believe and perceive to be 'true' is the basis of all wrongful behaviour and activity within the Earth today. The preceding verse implies that without truth, or if we deny the truth, we may be led into evil. Activities may seem right to us and good at the time and we often justify our acceptance of wrong doing. For Adam and Eve, this false perception created by Satan produced doubt and, as a result, they did not interpret the situation correctly. This misinterpretation led to a conclusion, from which they made a decision which produced an action. The action was disobedience; and rebellion against the Word of God. Throwing off Biblical laws and limits is known as sin.

We could summarize this simply by saying that sin comes through misinterpreting the *truth* of a situation and, consequently, what is actually best for us. For Adam and Eve, they saw that the tree *was* good. But in truth it was not good for them. They were much happier before, enjoying all of the many things God had given them in innocence and without guilt.

The devil continues to work in exactly the same way with humans to this day. He deceives us about who God really is and His attitude toward us, and then programs us with wrong beliefs about our own identities. Through this he manipulates humanity to serve and submit to him. His deception is behind every problem and area of suffering that is known to man.

Truth then, becomes the basis of freedom from captivity; it is the basis of faith which releases all of God's provision. It is the tool that sets us free and places us back over the influence of the deceiver that man has submitted to and come *under*.

Saul, later known as Paul, received direct instruction from the Lord that his ministry was going to be opening the eyes of those to whom he was to minister. They were under the power of Satan through deception, and they needed to correctly see and interpret their situation as the *beginning point* in turning back to God. The book of Acts records that the ministry would be

"... to open their eyes, in order to turn them from darkness to light, and from the power of Satan to God, that they may receive forgiveness of sins and an inheritance among those who are sanctified by faith in Me." (NKJV, Acts 26:18).

When we are converted, I believe we receive truth in our human spirit and something changes in us and in our relationship to God. We *know* we are children of God. And yet sometimes we don't feel like it. Our minds are not yet renewed and we struggle with our programming. Jesus said in John's gospel that the truth would make us free.

Specifically, *"And you shall know the truth, and the truth shall make you free."* (NKJV, John 8:32).

In practice I have found that we need truth in every area of our being, not just our minds. I will explain this in detail as we continue. In addition, Jesus promised that we are going to be freed with truth through the ministry of the Holy Spirit. He was going to want to inhabit every part of our person with truth, *all truth*. We could say then that one aspect of being 'filled with the Spirit' is to be filled with truth. Specifically,

"When the Spirit of truth comes, he will guide you into all truth" (NLT, John 16:13).

Section 1: Truth Encounters: A Biblical Perspective

CHAPTER 2
Why Grace?

When we are led *"into all truth"* (NLT, John 16:13), we come to new understandings of the grace of God. From Adam and Eve on, we are all born under the deceptive power of Satan. I think that we can accurately state that nobody asked for this to be the case. We need to remember that God is a *just* God. As a consequence, we see Jesus going to the cross and asking the Father to

"... forgive them, for they do not know what they are doing" (Luke 23:34).

That is, forgive *us* for the things that we do that have put Him in the place of needing to pay the price for our sin. He was seemingly speaking of the people who were physically putting Him on the cross at the time, but it rings true of all sinners who made His crucifixion necessary for their redemption.

So, if I can paraphrase His request in light of the lack of truth that we have just discussed and note this as being the root of our behaviour and sin. He appears to be saying; 'Father, forgive them, for they have no knowledge of what is behind what they are doing.' In other words, they/we do not understand the beliefs that have led them to interpret the situation in the way they have, or what has caused them to take the actions that they have. He knows full well why we do what we do! So, we see Him asking for grace for us in our sin.

"For the law was given through Moses, but grace and truth came through Jesus Christ" (NKJV, John 1:17)

I propose then, that the implications of the grace of Jesus going to the cross for us is a rationale something like;

'I will fulfil your will Father and take care of their behaviour and resultant sin, but I will also send the Spirit of truth to guide them into understanding as to why they do what they are doing.'

He was making us perfect and presentable to the Father while sanctifying us through a continuing journey of receiving truth in the inner parts. We see this confirmed in Hebrews (10:14), which states that we were perfected, past tense, through the sacrifice of Jesus. *"For by one offering He has perfected forever those who are being sanctified"* (NKJV). Amen.

We are however on an ongoing journey of being made Holy through sanctification, which is postured as continuing in a present tense.

Many people confuse redemption with sanctification. Redemption is the finished work of Jesus in making us perfect before the Father. Many people somehow think that everything was finished at the cross, including healing and sanctification. The evidence is that churches are full of sick people with all sorts of emotional and behavioural problems. To support their doctrine, we would have to assume that these believers are not actually in the Kingdom and are therefore unsaved. It would also mean that the gifts that the Holy Spirit works through believers are also not necessary to facilitate promises such as healing that Jesus won for us. The truth is that, as we have been alluding to, redemption came through Jesus Christ and, through the cross, all of God's blessings are paid for and now available to us. His mission was finished but the era and work of the Holy Spirit was just about to begin. Sanctification then is the ongoing work of the Holy Spirit to us and in us.

Some people seem to believe that if we just think of ourselves as being a 'new creation' then we will be completely whole. And yet, there are many Christians who struggle with sin, sickness, wrong reactions, damaged emotions, addictions, imperfect relationships, areas of deception, fear and anxiety etc.

We are indeed a new creation, in the sense that we are spiritually connected with, and in a new place with God. We now have a heart that is sensitive to God and is desiring relationship with Him. The old life that had no interest in God has passed away. Through the sacrifice of Jesus on the cross we are now back in direct relationship with God, our potential is now unlimited.

Healing, freedom, and sanctification are now available, along with the gifts of the Spirit, to facilitate the work of God. An example of this would be; God so loved the world and Jesus died for the sins of all. Are all people in the World saved? No, although He loves the World and desires that none perish, not all love God, so not all are saved because not all access the provisions of the cross through faith. In the same way, not all believe that healing, deliverance, or the healing of a broken heart are for today or for them personally. Consequently, they do not receive the fullness of their redemption.

Mankind fell from grace as the result of doubting the integrity of God's word to us; by implication, His good intentions, love, and plans for us all. God has now limited Himself to faith to access all of His provisions. The evidence reveals that we will only receive what we believe that God has provided for us. In the event that we believe that the Word of God says what it means and means what it says, we can perhaps summarize our New Testament relationship and interaction with Him in the following way;

Redemption	=	that which God does **for** you
Sanctification	=	that which God does **in** you
Mission	=	that which God does **through** you.

After we understand what God has done for us, we can then work with Him in allowing and pursuing that which He wants to do in us! The final outworking of this will see us positioned to serve God in whatever works He has predetermined to do through us.

Grace that produces a heart response

Strong's concordance states that an aspect of the Greek word *Charis*, which is translated *grace*, is an effect of His grace as 'the divine influence on the heart.' What a beautiful picture of the work of the Spirit of truth in encouraging us to seek out God's truth for our growth as a response to all that He has done for us. Grace is given, not taken; it is not something that we should receive without thanksgiving. It should elicit in us a heart of praise and a life laid down and dedicated to God. Sadly, many miss this and, having been forgiven, return to a self-centred life as 'Lord' of their own lives.

A wonderful illustration of redemption and grace

I recently read a story about one of New York city's most popular mayors by the name of Fiorello LaGuardia. His 3-term service was during the 1930s and 40s. He reportedly was not happy about people who exploited the poor. One bitterly cold night the mayor decided to preside over night court. An old woman was brought in charged with stealing a loaf of bread. She explained that her family was starving. LaGuardia's response was, "I've got to punish you. The law makes no exception. I must fine you ten dollars." (I worked out that in today's money, in Australia, that would be close to $300). Having said that he reached into his own pocket and paid the fine for her trespass, placing the $10 into his own hat. He then declared, "I'm going to fine everybody in this courtroom fifty cents for living in a town where a person has to steal bread in order to eat!" *As the story goes, the incredulous old woman left the courtroom with a new light in her eyes and $47.50 in her pocket to buy groceries. This could be as much as $1,500 today; a lot of groceries indeed.

It is a great picture of the Gospel. The law demanded that she be punished, but grace insisted on blessing. Indeed, the price for her trespass must be paid. But the person presiding over the law paid the price himself. The law held her accountable, but justice and righteousness held her environment and circumstances accountable.

As it is written, **"Righteousness and justice** are the foundation of Your throne; **Mercy and truth** go before Your face" (NKJV, Psalm 89:14).

What did she do to earn the great blessing and forgiveness that she left with? Nothing at all, she surely sinned. We come to God with our sin, and we walk away with so many blessings; it's amazing. Fiorello LaGuardia was looking past the sin as to why she sinned.

All have sinned but God was looking at *why* we sin. As we have just seen in Psalm 89, the very foundation of God's throne is justice. He would be denying His very nature to not extend grace and help in freeing and sanctifying a fallen and suffering humanity. Jesus paid the penalty demanded by the law, and then sent the Holy Spirit to ensure the provisions of God are received and to resolve the reasons for the offense to begin with. The mission of the Church therefore, is to serve the Father as Jesus did. We do this by ministering God's grace, co labouring with the Holy Spirit in bringing truth, freedom and healing to the captives.

Note: The basic deceptions that Satan proposed in relation to the tree of the knowledge of good and evil stand fast today as the basis for mankind agreeing to cooperate in sin. Let me summarise them as follows:
'This is what you need, this will make you happy.'
'You're missing out, good things are being kept from you.'

The tree of the knowledge of good and evil in that sense is alive and well today being strongly presented through channels such as media. In the Garden of Eden this had the added element of doubt that God really had their best interests at heart, and therefore was not really a good, loving God. Sin means to 'offend' or an offence. It is not surprising therefore that the first offence against God was doubting His person, and consequently the only way to now please Him and access His provisions is the reverse of doubt, faith.

*Gods Little Devotional Bible   HB HONOR Books

- Section 1: Truth Encounters: A Biblical Perspective -

CHAPTER 3
Understanding the Biblical meaning of the 'Heart'

Before we can fully appreciate the ramifications of receiving truth in the processes of sanctification, healing and freedom, we first need to study where truth needs to be applied.

The ministry of Jesus
John 16 says that *"however, when He, the Spirit of truth, has come, He will guide you into all truth"* (NKJV, John 16:13).

The application of this passage relates to the Holy Spirit guiding us into 'ALL' truth. *All* means every area that requires truth. We tend to read this as meaning doctrinal truth, revelation, and understandings for our minds. This is certainly *a part* of how we will know the truth that will set us free. For example, hearing the good news of Christ Jesus can bring us redemption. Renewing the minds of believers is a high priority for the modern church in an information-based world. There is no doubting that this is very important for learning and following the ways of God. The disengaging of the World is, no doubt, the responsibility of the believer in disciplining their mind to the things of God. We certainly need to be *hearers* and *doers* in terms of knowing how we should live and act. We have a mandate as follows:

"And do not be conformed to this world but be transformed by the renewing of your mind" (NKJV, Romans 12:2).

The heart
There is another area of our being that is however largely neglected by the modern church. This part of our person also requires truth, and is often directly related to us receiving wholeness and freedom. Once He had received the Holy Spirit, Jesus announced amongst other things that He was going to 'Heal the broken hearted,' and 'set the captives free.' He was quoting Isaiah 61 where the Old Testament prophet had listed what the activities of Jesus would be when the Holy Spirit came upon Him. Notably these words had not previously been fulfilled; it required that there was a person aligned with the Word and will of the Father whom the Holy Spirit

could work through. With the coming of Jesus as Christ the result was that the Isaiah 61 Word became flesh and had a manifestation and expression in the Earth.

We read in Luke 4, "*¹⁸ The Spirit of the LORD is upon Me, Because He has anointed Me To preach the gospel to the poor; He has sent Me **to heal the broken-hearted**, To proclaim liberty to the captives And recovery of sight to the blind, To set at liberty those who are oppressed; ¹⁹ To proclaim the acceptable year of the LORD"* (NKJV, Luke 4:18-19, emphasis mine).

Jesus modelled to us how to walk in the Spirit in terms of behaviour and attitudes, as well as how to minister in the Spirit, expressing the gifts of the Spirit. He did no works of His own ability and began His own ministry when He received the Holy Spirit and began to be led by the Spirit.

What He introduced to us was meant to be the beginning of the Luke 4:18-19 ministries for mankind and not the end. The plan was that Spirit led believers would continue the works and example modelled by Jesus. This is very much the reason the Spirit of the LORD is upon us today. We read,

"So Jesus said to them again, 'Peace to you! As the Father has sent Me, I also send you. And when He had said this, He breathed on them, and said to them, 'Receive the Holy Spirit" (NKJV, John 20:21-22).

The Gospels do not directly tell us how He healed the Broken Hearted. We do understand that the words that He spoke to people were powerful to heal, in that He was and is God Himself. Today, we still see people receive their healing when they receive a word from the Spirit of Christ. Some people struggle with this concept, but it is as simple as; 'my sheep hear my voice.' In fact, believers will seek to listen diligently knowing that His words are Spirit and life. John states,

"It is the Spirit who gives life; the flesh profits nothing. The words that I speak to you are spirit, and they are life" (NKJV, John 6:63).

Further, Jesus promised that when we know *the* truth it will make us free. Specifically,

"And you shall know the truth, and the truth shall make you free" (NKJV, John 8:32).
What is the Biblical function of the 'Heart'?

*"And you shall love the LORD your God with all your **heart**, with all your **soul**, with all your **mind**, and with all your **strength**. This is the first commandment"* (NKJV, Mark 12:30, emphasis mine).

Here are four clear and distinct areas that the Bible reveals as individual in function. Your *strength* is considered to be your forcefulness, ability, might or power. Your *soul* is generally accepted to be your mind, will and emotions in terms of the sum of whom you are as a person; I think, I will and I feel.

In this passage your *mind* is also singled out and the word that it is translated from, means, your capacity and faculty to be able to reason, understand, and imagine. It has the ability of conscious thought leading to conclusions. For example, it has the function of being able to compute and think through a mathematical problem and to produce an answer. It is very much a conscious activity and would include deliberately memorizing and voluntarily storing information. We could summarize the *mind* as your thinker or your computer which has the ability to store or access information.

We come now to what the Bible refers to as our *heart*. For the sake of the study, I will quote the function and operation of the *heart*, as translated from the Greek directly from the very reputable Strong's Concordance.

2588. kardia; the heart, i.e. (fig.) the thoughts or feelings (mind); also (by anal.) the middle: --(+ broken-) heart (-ed) (Emphasis mine).

It appears from the original language that the scripture is referring to a deeper area of the personality that holds thoughts which produce feelings and behaviour. I am proposing that these thoughts and feelings are coming from beliefs that were once conscious thoughts or beliefs involuntarily learnt by experiences and events. They were significant conclusions or interpretations arrived at in the past that are stored or *taken* to heart. These thoughts, beliefs or feelings have usually come as a result of the programming of life, as deliberate training or experiential beliefs stemming from events.

We may no longer know them as beliefs or thoughts but rather as feelings, behaviour or responses to particular situations. This is further confirmed in the Bible with the statement that the word of God is able to access this deeper place. Hebrews 4, verse 12 states,

*"For the word of God is living and active. Sharper than any double-edged sword, it penetrates even to dividing soul and spirit, joints and marrow; it judges the thoughts and attitudes **of the heart**".* (NIV, Hebrews 4:12, emphasis mine).

So evidently our *hearts* have thoughts and attitudes that need to be discerned or judged. Jesus actually named one means of doing this as listening to what people are saying. We can measure this against the word of God to see if the thought, intent, motivation or attitude is correct. For example, someone may be heard saying; "that's just how it is with me, I'm never going to be good enough." And yet, the word of God says that we are His creation and through Jesus we are just fine as we are! However, we discern that the preceding thought and statement is sourced from the heart. Scripture says,

*"You brood of vipers, how can you who are evil say anything good? For out of the **overflow of the heart** the mouth speaks"* (NIV, Matthew 12:34, emphasis mine).

It is a principle that often the words that come out of us locate us in terms of what our inner beliefs are. The New Living Translation presents it in this way:

"For whatever is in your heart determines what you say" (NLT, Matthew 12:34b).

Our heart, or *middle* as Strong's concordance describes, has a lot to do with how we live, act and react. Consequently, it is vital to have truth in our hearts in order to experience wholeness and abundance in our lives. 1 Corinthians 4:5 says:

*"Therefore, judge nothing before the appointed time; wait till the Lord comes. He will bring to light what is hidden in darkness and will expose the **motives** of men's **hearts**. At that time each will receive his praise from God"* (NIV, 1 Corinthians 4:5, emphasis mine).

Let me suggest some of the outworking's and implications proceeding from the beliefs held in the heart. In fact, we have found that every kind of problem known to man can be found *beginning* here. As a sweeping statement, this includes things that we suffer as a result of the condition of other people's hearts. This is clearly confirmed in scripture:

"Above all else, guard your heart, for it affects everything you do" (NLT, Proverbs 4:23).

Above all else, protecting what goes into your heart is a compelling and vitally important instruction; this includes whatever we allow in through our conscious decisions. We can consistently and deliberately expose ourselves to the things of God through voluntary activities such as storing up the word of God, or we can be conformed to the World by various forms of media and exposure to negative influences. May I suggest that perhaps the 'heart' is the middle, central point or junction of the soul. That is the mind, will and emotions, and consequently it has a direct affect and influence on the function of them all.

- Section 1: Truth Encounters: A Biblical Perspective -

CHAPTER 4
The role of memory

Voluntary and involuntary memory

Voluntary memory
Permit me to introduce some terms that we can use to help us understand the different ways that we can have things *stored up* in our hearts. One way is that we have information that we have decided to consciously learn and then retain through repetition. This could include the 10 times table or the scriptures. We could also have memory that affects us from Worldly things that we have decided to expose ourselves to. These things which we have taken into our hearts will have an influence on how we live by way of future decisions, motivations, activities and behaviour. This kind of memory or *heart belief* is to do with how we shape what we understand and perceive about the world around us. It pertains to things such as our morality, skills, and functionality.

Automatized thinking
As an adult, most likely if you exit your shower or bath and begin to dry yourself with a towel, it will not be a deliberate conscious exercise. You are possibly thinking about how your day will go or something else. At one time when you were learning how to dry yourself, it was a deliberate conscious effort involving your mind. Now if you involve your conscious thought with something like, "do I dry this arm or this arm next?", you might find that your minds involvement creates confusion with your processes that are now automatic.

I quite like music, and as an adult I will sometimes memorize a song in order to be able to just play it. I find that if I just let it come out of my heart it happens automatically, but if I begin to consciously think about which note is coming up next, I almost always mess it up.

Many of the feelings, responses, decisions and activities that we go through are done automatically in this way. For example, the mental activity of deciding what is suitable for us to watch on TV. It was once something that we worked out with our conscious mind, but now our responses and actions come automatically from the conclusions and interpretations about life that *we already* hold in our hearts. Jesus very emphatically stated that many of our actions come from the prior encoding of this deeper place.

Matthew says, *"But the things that come out of the mouth* **come from the heart**, *and these make a man 'unclean.'* **For out of the heart** *come evil thoughts, murder, adultery, sexual immorality, theft, false testimony, slander"* (NIV, Matthew 15:18-19, emphasis mine).

We could quite easily add a large number of good and bad deeds that come from the heart to that list. Jesus was just giving us a sample of negative activities that come from what has been stored in the heart. It is worth considering as the modern church that Jesus really took the Pharisees to task for focusing on outward appearances and neglecting dealing with *the issues of the heart* in the people they were responsible for. They were giving them religious rules on how they should look and what they should do, instead of helping them find freedom by a relationship with God and accessing His provisions through the Holy Spirit. That is not to say that we don't want to present well as a church, but we need to major on ministering to the broken hearted as Jesus did.

"Then the Lord said to him, "Now you Pharisees make the outside of the cup and dish clean, but your inward part is full of greed and **wickedness**""* (NKJV, Luke 11:39, emphasis mine).

A little later he admonished them for giving them outward religion and rules without setting them free from the problems that have caused their negative behaviour to begin with. Religion is seen as follows; 'This is what you do to be right with, or please God!' or 'This is how you do it, how you should look, what you should say!' These are human created standards and efforts for practicing Christianity.

"Yes," said Jesus, "how terrible it will be for you experts in religious law! For you crush people beneath impossible religious demands, and you never lift a finger to help ease the burden" (NLT, Luke 11:46).

Involuntary memory
Involuntary memory is beliefs that you have taken into your heart that were not intentionally or purposefully learnt. These beliefs

have also become 'automatized' and so we no longer know them as conscious thoughts or beliefs; we may now know them as only feelings, emotions or responses and behaviour.

Remember our definition of 'the heart' as being *thoughts and feelings* from our *middle or central part*. These may come to us involuntarily through experiential learning in, for example, feelings of rejection received in a historical event, or perhaps fear, anger or inferiority learnt through life.

We have already stated that the conscious mind interprets events and comes to conclusions which then become beliefs that are stored in our *hearts*. These beliefs that are in our hearts are recorded there usually through repetition or significant events. In terms of critical matters such as our identity and how we think others view us, the Bible tells us that we are most influenced as children. Science confirms what the Bible has always said, that a child's brain is plastic and formative in terms of self-awareness and identity up until around 10 years old. In Hebrew, **a child** is regarded to be between infancy and adolescence. Adolescence is considered to begin at around 10 years old, so biblically a child is less than 10 years old.

"Train a child in the way he should go, and when he is old he will not turn from it" (NIV, Proverbs 22:6).

20 years and thousands of hours of ministry have confirmed that most people's identity beliefs, proceed from situations, that have been found in the heart and are sourced in memories before the age of 10 years old. An *identity belief* is one that has to do with who you 'are' and how you perceive that others see you. It is *your* reality or *truth* about your- 'self.' Very often a spirit other than the Holy Spirit has helped you interpret life and come to the conclusion that you now hold about yourself. Even in a Christian household those who were meant to help *guard our hearts* may have unintentionally been the source of our programming.

Many people have grown up in households where as a child you were informed that; 'little children should be seen and not heard!' At that moment you have had fed into your heart that you are some kind of lesser humanity that should not have a voice.

Situational beliefs

A *situational belief* is one that has come from an event or theme in life that has programmed you to believe something which could affect how you perceive your identity, but also how you feel about life in general. Many children today are in a situation where a parent has left them and gone out of the home. Their experience has perhaps taught them that, 'people cannot be trusted to care about you, you are not safe or important.'

A *sample of identity beliefs includes*: 'I am not loved/lovable, I am worthless, not good enough, not important, I am a nothing, I don't matter,' etc. etc.

A *sample of situational beliefs includes*: 'There is no one there to protect me; no one cares about me, nobody wants me, I am not as good as others, I won't be able to do it,' etc.

Repetition

Reportedly the brain has little cells called 'Microglial' cells which account for 10-15% of all of the cells found in the brain. A part of their function is to clear up cellular debris. They are like little vacuum cleaners that go through your brain and suck up and dispose of useless information that is not reinforced within 24 to 48 hours. General information is considered important enough to be kept *through repetition*. We see this with the ten times table, or perhaps repeatedly being dealt with in a particular way while growing up. This will program and reinforce what you believe to the point of it becoming a permanent belief.

A Biblical example can be found with God telling Joshua five times to be strong and courageous. He seems to be saying; 'you need to meditate on this, take it to heart, and make it your default position, because when you see those angry guys with spears coming over the hill you will need to have your default position and response settled way down deep inside of you. Then you don't need to think about it because you have it as an *automatic* response.

Critical moments or events

Information deeply encoded in *significant* emotional or traumatic events, including moments of weakness, or episodes containing fear or extreme stress, are taken to heart and remain. Most seventy-year old's will not remember what they had for breakfast on their first day of school. There is no reason for your brain to store in memory that information as it has no real bearing on your life. They may however remember beliefs recorded through interpreting events related to the anxieties of the day, and the acceptance of others in a new environment.

We have found that anything that you can remember from your childhood was a significant moment in either a positive way or negative way. It may have been a time where you were coming to some conclusion about yourself or your situation. Once you have decided that you are, for example, inferior you are going to interpret future situations in the same way. It is a *heart belief* that you now carry and you are, in a sense, what you think you are in your heart. You will make your decisions based on those beliefs. For example, if you have learnt through experience that you are not very smart with remembering words you will probably avoid spelling contests like the plague. They will only potentially confirm what you already believe about yourself and expose that perceived weakness to everyone else.

Significant emotional or traumatic events are burned deeply into your memory through an electro-chemical process called protein synthesis. This could be events such as being embarrassed in a school room, a fearful event of perhaps nearly drowning, and range through to the trauma of seeing porn on a smart phone where the deeply recorded images can reportedly last a lifetime.

CHAPTER 5
Grasshoppers and faith

"For as he thinks in his heart, so is he. "Eat and drink!" he says to you, But his heart is not with you" (NKJV, Proverbs 23:7).

Notice that this passage does not state *as the man thinks in his mind*. The passage suggests that the man has invited you for a meal and that is the good intention that he has towards you. But he has a conflict between his conscious choice and what is going on for him at heart level. Perhaps he heard a great message about hospitality at church and is trying to live it out, however he grew up in a poor household where they often didn't have enough to eat. That which he now wills to do is in conflict with the anxiety coming from his previous experiences and the beliefs held inside him about there being enough. The reality may well be that he has plenty but he is going to default to his previous programming every time.

As he thinks in his heart, so is he. A profound old saying puts it this way: **'It's not what you think you are, but WHAT YOU THINK, you ARE!'** In other words, you will live your life according to what you think about yourself. Let us reinforce this thought by repeating the scripture from Proverbs,
"Above all else, guard your heart, for it affects everything you do" (NLT, Proverbs 4:23).

A great example of this in the scriptures is that of the Israelites. While God was doing everything, they were doing fine. It is the picture of redemption where God performs the complete activity for them in delivering them from the slavery and the subservience that they were under in Egypt. In the same way God does everything through Jesus and delivers us from the slavery of the law and sin.

God was then looking for them to participate with Him in occupying a land that He had set apart for them. He even tells them that He had gone before them and had given them the land. By faith they can walk into their inheritance. It would be wonderful, and they all agree that it is a good land. So, what is the problem, what holds them back from entering into this promised life walking in the provision

of God? Numbers 13:33 records the problem as a reconnaissance report stating,
"We even saw giants there, the descendants of Anak. We felt like grasshoppers next to them, and that's what we looked like to them!" (NLT).

The Israelites had grown up as slaves. They had grown up with low self-image and inferiority as they were being treated as some kind of lesser beings. This lack of confidence now emanated out of them and was discerned by their potential opponents.

Often people criticize the modern church for its lack of faith and power. Remember that many have grown up in a broken, rejective family and society. Like the Israelites, they would like to move into the Promised Land but they have been taught that they are not good enough, or not worthy to carry God's power and provision. They need first to be set free at a heart level.

The Promised Land for believers is the 'abundant life to the full' that Jesus announced He came to bring. Sadly, just as with the Israelites, many never come into it because of their **unbelief**, that is, **wrong belief** about themselves and how God sees them. They give mental assent to the scriptures but can never exercise heart faith and trust in God to live the life that He wants for them. It is noteworthy that Jesus said that we can have whatever we believe in our hearts as opposed to what we believe with our minds.

Mark 11:23 says, *"For assuredly, I say to you, whoever says to this mountain, 'Be removed and be cast into the sea,' and **does not doubt in his heart**, but believes that those things he says will be done, he will have whatever he says"* (NKJV, emphasis mine).

Doubt comes from a wrong belief about God. It began with Adam and Eve who doubted God's integrity and genuinely perfect intentions for them. It started with 'did God really say?' When we hold wrong beliefs about God at a heart level, we may hear a great inspirational message about what we should be doing, and then decide as a mental activity to try, having been convinced in our minds, only to be disappointed because we do not really believe God for the outcome.

Genuine faith is not about what you can get God to do for you by believing Him for something. True faith is about having a correct picture of who He is and His plan for you. Often, we need to hear His voice, as Jesus did, before He began His ministry confirming that you are His child and that He is pleased with you. He may not be pleased with everything you do but He is most likely pleased with who you are. He understands why you do what you do even though you do not. If your heart condemns you, God is greater than your heart.

People often quote that faith comes through hearing, and hearing the Word of God, and encourage you to read your bible more to grow in faith. In the Greek language there is the word 'logos' which is the written word of God, and the word 'Rhema' which refers to the spoken word of God. The Romans passage that we are discussing uses the word 'Rhema.'

Romans 10:17 says, *"So then faith comes by hearing, and hearing by the word (Rhema) of God"* (NKJV, emphasis mine).

So, faith or trust in God comes to us when God speaks to us in some way. This could include reading the Word at times if the Holy Spirit is highlighting a passage. But in regards to bringing truth to your heart, it is when God speaks to what you believe that your picture of God and yourself consistently changes. This releases true trust and faith in Him.

- Section 1: Truth Encounters: A Biblical Perspective -

CHAPTER 6
'Strongholds' and spiritual warfare

Many years ago, we were ministering through Micronesia and our host took us for a tour around the Island of Guam. He showed us the concrete bunkers that the Japanese had built before the coming battle in order to hold the ground or territory that they occupied. The Bible says in Ephesians chapter 4 and verse 7 to not give the devil a place. The Greek word translated as 'place' is the word, topos. It means a place, a location, a position, a spot or a home.

In much the same way as the Japanese made strongholds **before** the battle began, the devil establishes **a place** in our belief systems through deception and misinterpretation. Later, as the Apostle Paul found out, when the Spirit of truth comes on the scene there is an internal battle and conflict for the ground or place of the heart that has already been occupied.

Many people believe that when they are feeling bad or anxious that they are under some kind of spiritual or demonic attack. Most times what is actually happening is that beliefs that the person already holds are being stressed or triggered through the environment or situation that they find themselves in. Perhaps they are confused by Paul's later statement in Ephesians regarding wrestling spiritual powers which states

"[11] Put on the full armor of God so that you can take your stand against the devil's schemes. [12] For our struggle is not against flesh and blood, but against the rulers, against the authorities, against the powers of this dark world and against the spiritual forces of evil in the heavenly realms" (NIV, Ephesians 6:11-12).

In fact, he is more likely to be making reference to the fact that, although you are dealing with humans, flesh and blood, it is the negative spiritual dynamics projecting from them onto you that is your problem. In other words, it is not the people themselves that are attacking you. It is the spirits manipulating the people through their areas of deception which give place and cooperation with the powers that you are actually dealing with.

Jesus floated the concept of human participation with spiritual inspiration at various times in the gospels. It is wrong believing that opens us to being potential unwitting hosts to unholy spirit. This is exemplified in the following passage:

"⁵⁴ *And when His disciples James and John saw this, they said, "Lord, do You want us to command fire to come down from heaven and consume them, just as Elijah did?"* ⁵⁵ *But He turned and rebuked them, and said, "You do not know what manner of spirit you are of"* (NKJV, Luke 9:54-55).

In other words, James and John were not aware of what type of spirit they were cooperating with. Peter was inspired by the Spirit of God but was soon found to be working for the other side. This is true of all of us. People can do something wonderful in the love of God, and later be heard gossiping, criticizing or judging another believer. The truth is that, if we don't get our hearts cleaned out, we can at times be found to be double agents and on occasion working unintentionally for the other side! In contrast,

"He said to them, "But who do you say that I am?" Simon Peter answered and said, "You are the Christ, the Son of the living God." Jesus answered and said to him, "Blessed are you, Simon Bar-Jonah, for flesh and blood has not revealed this to you, but My Father who is in heaven" (NKJV, Matthew 16:15-17).

Peter had a wonderful Rhema word from the Father. A few short verses later, his inspiration was coming from another source which he was open to, through his previous programming in life. I am fairly sure that Jesus, much to Peter's dismay, was addressing the spirit behind the idea. This would have been quite confronting for Peter to be exposed for his co-operation and deception.

"²² *Then Peter took Him aside and began to rebuke Him, saying, "Far be it from You, Lord; this shall not happen to You!"* ²³ *But He turned and said to Peter, "Get behind Me, Satan! You are an offense to Me, for you are not mindful of the things of God, but the things of men""* (NKJV, Matthew 16:22-23).

It is clear that very often the things that men have in mind are inspired by Satan. Nothing spiritual happens on Earth without human participation, this includes the works of God. There will be prayers and deeds motivated by faith behind Gods activities as well. When people are rejective, competing or putting you down for example, and you are feeling anxious or depressed it is most likely tapping into a belief that you already hold and not a spiritual attack.

CHAPTER 7
Beliefs produce feelings or what we term emotions

We have seen that the Israelites were unable to take up their destiny because of beliefs of inferiority which produced feelings of fear and inadequacy. If they had instead been programmed by life that they were equal or if they had received healing from their previous beliefs, they would have felt confident and full of faith! Sadly, the covenant that they were under did not include the ministry of the Spirit of truth, so they did not have the opportunity for freedom from their inner thoughts that we find ourselves with.

Thoughts and feelings

A feeling or emotion is the result of a belief that has been accessed. In fact, it is your chemical bodies' version of what you believe. So, a thought or belief and feelings or emotions are one and the same. Some time ago I was reading a book where Charles Finney made the statement that 'feelings follow thoughts.' This is a profound statement in its application to what we are discussing about the heart. You do not simply have a feeling because you have a feeling. It is emanating from something that you already believe:

- If you believe that nobody loves you, then you will feel sad.
- If you believe that no one cares about you, you may feel angry.
- If you think that there is no protection for you, your emotion will probably be anxiety.
- If you believe that you will never ever be able to be what people expect you to be, then you will feel overwhelmed and hopeless, which is the basis of endogenous depression. Endogenous meaning, having an internal origin.

Proverbs 12:25 says, *"Anxiety in the heart of man causes depression, But a good word makes it glad"* (NKJV, emphasis mine).

A feeling or emotion is a chemical elaboration of a belief through the release of hormones or neurotransmitters. It is a thought or belief that your body makes into a feeling or emotion through these chemicals. For example, a fear belief will release particular hormones such as adrenaline and the stress hormone, cortisol, so that your body can make your thoughts something that you can feel. These hormones have other functions in your bodies so when you have long term negative emotions, they become imbalanced, and this is the basis for disease.

Two little boys
In order to help people understand this principle, I often use the following story when I am preparing them for ministry. There were two little 5-year-old boys walking down a street in their town. One of them noticed a motorbike across the road and went over to look at it. As the other boy continued down the road a dog came out of the gateway of a nearby house and bit him on the leg. In that moment of trauma, it was deeply encoded in him that dogs can hurt and frighten you. His mind has made a very good memory of the event, and he is now on guard against the possibility of it happening again. In order to counteract this ever-present fear, he reads numerous books about how dogs are man's best friend and that most of them will never hurt you. He is trying to counteract his involuntary heart belief with voluntary information from his mind.

This is often what we do in church and wonder why people never change or have limited growth. We give them lots of information to learn for their problems and tell them how they should think, perhaps sometimes not unlike the Pharisees. The Jesus model was to heal their broken hearts and set the captives free. I will explain what I mean by this statement a little further on, but back to our story for the moment.

As he grows up and becomes a teenager he is often invited to his friends' houses and really wants to go, but underneath there is a nagging hesitation and anxiety. He is not consciously thinking it but underneath the thought that there may be a dog at their house is producing the anxiety. So, his inner beliefs are beginning to affect his life choices.

Many years later the 5-year-old boys are again together walking and are now 40 years old. As they go along a small dog comes out of a laneway near them wagging his tail. The man who was bitten has an immediate physical fear response, even though with his mind he is trying frantically to apply the knowledge that he has about dogs and is telling himself how it looks so friendly. His heart belief that dogs sometimes bite you is greater than his logical conscious knowledge that the dog looks really friendly. The outworking is the release of fear hormones and a very uncomfortable feeling in his physical body.

His friend on the other hand has an entirely different response. He feels happy, warm and 'fuzzy.' What is the difference; it's the same dog? Growing up as a small boy, his family had a friendly dog that played with him, climbed all over him and licked his face. The emotions that he was feeling were coming from different beliefs about the situation stored in his heart. So, the same situation was producing opposing responses based on what they already believed.

Captivity

Many people are tormented and held captive to beliefs that they hold about themselves, their worth, or their situations. For example, a number of years ago we had a black dog we called 'Misty.' As a pup she used to go out of the yard and get lost if we weren't home. As a result, if we went out, we would tie a rope to her collar and connect it to a fence post to keep her from running away. Of course, she tried to get loose for a while but eventually gave up. When she was older, I would tie the rope to her collar but not bother to tie up the other end. She no longer tried to get away; she had attempted to before and learnt that it was impossible. She was captive in her thinking to her previous situation.

This was now belief-based behaviour or responses. This was not necessarily an emotion for her anymore although originally it may have been frustration. Now it was belief-based behaviour that she was captive to.

Many people are held captive to what they perceive to be true. These inner thoughts indeed may come from an episode or training that at one time was true. A lot of actions, activities and responses come from previous programming, and although consciously with our minds we want to do something, we find that we cannot do what we want to do, there is something opposing us.

The Apostle Paul came to understand this clearly in his own walk. Many people like him wish to follow the things of God as they come into a New Creation potential, being on a new footing with a reborn spirit. They now have the Holy Spirit to guide them, and the word of God to instruct them. Just like Paul however, they often find themselves with one foot on the accelerator and one foot on the brake.

A program behind the program

In our early days of teaching this ministry I was operating one of the first versions of Microsoft PowerPoint from my Laptop computer to facilitate the presentation. My computer was not running properly and was taking a very long time to perform normally simple tasks. The man who had sold me the computer was actually in the congregation and so I invited him up to the platform to resolve the issue. He took one look at the computer and pointed to a little green light that was flashing. "There," he said, "there is a program running behind the program, and that is why it is not functioning properly!" With that he, with a blur of hands across the keyboard, far too fast to ever remember what he did, turned off the 'scanning' program that was operating in the background. It was going on underneath, with no obvious evidence on the screen other than its poor operation and the little green light flickering. This was a light bulb moment for me. I suddenly understood Romans 7 and the Apostle Paul's dilemma in a new way. Not only his discomfort but also many other Christians who want to live according to the word of God.

There is something going on in the background that is affecting the operation of the will. This other 'program' needs to be switched off by the Holy Spirit before you can be all that you can be and do all that you choose to do without hindrance.

If you can imagine the screen as the conscious mind which will only display what you actively choose to think about. If you think about fruit or perhaps a hot dog, you will now have something on the screen of your conscious mind. But while you think about what you have decided to think about, behind this may be feelings of anxiety or depression coming from a deeper place, your *heart*, that are not conscious. These are other programs behind what you are deciding to do with your mind need to be addressed. You want to think and react in all of the ways that you see in scripture with your conscious mind but something else is in play.

I sometimes think that we read in the Bible, for example, about the fruit of the Spirit as ways that we should decide to act. This is certainly true in the sense of our conscious decisions, but in practice these fruits are more often the results of the work that the Holy Spirit has done in our hearts. We could use the example of choosing to be joyful, but for many, this will be impossible without being made free from beliefs producing guilt, shame, inadequacy or anxiety.

CHAPTER 8
The example of the Apostle Paul's Dilemma

In Romans chapter 7:15-25, we see a battle going on in the 'members' or different areas of the Apostle Paul's being. This is the case for many people in the church today. Let us summarize the problem in this way. Their spirit is reborn of the Holy Spirit, (John 3:5-8) so they are now connected to the Father and the Kingdom of God, but there are areas where wrong believing still has 'a place.' They are hungry for the truth and want to live out the Word of God as a response to the leading of the Holy Spirit. So spiritually they are willing, and in their conscious minds they want to walk after God. However, pulling against them is their old programming. They have what they know and confess to be true from the word of God, but it is not setting them free. They appear to be double minded. Their confession, and their responses, behaviour and actions do not match.

These people are on a journey of renewing their minds with truth, but another part of them is defaulting to their old ways of acting. Their bodies and hearts want to continue to conform to the responses, attitudes, motivations, habits and associations that have been programmed into them through life in the World.

In order to understand this clearly, in the following verses from Romans Chapter 7 let's make **his renewed spirit man, under the influence of the Holy Spirit** to be in bold letters to make a distinction. In order to see the opposing nature of his 'flesh' person we will underline it where it presents.

(Note: We understand that his 'flesh' or Sarx in the Greek language is what I propose is largely his unsanctified and previously programmed heart. As we have already alluded to, this is where Jesus says that the nature of sin proceeds from. See Mathew 15:18-19 and Luke 11:39. This is also sometimes translated or referred to as the sin nature, Adamic, Carnal or fallen nature. I like to think of it for the sake of simplicity as; the fallen self-life, or the old life.)

"I don't understand myself at all, for I really want to do what is right, but I don't do it. Instead, I do the very thing I hate" (NLT, Romans 7:15, emphasis mine).

It is like that person in church who hears a message on forgiveness. A part of them wants to forgive and be in line with the Kingdom, and they even know that they should. But another part of them wants to justify itself and hold on to the resentment. Internal peace is gone as flesh clashes with spirit.

Mostly, the truth in this case is that whatever the person who is not being forgiven is doing or has done is not the main problem. The issue is usually that something that is offending is touching a belief that the person holds, and this causes some kind of emotional reaction. For example, you may not be forgiving a spouse for seeming to not care about your needs. The probability is that somewhere in your history you were treated as though you do not matter or are not important. So, the real issue behind the resentful response that you are trying not to have, is the pain of believing that you do not matter for some reason. The unforgiveness is the *fruit* of the hurt that is held and not the actual root of the behaviour.

The problem then is the belief that is held in the unsanctified or unhealed part of the heart. The Spirit of truth has to bring truth, healing and sanctification to this belief before that area of the heart can come into harmony under the covering of the Spirit. Otherwise it will continue to contest what kind of behaviour is most appropriate as a response to life situations. This appears to be the kind of dilemma that Paul was found in.

"*²² For I delight in the law of God according to the inward man. ²³ But I see another law in <u>my members</u>, warring against the law of my mind, and bringing <u>me</u> into captivity to the law of sin which is in <u>my members</u>*" (NKJV, Romans 7:22-23 emphasis mine).

Let us try to give another picture of what this could look like in practice. A person is waiting for the Sunday church service to begin. The Pastor or minister comes in and walks right past them without the least sign of recognition. The person feels quite upset but tries to tell themselves that it is ok, and not to worry about it. It's all good, after all they have lots of friends. It happens again the next week and they have a little anger and begin to notice little faults with the minister and shares them with others. **They** know that *they* should not be doing this, but what **they** know *they* should not do, *they* do. What is happening here?

The person knows that they should forgive the minister. If they looked at and identified that upset feeling they would find that they are being made to feel unimportant. An area that does not yet have truth, that has previously been programmed, teaching them that they are unimportant is being accessed. Out of them are coming retaliatory responses that they know are wrong but that they cannot seem to stop. The *truth* is that they have misinterpreted the situation, believing and holding a perception that the minister did not value them. In actual fact the minister considers them a valuable part of the church family, but immediately before the service he is trying to make sure that all the music is in order, the preaching is ready to go, and the equipment is all working and so on.

Is this resolved by the person trying harder to solve their concern? They are already trying as hard as they can to go with their convictions from scripture about how they should be, and they are feeling condemned because they cannot seem to resolve it with their good intentions, knowledge of scripture, and their own efforts to work it out with their minds.

"*24 Oh, what a miserable person I am! Who will free me from this life that is dominated by sin? 25 Thank God! The answer is in Jesus Christ our Lord*" (NLT, Romans 7:24-25).

The answer is Jesus Christ our Lord. So how can we be free?

King David made a profound statement in regards to God's intentions and method for healing, sanctifying and freeing us. When he talks about God's desire for truth in the inner parts, you will see how this lines up with healing broken hearts, setting the captives free and working through the process of sanctification. *Inner parts* in the Old Testament scripture that we are about to quote can, according to Hebrew scholars, also be translated as *the heart*. The *inmost place* refers to the human spirit. Personally, I believe that our re-born human spirit already receives and witnesses to the truth of God's word by the work of the Holy Spirit. However, our hearts or inner parts need the truth that God wants us to know in order for us to be set free.

Psalm 51:5-6 says, "*5 Surely I was sinful at birth, sinful from the time my mother conceived me. 6 Surely you desire truth in the inner parts; you teach me wisdom in the inmost place*" (NIV).

Noteworthy, King David acknowledges the passing of the sin nature through the generations to him right at the point of conception. The King also acknowledged that it was his heart that needed cleaning. Psalm 51 was written following David's sin with Bathsheba. Somehow, he had for some time managed to deny his sin and contrived some way to justify his behaviour. Many people seem to be content to live on the surface of their being not seeking out the root reason for their activities. As Jeremiah 17:9-10 states,

"[9] *The heart is deceitful above all things, And desperately wicked; Who can know it?* [10] *I, the LORD, search the heart, I test the mind. Even to give every man according to his ways, According to the fruit of his doings"* (NKJV).

It becomes very apparent that each of us need to let the LORD search our hearts, as most often we are not aware of why we do what we do, or where it is coming from. We can join with King David in inviting the Holy Spirit to help us find out what we believe at a heart level and set us free. It is like putting the anti-virus program on your computer to remove the corrupted files so that the machine runs how it was intended. Scripture says,

"Create in me a clean heart, O God, And renew a steadfast spirit within me" (NKJV, Psalm 51:10).

Adam and Eve ran *from* God. Through Jesus we can now run boldly to God for freedom through His truth in our hearts. Psalm 139:23-24 expresses this desire as follows;

"[23] *Search me, O God, and know my heart; test me and know my thoughts.* [24] *Point out anything in me that offends you, and lead me along the path of everlasting life"* (NLT).

CHAPTER 9
Sanctification, healing & freedom come through truth

We have already quoted the verse that *the truth will make us free*. This freedom begins by acknowledging that our captivity comes through what we believe that is not truth. Such as not understanding sound doctrine in regards to our minds but also importantly what we hold to be true at heart level. It is clear that sanctification comes through truth from God.

John says, *"Sanctify them by Your truth. Your word is truth"* (NKJV, John 17:17).

That is a fairly unchallengeable and straightforward statement. Our minds are renewed by truth and our hearts are healed and released from captivity to wrong beliefs in the same way. If then, sanctification comes through truth, it is fair to deduce that being guided into truth by the Spirit of truth is the way of sanctification at every level.

"When the Spirit of truth comes, he will guide you into all truth" (NLT, John 16:13).

This is why we have come to refer to this ministry as 'Truth Encounters.' It is when we have an encounter with the Holy Spirit and He reveals truth to us. He speaks to us as sheep who hear His voice and we are changed. The Holy Spirit has been sent to us through Jesus, who has extended us grace for our sins, but also is influencing our hearts to seek and walk in the truth. As previously stated, Strong's concordance presents Charis, the word from which grace is translated in the following manner.

485. charis,; from G5463; graciousness; lit., fig. or spiritual; espec. (the divine influence upon the heart) acceptable, benefit, favor, gift, grace

It appears from the Bible that the very reason for the coming of Jesus was to bring us the grace of God, and then restore us to wholeness through the truth. The ministry of the Holy Spirit then in this era is vital in every way.

"For the law was given through Moses, but grace and truth came through Jesus Christ" (NKJV, John 1:17).

CHAPTER 10
What is a Broken Heart and who are the broken hearted?

Let us first examine God's priority regarding those suffering in this area. We have already identified from the Greek language in the New Testament that the *heart* is beliefs or thoughts that are manifested or matched by corresponding feelings or emotions. In the Old Testament the word that is translated as *heart* from the Hebrew language *Leb* also relates to your centre, your intellect, will and is widely used for feelings.

The central place of motivation for your inner thoughts, which produce feelings and influence your decisions and responses, is your *heart* and the *beliefs* held there. This is well supported by the context of the Psalms of David that we have recently quoted. So, when this area is out of order, not whole, or not as God intended, it means problems for us.

Broken?

In the Gospel of Luke chapter 4 we see the statement that the Spirit of the Lord is upon Jesus to Heal the Broken Hearted. I think that we have thoroughly dealt with what the heart means, but what does it mean for a heart to be 'broken?' Luke 4:18 speaks to this brokenness as follows:

"The Spirit of the LORD is upon Me, Because He has anointed Me To preach the gospel to the poor; He has sent Me to heal the **brokenhearted***, To proclaim liberty to the captives"* (NKJV emphasis mine).

If our hearts are our *central beliefs that produce emotions*, then how does that relate to being broken? I think that we can deduce that if our thinking and feelings are not whole or as they were intended to be, then they are broken and need healing/fixing. We have already established that this is done by receiving truth from the Spirit of truth. The Greek word 'suntribo' translated *'broken' literally means broken, crushed, shattered, or bruised.*

If you have a clock and it has a slightly bent hand on it you would call it broken. If it is smashed to pieces you would also consider it to be broken. Whether you are a little bit broken or you are completely shattered, you are still broken because you are not in the working order that the designer intended. You are not whole. The application here is relating to the state of your heart. So, if your beliefs and feelings are in any way not as they were intended to be, then you are broken.

None of us have perfect truth about ourselves, or about how God really feels about us, therefore we are ALL broken hearted. The only question is how broken, and where are we in the process of sanctification and healing? Now we can see clearly why God desires truth in our hearts. It relates directly to our journey into wholeness and freedom from captivity in every area of our lives.

Many people have had their self-image *broken* down through negative statements and constant criticism. Others are *crushed* under the burden of expectations to perform and please others. Some have had their lives *shattered* through such traumas as physical or sexual abuse. Still more have had their sense of well-being *bruised* through anxiety about being loved and valued. All of the beliefs resulting from this treatment and programming, constitute the brokenness of the human person in *the heart*.

The Greek word 'sozo', normally translated as 'saved' on examination carries a much fuller meaning. As well as saved, it includes; *to be healed, to be delivered and to be made whole*. God did not save us for eternity only, He had in mind for us to be transformed and bring Him glory through our lives on Earth. We have seen that as people are made whole and healed of their brokenness, others see the changes. In turn this proves the integrity of God and the promises in His Word.

Implications of a 'Broken Heart' and Captivity for wrong beliefs
Let me outline seven basic problems that assail mankind. I will not address them in detail here but you will see that each of them is directly impacted by what we believe.

1. Spiritual bondage
This relates firstly to remaining unsaved and a slave to the ruler of this world. Our blindness and lack of knowledge regarding our situation keeps us submitted to this spiritual being. Secondly, we often see areas of demonic strongholds as a part of the mechanism of serving or being held in sin. It is often an undiagnosed element and result of giving *ground* and permitting the *strongman goods*. So, giving place to, and co-operating with unholy spiritual entities, is also based on our bad solutions to our problems which stems from our wrong beliefs.

2. Mental soundness
Beliefs producing fear and anxiety are tormenting and can lead to all kinds of *masking* behaviour. The vast majority of mental problems that are observed begin with beliefs at a *heart* level with chemical imbalances being the outworking. It is also true that some people are born mentally handicapped in some way and others have mental impairment through events such as damage from an accident or drug abuse. In the case of belief based mental issues, there will usually be coinciding emotional and physical implications.

3. Emotional peace
If our minds and thoughts are not at peace then our feelings and emotions will also be out of order. You do not simply have an emotion; remember it is a thought coming from a belief first.

4. Relational wellbeing
If you have mental inner thought issues along with emotional damage, your responses will also be out of order in relationships. Typically, your wrong belief-based hurts will react with the faulty inner thoughts of others making it very difficult to have harmonious interactions.

5. Sexuality
We have even found that in order to come together fully in sexual union there are usually beliefs that need to be dealt with first. This can be basic inner thoughts that affect other areas of life such as; "You don't really care about me; what I want is not important!" Other kinds of brokenness stemming from feelings proceeding from sexual abuse commonly need to be rectified.

Another way that sexuality can be out of order is through belief-based gender confusion. Sexual sin such as adultery or fornication usually proceed from emotional issues such as looking for acceptance, so again all of these things as Jesus stated are *heart issues*.

6. Addictive problems and besetting sins
Addictions are usually related to masking behaviour or coping mechanisms for heart based unresolved emotional issues. They are in effect our solution to our pain or anxiety which lay us open to setting up chemical cycles, associations and bondage to habits to cover our feelings.

7. Physical health
Our bodies are the end of the line in terms of our thought life. How you think about yourself and life will have a direct effect on your health in either a positive or negative way. Your body will flag or play out your inner thought life as your physical feelings are the chemical elaboration of the thoughts. It begins as a thought, becomes a feeling, which in terms of your body is a chemical release. We could say then that if your inner and outer thoughts are positive then it will be reflected in your body, hence the mind/body connection. We can say then that in many ways your physical state begins in your thinking and ends in your body.

CHAPTER 11
Physical healing through healing the broken heart

When we have a thought or belief it goes to the part of the brain called the hypothalamus. This part of the brain oversees, amongst other systems, the central nervous system and the endocrine or glandular system. These glands release hormones into our bodies that are involved in many body functions. In terms of your chemical body, hormones make your world go around.

Perhaps this is most easily demonstrated in some basic life activities. If you begin to think about your favourite food, your hypothalamus will begin to perform the relevant functions to get your body ready to eat. You may now find your stomach grumbling as the hormones involved begin to wind up your gastric system. If you think about a sexual encounter your body will release the appropriate hormones to prepare you for the physical act. Men are far more likely to have a rapid response to these thoughts because, according to the scientists, they have on average 20 to 25 times as much of the sex hormone testosterone. So, guys, it is advisable to avoid potential discomfort, by not thinking about sex before you have cleared the appointment with your wife.

So, we can see the fundamental outworking of our thoughts in our bodies through these simple illustrations. A cheerful or happy heart that is content with life and at peace with self and God will release hormones that promote health and well-being. The word of God says,

"A cheerful heart is good medicine, but a crushed spirit dries up the bones" (NIV, Proverbs 17:22).

A heavy heart, loaded down with negative beliefs will produce hormone imbalances which lead to disease. We say that if your mind is not at peace or at *ease*, you are open to *dis-ease* in your physical body.

A bull in a field

As an example of how this can play out in our bodies, let us look at two hormones in the hormonal cascade that affect each other and need to be in balance with each other. One is called cortisol, which is a stress hormone. It has anti-inflammatory properties and helps mediate actions such as blood sugar balances and so on. There are a number of other hormones that we need to function and be healthy that are in turn made from cortisol. There is another hormone on the other side of the cascade known as DHEA (Dehydroepiandrosterone) also from which many other hormones that we need are made. Amongst other things DHEA is implicated in mood and a sense of wellbeing.

Imagine finding yourself in a field with a snorting bull staring you down. Might I suggest that in that moment you do not need to be in a good mood and feel that all is right with the World! You actually need to have a stress response and go into flight fairly quickly. This is typically what happens with such a threat. Hormones that you need to get you out of the situation such as cortisol rise rapidly and hormones that give you a sense of well-being or are not important in the moment diminish. After the situation is resolved these levels go back to normal.

But what if your stress is coming from a fear related to people such as fear of rejection, failure, or performance anxiety to do with the expectations of others? It is very hard to avoid all humans. There are billions of them and invariably you will need to deal with some of them at some point in time. Anxiety issues related to whether you perform to expectations, or receive acceptance or not, are ever present, daily stressors. Hormonally, this means that your chemicals stay out of balance long term, and usually become more exaggerated over time. This is a common phenomenon in a society founded on achievement, conformity to expectations and success in return for value, significance and worth.

So now you have too much of one hormone and not enough of the other as an outworking of your way of life and culture. Normally, over time, the imbalance of these hormone values become more and more exaggerated. Simplistically this is a typical example of the pathways to disease. Each negative emotion will have some kind of unhelpful effect on your physiology.

Scientific statistics

Modern science confirms what the Bible has always stated, that if our soul is functioning well then the outcome will be health. The most recent statistics that I have heard is that around 90% of diseases proceed from emotionally rooted chemical imbalances. I would suggest that possibly the other 10% are to do with our bad solutions to our emotional problems such as drugs, alcohol, excessive food or even at times prescription medication which can carry a considerable number of side effects. I am not sure that we can lay all of our diseases at the feet of cultural issues, such as a high sugar diet as some do. However, these and other substances that we ingest certainly create an environment for disease to prosper and proliferate.

3 John 1:2 says, *"Dear friend, I pray that you may enjoy good health and that all may go well with you, even as your soul is getting along well"* (NIV).

The preceding passage confirms that if our souls, that is our mind, will and emotions, are in good order then our bodies will also be healthy. As we have seen, the state of our souls and physical well-being are directly linked to the condition and beliefs of our heart. In practice we have seen this to be the case over and over again. If our thought life is conformed to the word of God, both at the voluntary conscious level and also in the heart, we can expect the result to be health. Proverbs 4:20-23 puts it this way,

*"[20] Pay attention, my child, to what I say. Listen carefully. [21] Don't lose sight of my words. Let them penetrate **deep within your heart** [22] for they bring life and **radiant health** to anyone who discovers their meaning. [23] Above all else, guard **your heart**, for it affects everything you do"* (NLT, emphasis mine).

I have read somewhere that there is an area of modern medicine known as bio psychiatry. The premise of this model is that if they could get people to think correctly then nobody would be sick. The concept is correct, however without the power and ministry of the Holy Spirit I suggest that it is impossible for them to attain.

The New King James version translates this passage as the 'issues of life' that come from the heart. Health is certainly an issue that many have to deal with.

"²⁰ *My son, give attention to my words; Incline your ear to my sayings.* ²¹ *Do not let them depart from your eyes; Keep them in the midst of your heart;* ²² *For they are life to those who find them, And* **health to all their flesh**. ²³ *Keep your* **heart** *with all diligence, For out of it* **spring the issues of life**" (NKJV, Proverbs 4:20-23 emphasis mine).

The example of a thyroid gland healed

A young lady in her mid-20s came for ministry with a presenting problem of her thyroid counts being, as she put it, *off the charts*. Her doctor was going to start her on hormone treatment immediately. I suggested that we work on the anxiety beliefs that she held that were producing the problem. We spent about an hour investigating and ministering to her anxieties. The next week she returned to her doctor reporting that she was well. His response to the blood test that followed was; *that can't be right, it is all in balance*. And so, he ordered another test which also proved to be perfect. An unexpected bonus from the ministry time was that she reported delightedly, that *the best part was that she didn't have a panic attack*, as she normally would when they did the blood test. Even her anxieties about the blood test were belief based.

A Broken Heart healed, leading to release from a physical malady

A number of years ago we were ministering in a large church in a rural city in Australia. A lady in her 50s was on the list to come for help and she was suffering from a variety of emotional problems. She was very eager to be set free and so her session went unusually quickly. Most of her problems were as a result of a considerable amount of sexual abuse in her early life. After around 45 minutes she reported that she was completely at peace and so we concluded our time together.

About 2 to 3 weeks later I received a message from her reporting all of the many benefits from the session. Unexpectedly she also reported that she no longer had to be hospitalized weekly for treatment to her liver and kidneys. I was not even aware that she had a problem as she had not mentioned it. Consequently, I had not prayed for her healing, it was simply a by-product of her broken heart being healed by the Spirit of Christ.

At times we deliberately target beliefs that produce disease, and other times it happens unbidden as a result of the healing and release from captive thoughts and feelings taking place. We have seen various problems, such as arthritis or asthma, being healed without direct prayer. Somewhere in the process of an emotional release, the body comes back into order and they simply disappear. That is certainly not to say that God does not heal the body in a number of other ways, it is a way that we see God healing the sick.

The power of life and death
Proverbs 18:21, *"The tongue has the power of life and death, and those who love it will eat its fruit"* (NIV).

This proverb suddenly becomes very powerful in its potential power to break a heart. For example, in its simplest form, when a child is told that they are stupid, useless or in some way inadequate, it becomes part of the programming of the identity or self-beliefs within their hearts. The echoes of these beliefs are literally a breeding ground for negative emotions eventually leading to disease and finally premature death. Not only might they impact on the length of life, they will almost certainly have an effect on the quality of life. Fortunately, Jesus promised us that He came to set the captives free in order for us to have abundant life to the full.

If we have been crushed by negative words, it will be difficult to have a cheerful heart that releases healthy hormones. A heavy heart that has been crushed this way will load our human spirit down in its ability to empower our bodies to function properly.

Proverbs 18:14 says, *"A man's spirit sustains him in sickness, but a crushed spirit who can bear?"* (NIV).

The heavy weight of a broken heart will sap away the life-giving function of the human spirit. We have already seen that a crushed or broken spirit dries up the bones. Other authors have already documented that the blood cells making up the immune system are manufactured in the bone marrow. If this is dried out it becomes pretty obvious that this can lead to some pretty serious diseases that have their Etiology or causation in immune cell production or disruption.

Autoimmune disease

Statistics vary, but a general figure of 1 out of every 7 to 10 people in the U.S. suffer from what is termed autoimmune disease. I imagine that the numbers would be similar across the developed World. There are more than 80 of these diseases listed. Some Christian commentators consider the root of the autoimmune component of diseases to be self-rejection, and we have found this to be the case.

Remember your body is the end of the line for your thought life. If, at a heart level you do not accept yourself then, your body will play out those thoughts. In essence you yourself become the enemy of your own acceptability because of some kind of perception that you hold about your worthiness. Your body then follows your thoughts by attacking itself. Some state that your immune system will then attack the weakest link in the chain. If you have stress, fear or anxieties this may be your thyroid or your adrenal glands for example. If you are overweight and your pancreas is overworked you may be a candidate for diabetes. At times we see people who are enormous and massively overweight or morbidly obese but they are not diabetic. They certainly have created an environment for the disease but emotionally they do not hold inner beliefs that make them predisposed.

Everything starts with a thought

I have come to the conclusion that everything begins with a thought that is shaped by what we believe. Further, the beliefs of the heart are most powerful in terms of their implications because we do not usually know what they are or how to rectify them without the Holy Spirit. The outworking's of these range from your own personal inner health and relationships, right through to world leaders with low self-image making decisions based on their emotional needs and beginning world wars. The thoughts of the heart are the principle issue with implications for everything. How we are programmed becomes critical. 1 Corinthians 2:10-11 states,

"10 But God has revealed them to us through His Spirit. For the Spirit searches all things, yes, the deep things of God. 11 For what man knows the things of a man except the spirit of the man which is in him? Even so no one knows the things of God except the Spirit of God" (NKJV).

CHAPTER 12
Gods own perspective for those suffering in this area

Before we begin with how to practically work with the Spirit of truth in applying this ministry, let us examine God's position and provision towards this ministry. Do we need to talk God into helping us, or is it His idea?

Do you want more of the presence of God, or anointing on you?

Let us begin with a couple of Old Testament passages firstly encouraging our involvement and commitment to the ministry, and then a prophetic account of what those who respond to these passages will be doing.

Isaiah 57:15 states, *"For this is what the high and lofty One says-- he who lives forever, whose name is holy: "I live in a high and holy place, but also with him who is contrite and lowly in spirit, to revive the* **spirit of the lowly** *and to* **revive the heart** *of the contrite"* (NIV, emphasis mine).

We have to 'tease out' the exact meaning from the Hebrew that this passage comes from. He is saying that, He is with the contrite (Heb. Dakka - meaning, crushed or destroyed) and the lowly in spirit (Heb. Shaphal - meaning depressed). He is with them to revive them (Revive Heb. Chayah – meaning, to make alive, quicken, recover, repair, restore (to life), revive, save, to make or be whole).

This is much the same meaning as the NT Greek word 'sozo'. His promise is also to revive their *hearts*, which coming from the Hebrew word *Leb*, as we have pointed out means the feelings, intellect and will. Or perhaps we could suggest the feelings proceeding from our beliefs which affect our choices.

In the New Testament we have words such as 'Anapsuksis' which is normally translated as 'refreshing' but in the Greek it is actually, 'recovery of breath' or 'revival.' So, whatever you think about what 'revival' is, from a Biblical perspective, it is bringing life back to an individual's spirit and heart. *A revival* is when enough people are revived to change a community, city or even a nation.

Acts 3:19 says, "Repent, then, and turn to God, so that your sins may be wiped out, that times of **refreshing** (Anapsuksis, - recovery of breath, revival) may come from the Lord" (NIV, emphasis mine).

The basis of this is **repent**. This literally means to 'think differently,' or 'reconsider how you think.' Once we have changed our minds about how we regard God and His kingdom, it falls to Him to revive us and bring us to wholeness. As we know, in Luke chapter 4 and verses 18-19, Jesus unravelled the scroll of Isaiah and quoted from chapter 61 regarding what He was now about to do. However, in Isaiah 61 the chapter goes beyond what Jesus reads and details what those that had received healing of *their* broken hearts and freedom from captivity were going to do. Isaiah 61:1-3 notes that,

"¹ The Spirit of the Lord GOD is upon Me, because the LORD has anointed me to preach good tidings to the poor; He has sent Me to heal the brokenhearted, to proclaim liberty to the captives, And the opening of the prison to those who are bound; To proclaim the acceptable year of the LORD, and the day of vengeance of our God; ² To comfort all who mourn; ³ to console those who mourn in Zion, to give them beauty for ashes, the oil of joy for mourning, the garment of praise for the spirit of heaviness."

Up until this point He is talking about what He, in the first instance, will do for us. Next, He shifts to what the results of this ministry to us will be, and the passage moves on to what we who have received from Him will be doing:

*"³ That **they** may be called trees of righteousness, the planting of the LORD, that He may be glorified. ⁴ And **they** shall rebuild the old ruins, **they** shall raise up the former desolations, and **they** shall repair the ruined cities, The desolations of many generations"* (NKJV, Isaiah 61:3-4, emphasis mine).

I believe that in type, the ruined cities refer to the broken human personality. Jesus referred to His own body as being a temple. The Bible also states that we are the temple of the Holy Spirit. So, the picture of the temple, or a city is not an uncommon portrayal of the human personality in the scriptures. This position is strengthened from other passages which refer to setting yourself on helping people receive the promises, such as Isaiah 58. Another example is that found in Proverbs 25:28.

"Like a city whose walls are broken down is a man who lacks self-control" (NIV).

This passage refers to the ability of a man to resist and defend his person from participating with outside spiritual pressure. For example, normal emotional control being compromised through drugs or alcohol abuse.

As we round out our thoughts on the subject of Truth Encounters from a Biblical perspective, we can be encouraged to note in the following passage some powerful promises for our own healings as we set and position ourselves to free others. My wife and I can confirm that God is faithful to His word. We have progressively received healing and freedom ourselves as we have dedicated our lives to ministering to others.

Isaiah 58:6-12, *"[6] Is not this the kind of fasting I have chosen: to loose the chains of injustice and untie the cords of the yoke, to set the oppressed free and break every yoke? [7] Is it not to share your food with the hungry and to provide the poor wanderer with shelter-- when you see the naked, to clothe him, and not to turn away from your own flesh and blood? [8]* **Then your light will break forth like the dawn, and your healing will quickly appear;** *then your righteousness will go before you,* **and the glory of the LORD will be your rear guard**. *[9] Then you will call, and the LORD will answer; you will cry for help, and he will say: Here am I. "If you do away with the yoke of oppression, with the pointing finger and malicious talk, [10]* **and if you spend yourselves in behalf of the hungry and satisfy the needs of the oppressed, then your light will rise in the darkness, and your night will become like the noonday.** *[11] The LORD will guide you always; he will satisfy your needs in a sun-scorched land and will strengthen your frame. You will be like a well-watered garden, like a spring whose waters never fail. [12] Your people will rebuild the ancient ruins and will raise up the age-old foundations;* **you will be called Repairer of Broken Walls**, *Restorer of Streets with Dwellings".*

It is clear in the New Testament that Jesus discipled His followers into doing what He did. The Father's Will shall always involve ministering to, or supporting, those who are helping people to receive salvation, healing and freedom. If the Father is all about meeting the needs of the people He created, then it is inevitable that His children will be dedicated to the same activities.

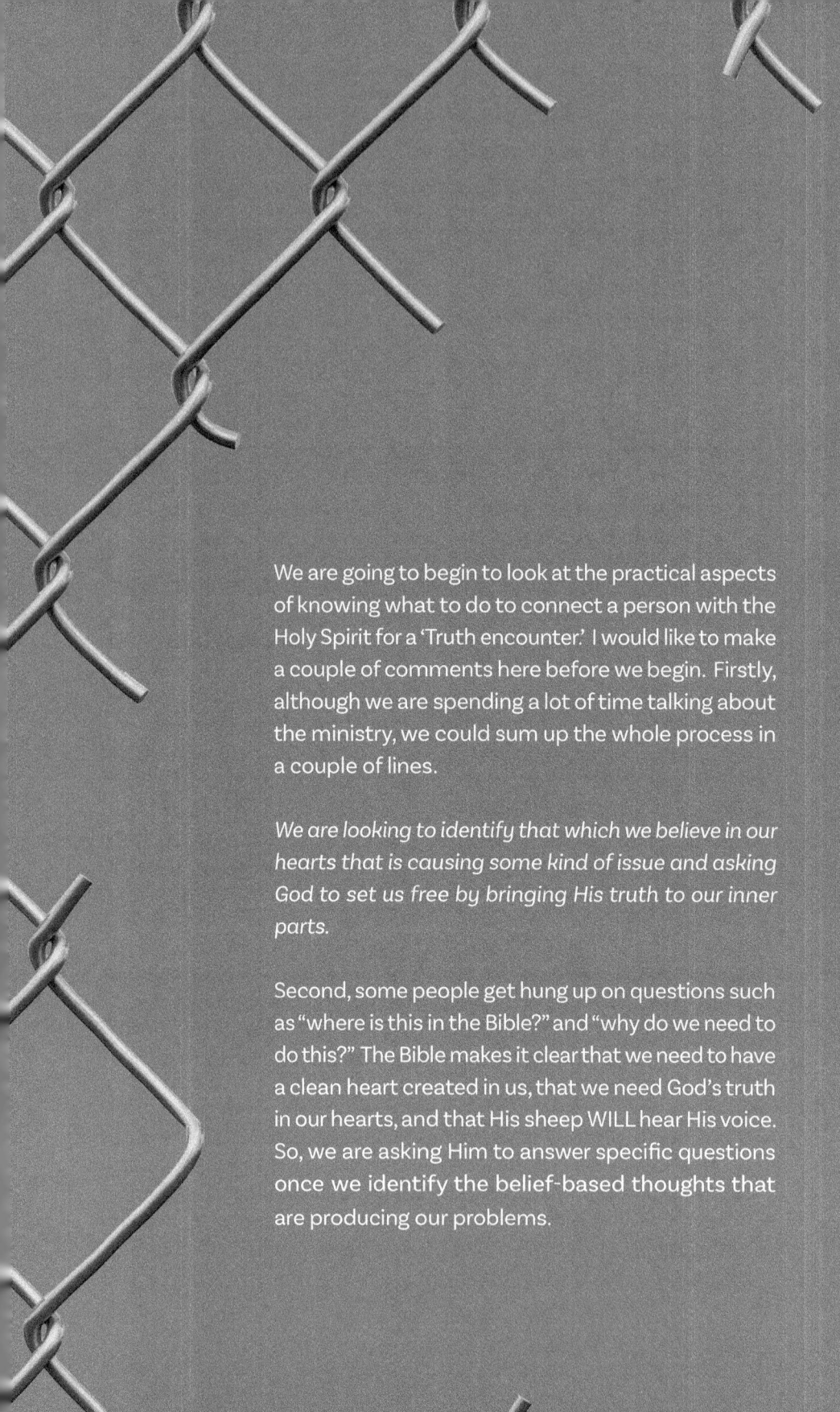

We are going to begin to look at the practical aspects of knowing what to do to connect a person with the Holy Spirit for a 'Truth encounter.' I would like to make a couple of comments here before we begin. Firstly, although we are spending a lot of time talking about the ministry, we could sum up the whole process in a couple of lines.

We are looking to identify that which we believe in our hearts that is causing some kind of issue and asking God to set us free by bringing His truth to our inner parts.

Second, some people get hung up on questions such as "where is this in the Bible?" and "why do we need to do this?" The Bible makes it clear that we need to have a clean heart created in us, that we need God's truth in our hearts, and that His sheep WILL hear His voice. So, we are asking Him to answer specific questions once we identify the belief-based thoughts that are producing our problems.

SECTION 2

MINISTERING TRUTH ENCOUNTERS

"Why do we need to do this type of ministry?"
In our modern society we are flooded by all kinds of media. For many people, a few spare minutes means an opportunity to check their emails or Facebook, or perhaps relax in front of the Television. Added to this is the complicated, activity-based lifestyles that we lead. I propose that by the time evening came, one hundred years ago, saints such as Oswald Chambers most likely had their Bible and a candle to fill in their nights. So, to sit with God and relate with Him regarding the source of their issues would have been a comparatively uncomplicated endeavour. Most of us can point to times where the Holy Spirit has communicated something to us that has brought some kind of change. In fact, we are in a time of the outpouring of the Spirit of Truth as never before in history.

So, this ministry is aimed purposefully, deliberately and diligently at bringing specific areas, issues and hurts to the feet of the Father for His truth. Most Christians want to be free to be all that they can be in service to God. They want to bring Him glory by modelling and giving evidence to His provision and love by seeing it manifested in their lives. Let us look at how we can receive truth for ourselves and then help others.

Section 2: Ministering Truth Encounters

CHAPTER 13
Accessing the Heart via the mind and emotions

Screens, icons, programs

For the sake of an illustration, let us imagine your conscious mind as a screen; perhaps as a television (TV) screen. In today's world there can often be up to 100 channels or more on our TV. On a normal TV set you can only view one channel or program at a time. We described in Chapter 7 how in much the same way, if I begin to talk about a hot dog or your favourite meal you may now have a picture on the screen of your mind. To access that picture of food you had to put whatever else you were thinking about to the side and change channels briefly. Your conscious mind is much like a computer in this respect, having been designed to be a sequential processor, or in other words to focus on one task at a time.

In a ministry session then, we are tuning into the fear, rejection or whatever other channel in order to view and connect with it. Thinking now of a hot dog, if we focus on it long enough, we will begin to have something happen in our stomachs as a reaction to the thought. In the same way as we begin to concentrate on, and embrace our fear or other issues, bringing them onto the screen of our conscious minds, we will have a chemical bodily response that we call emotion or feelings.

We can now begin to look for the belief and inner thoughts producing the emotion. Whether we present with a negative emotion and identify the belief producing it, or have a negative belief and let ourselves feel it, is immaterial. The important thing is that we connect them both on the conscious screen of our minds. Usually people will come presenting with negative emotions such as anxiety, fear, anger, rejection, bitterness and so on. Some people will look for help because of how they are reacting in relationships or to life.

As you listen to their story or problem you will most likely hear the beliefs behind the emotions come out in words. I usually have a piece of paper or a notebook with me, and record statements that I believe may be connected to beliefs. Jesus said that we will hear the overflow of the heart from the mouth: Matthew 12:34b states,

*"... for out of the overflow of the **heart** the **mouth** speaks."* (NIV, emphasis mine).

For example, in the course of telling their story, somebody might say something such as; 'school was a difficult time for me, but that's not surprising, I can never keep up with the other kids!' When the time comes for ministry, we could say to them something along the lines of, 'I heard you say before that you can never keep up with the other kids; is that true?' Now, as they concentrate on that statement and connect with the feeling that goes with it, we can ask a further question to find out the belief of the heart. 'What does that make you if you can't keep up with the other kids?' Their possible answer may be something such as; 'I must be dumb!'

The next thing that we want to do is find the place where they first learned this; the critical moment when they 'took it to heart.' There is always a historically matching memory. They may report something along the lines of, 'when I was in grade 3, I could not do my times table and the teacher embarrassed me in front of the class.' So, I would probably say something along the lines of, 'so in that moment you believed that you **are** dumb because you could not do the times table?' Response 'Yes.'

Then I would say something such as, 'Lord, Fred believes that he is dumb and can't keep up with other people because he could not do his times table. His truth is that *he is dumb*; what is your truth for him?' As 'Fred' now has the belief, the matching negative feeling, and the historical event pulled up onto the screen of his mind it is time to ask God to reveal *His* truth to set him free. Whatever, God does in that moment will set 'Fred' free simply because He is God. The key for *us* in helping Fred is finding what is believed in his heart.

We tend to remember whatever is stored in the moment of emotional weakness and vulnerability. Surrounding details are not necessarily a part of interpreting the event so much as what is happening in the moment. God could remind him that he had been off sick and was not present when the instruction to learn those times tables was given.

Remember, this whole event including beliefs were beneath the surface in the heart all along. They needed to be deliberately accessed and brought into the conscious mind to be processed. It is necessary to know what you believe before you can present it to the Lord to address it with His truth.

Dealing with multiple beliefs

Rounding out our illustration of a television screen, let us consider the multiple channels again. When we first began this ministry, people would come to us for help, and in a session, we might work through 2 or 3 beliefs and feelings that were a problem. They would usually report how free they felt, and we would be thinking that we had just worked with the Lord to fix up their whole lives! In some cases, people were happy with their new freedom, but many times we would be contacted with a report that they were struggling again. Upon investigation we would find out that everything resolved in the previous session was still settled, but there were other new issues. We have found this to be the case in ministering to others as well as receiving healing for ourselves. Most of us have a significant number of *channels* that need to be *reprogrammed*.

By way of example, someone may come presenting a problem of fear. They may have a fear of rejection, failure, flying, abandonment, or lack of protection or provision and so on. Each of these fears is a different belief and stem from various historical events. You can only have one of these *channels or programs* running in your conscious mind at a time. It is necessary to go through them one at a time and switch them off individually, so to speak. You only need one fear program still running to feel, for example, anxiety. Typically, as you go through ministering to each belief the intensity becomes less and less until they are completely free.

That is not to suggest that every fear needs to be dealt with before your anxiety is completely gone. It is usually fear related to people that is ever present, such as fear of rejection. It is difficult to not deal with people as there are billions of them on the Earth. A fear of flying, for example, may produce no anxiety at all because you simply choose not to fly. However, if you have to fly for some reason, your belief-based anxiety will quickly be present and need to be resolved.

The 'Golf' principle

I once saw a picture of the famous golfer Tiger Woods standing beside a pile of golf balls that would fill a shopping trolley. He was basically practicing producing the same swing over and over. The courses may change, the competition varies, the conditions will be different, but he is doing the same thing over and over. In much the same way we have a handful of questions that we use over and over to help people identify that which they believe. Sometimes we will be visiting fear channels, other times switching of all of the rejection or bitterness channels. On occasions we will be finding the beliefs behind sin.

Some people will be very emotionally connected and receive the ministry easily. Others will have defences and objections or be people who want to resolve their own problems with their minds and have not been able to. Whatever comes to us, as co laborers with the Holy Spirit, we patiently and graciously give our time, repetitively, asking the same handful of questions!

After a while, once you become familiar with the process you will find yourself ministering a *truth encounter* driving with someone in a car, across a table at lunch, in a prayer line or more purposefully in a prayer room at some location. The point is that once you learn the simple process you will be applying it over and over to different cases. It is very rewarding to see God setting people free, and Him allowing us the privilege of being involved.

'Icons' and 'shortcuts'
Before we move on, I want to push out the parameters of the *screen* in the conscious mind analogy. Up to this point, we have discussed it as a television screen in order to illustrate that some people may have many *channels and programs* that need to be worked through, and others just a few. It doesn't actually reflect on you as a person how many negative beliefs that you have collected. It is a bit like being clothed by life. Someone's clothing may be expensive and plentiful; another's may be dirty and tattered. In the end we are all the same, just people clothed by different circumstances and conditions.

We know that God looks at who you are and not the outer appearance, this includes weighing justly your circumstances and how you arrived where you are. We cannot then judge anyone's behaviour in any way. Something happened to produce the responses, everyone has a story, and if nothing negative happened to you then you can consider yourself blessed. You need to know though, that if you were the product of the same situations, then you would probably hold the same beliefs and produce the same attitudes and behaviour. These responses to beliefs I call, universal reactions. They are predictable reactions to beliefs that are held. I will illustrate these in a later chapter.

Computer screens
Most people today have seen a computer screen. We can use this as an analogy to further examine how our conscious mind operates. On most screens are little pictures called icons which have some kind of symbol depicting the program that they represent. The program is in the unit stored in a deeper place. On my computers you have to click a button twice with the pointer on the icon to open the program.

The point is that these icons connect you to programs that are there underneath whether you open them or not. In the case of operating the computer most of these are opened as a deliberate act. This can be the case with our minds. For example, we can purposefully open the *time to cook the dinner* program which holds all the information that we have stored and held as data about preparing food. It will come up onto our screen and we will access what we know to complete the task. In my case all there is when I open the *prepare dinner program* is, 'buy Pizza'.

Associations
With regard to our minds, these programs are often accessed by situations or circumstances automatically. We call these *associations*. Perhaps the simplest way to explain this would be something like the ringing of your telephone. Your brain associates the sound with somebody wanting to talk to you. It then opens the *program* containing information on how to answer the phone and most likely selects the most suitable response, depending on whether you expect it to be a friend or a grumpy employer.

Emotionally, we operate along much the same lines. Perhaps we are starting a new job in a crowded office. Without deliberately wanting to, we access an anxiety belief. Stored in the memory in the file along with the belief is *how do I react in this situation?* The belief could be something like, *people won't like me unless I do what they want and make them happy*, and this has been learnt from a historical event. The response to the situation, also stored in the memory, could be something such as, to entertain them and be funny. This may have been how they gained acceptance and fitted in as a child in similar situations. So, the behaviour coming from the *I need to perform to be accepted belief* is a mask.

People often present with these types of situations on their *shopping lists* for healing. They would most likely come into a session reporting anxiety in these environments. We have them *click on* the *I am uncomfortable in group situations* icon on the screen of their conscious minds. By that I mean, concentrate on this type of situation and how it makes them feel. Then, we identify a matching historical event with the same emotions in it and clarify what is believed that produces the feelings. Once we have these elements, we can invite the Spirit of truth to minister freedom to them.

Shortcuts
Before we move on from the screen analogy, I would like to point out that these icons are readily accessible shortcuts to the programs within the computer that bypass the normal pathways. This is a helpful picture for us in terms of resolving habitual sin cycles. Let us create a common scenario.

A married woman struggles with rejection having never had true love and acceptance in childhood. As a consequence, deep inside she believes that she is *not loveable or good enough to be noticed*. The spouse, because of their own issues, is always at work, playing golf or at the pub with his friends. He feels that he has shown love by getting her a nice house and a car. Along the way she meets a nice man at work who comments on her hair. Later he invites her for a coffee.

Up until this point the whole process is going through the normal pathways of feeling that this is wrong, knowing that you shouldn't be doing it, but at the same time, mistaking the good feeling of being cared about as love. Usually your emotional needs will be the greatest predictor of your behaviour and eventually she moves past the self-conflict into an illicit relationship. After the first time, the person no longer works through the normal pathways regarding whether or not the sin should be entered into. Now this is the apparent solution to their rejection and they *shortcut* the process and go straight to the sinful activity. Without being set free from the underlying rejection beliefs, she can easily fall into further affairs. Typically, with both men and women, when their rejection is resolved they struggle to see how they could have gotten into the situation to begin with.

Another example could be a man addicted to pornography. At one time he felt convicted and guilty. But eventually when the opportunity or situation presents for him to access the sin, it is now a shortcut and he goes directly to the sin without inner opposition. His heart is hardened and he no longer goes through any thinking process that would hold resistance or objection, he goes directly to the sin.

2 Peter 2:19b says, *"for a man is a slave to whatever has mastered him"* (NIV).

Many sins have an emotional need component as the original trigger which needs to be resolved. Christians are not any different to anyone else in terms of their humanity and emotional needs. They are not the same as other people, however, in that they have the opportunity to be set free.

In summary then, as a tool to help our understanding, we know that when people look to us to connect them to God for healing, we need to get them to go through the exercise of connecting, consciously and deliberately, with information that they hold in their hearts. Some are hesitant to do that and you may need to spend some time working through getting them to look at the problem and bring it up onto the *screen* of their conscious mind. Quiet rooms and a one on one session are ideal for this where possible. If they are prepared to, I have them focus on their thoughts or feelings, and go to what I term *periscope depth*. This is where they begin to concentrate on, and explore, what is underneath in the heart.

Note:
We can only minister to whatever a person is wanting help with. It is entirely up to them. God will not make them get ministry and neither should we. Our job is to offer healing if they desire it. We can encourage people to work through everything that they can

find. Some people will, for example, be pleased to get rid of a fear or the like, but are happy to keep their pride and rebellion. It's almost as if they go, 'thanks for that God, but I am taking over again and am satisfied with my own solutions!' This is between God and the person; it is not our place to judge, only to be equipped to help when possible. We can only work with whatever issue that they present with.

CHAPTER 14
Sources of & Influences on Heart beliefs

The Generational principle

Exodus 20: 5-6, states, "⁵ *For I, the LORD your God, am a jealous God,* **visiting the iniquity of the fathers on the children** *to the third and fourth generations of those who hate Me,* ⁶ *but showing mercy* **to thousands**, *to those who love Me and keep My commandments*" (NKJV).

Doing the mathematics, Almighty God offers mercy to one thousand generations for those who show their love by keeping His commandments. That is 250 to 333 times more that He wants us to be blessed; than He wants us to be disciplined! If there are no consequences then there is no fear of God. However, this passage makes it abundantly clear that He wants to encourage us and reward us for showing our love for Him. God's love language is obedience.

John 14:15, "*If you love Me, keep My commandments*" (NKJV).
John 14:15, "*If you love me, you will obey what I command*" (NIV).

The *visiting* in Exodus 20:5 is like a *drawing to*. On face value, it almost seems as if the father's sin in a particular area, becomes an area where the children will be tested to see if they love God and prefer His commandments and ways. Will they seek Him to be free from their sins and weaknesses?

Have you ever wondered why, in a neighbourhood, some of the residents are alcoholics, while others will never have a drink in their lives but are drawn like a magnet to horror movies, drugs, violence or pornography? This is the outworking of the *visiting* on the family line. Under the curse of the law this was the consequence of iniquity. It continues today for those who remain under the judgment of the law, not having believed that Jesus fulfilled the law and took the penalty of the curse in their place. Sin is defined by the law, it did not begin with the law; it began with Satan and entered the human generation line through Adam and Eve.

Positions on generational principles
Let me give you three distorted positions that Christians often hold pertaining to generational principles:

1. It was 'all done at the cross.'
This doctrine proposes that Jesus ended the penalty of the curse and so there are now no effects on Christians. This is a *positionally* true statement. Jesus did pay for our freedom from the curse of the law; hence all of His part was *done at the cross*. But we need to know that all of these promises are under the New Covenant which is mediated and accessed by faith. In the event that this were automatic and operative without the faith component there would be no sick Christians, no mental, emotional, relational issues or sin addictions to be dealt with. It is reasonably obvious that this is not the case. All of these maladies one way or another relate to the curse of sin through our generations all the way back to Adam.

The truth remains though, that Jesus did pay for the curse that passes through the generation lines, and largely we appropriate that provision of freedom through the ministries of the Holy Spirit. Water baptism is an ideal time to pray against dynamics coming through the family, as you are choosing to put the old life behind. We have seen evidence such as repeated accidents as a result of a family curse stop when we have prayed specifically against them at water baptism. But again, you will only be able to access by faith those things that you are aware of. As a consequence, many other areas are discerned later in further ministry settings.

Galatians 3:13, *"Christ redeemed us from the curse of the law by becoming a curse for us, for it is written: 'Cursed is everyone who is hung on a tree'"* (NIV).

Still others believe that traits passing from generation to generation simply do not exist. In a practical sense, observing even our physical characteristics and mannerisms and those of our parents and ancestors quickly dispels this thought. Even practices such as architecture or diet have a generational influence.

2. All of your healing and freedom will come through dealing with generational issues.
This group has you renouncing everything that you can possibly think of. Personally, I have not seen freedom come to many people

using this model. If your generational influences have become your personal sin then you need to confess, repent and be ministered to and set free. It can become an excessive practice that is meaningless. I have seen people with issues that could be easily ministered to endlessly and fervently going through books renouncing all kinds of sins of their ancestors.

The truth is that Jesus DID take the penalty of that curse for you. Now by faith and through the ministry of the Holy Spirit you can be set free. Self-effort in renouncing will not yield much without Him. A minister led by the Spirit may help you with the prayer of faith in these times. In the Old Testament we see that Balaam could not curse the people of God as they were protected. The method that was used to expose them and bring a curse on them was by getting them to participate in the sins of the societies around them.

3. The children eat sour grapes.

In arguing that generational influences are not relevant to Christians, people often quote the book of the major prophet Ezekiel in order to imply that generational principles are no longer in effect.

Ezekiel 18:1-3, "*The word of the LORD came to me again, saying;* 2 *"What do you mean when you use this proverb concerning the land of Israel, saying: 'The fathers have eaten sour grapes, And the children's teeth are set on edge'?* 3 *"As I live," says the Lord GOD, "you shall no longer use this proverb in Israel".*

If these people were to look further to the same account in the book of Jeremiah they would see a fuller explanation of this. Remember, they are both prophetic books speaking of a time to come.

Jeremiah 31: 29-34, 29 "*In those days they shall say no more:* **'The fathers have eaten sour grapes, And the children's teeth are set on edge.'** 30 "*But every one shall die for his own iniquity; every man who eats the sour grapes, his teeth shall be set on edge.* 31 "*Behold, the days are coming, says the LORD, when I will* **make a new covenant** *with the house of Israel and with the house of Judah;* 32 "*not according to the covenant that I made with their fathers in the day that I took them by the hand to lead them out of the land of Egypt, My covenant which they broke, though I was a husband to them, says the LORD.* 33 **"But this is the covenant that I will make with the house of Israel** *after those days, says the LORD: I will put My law in their minds, and write it on their hearts; and I will be their God, and they shall be My people.* ³⁴ "No more shall every man teach his neighbor, and every man his brother, saying, 'Know the LORD,' for they all shall know Me, from the least of them to the greatest of them, says the LORD. **For I will forgive their iniquity, and their sin I will remember no more**" (NKJV, Emphasis mine).

Clearly, the expanded Jeremiah passage refers to the new covenant of provision through faith which was established for us by Jesus. You will find this in the book of Hebrews Chapter 10 in the New Covenant directly quoting Jeremiah. (See previous and following underlined passages). So, we can deduce that the prophetic biblical statement that was made by Jeremiah and Ezekiel regarding 'sour grapes' referred to the covenant that we are now under. It was not something for their times.

Hebrews 10:16-17 ***"This is the covenant that I will make with them after those days, says the LORD: I will put My laws into their hearts, and in their minds I will write them,"*** ¹⁷ ***then He adds, "Their sins and their lawless deeds I will remember no more"*** (NKJV Emphasis mine. The same as Jeremiah 31:33-34).

How then should we regard generational principles?
As we have already established, Jesus paid the price for our freedom from generational influences. We consider co-labouring with the ministry of the Holy Spirit as a part of facilitating that freedom in a person's life. Because Jesus has already paid for their release then we can now simply consider generational influences as another potential source for their problem.

Let me give a very simple example of this. Imagine a parent has suffered from rejection from their own family. Remember the nature of God is always accepting. God did not reject man, man rejected God. Rejection then, not being one of the ways of God, can be considered as iniquitous or fundamentally, a sin-based activity. In this simple illustration then we see that the parents sinned against the child in not accepting them. Almost certainly they also suffered areas of rejection from their generations. Our sample parent then, having not received acceptance for their person will most likely continue the cycle, Christian or not, until it is broken.

Are we then getting them to renounce rejection when they come for help? No, we don't even necessarily need to know that it is generational. We are simply ministering to the beliefs that are now held as a result of the rejection. Now, as they have acceptance themselves on the inside, the cycle is broken and they will be carriers of love and grace. Their children may also need some ministry if they have already been affected by the rejection.

When we are dealing with emotional and heart-based healing, regardless of the source the ministry is the same, although we may observe that the source is generational. The ministry is actually appropriating the freedom from the curse that was promised under the New Covenant.

Deliverance from generationally transmitted weaknesses
Although not directly related to our 'Truth Encounters' subject, I will mention here that at times, deliverance of an evil spirit can go along with the ministry. A number of years ago I was ministering to an elderly lady who had suffered with guilt from an event early in her life. She eventually confessed that she had performed a sexual act with a dog. As well as ministry to the beliefs that she held relating to the event, she was delivered from a generational spirit drawing her to the bestiality act. She had never confessed this episode to another person prior to seeing me.

A few years later her middle-aged daughter also came for emotional healing. Towards the end of the session she confessed something that she had never told anyone before. When she was a young girl, she had also had sex with a dog. She also needed deliverance from the unclean spirit compelling her to this act.

Once you have seen a few of these cases there are no further doubts regarding generational influences. They were both lovely people, and both exemplary Christians, but there was an area of weakness that had come to them that they had not chosen.

Over the years we have seen many people set free from influences which cause them great guilt and condemnation. They are so relieved to realize that they are not inherently evil people, but something happened in their generations further upstream that they did not ask for. Their specific area of *visiting* was not something that they had read about in the will!

Hereditary disease
If you attend doctors for some kind of chronic illness or disease, they will usually ask you if it is in the family. Physiologically they may test and observe some kind of genetic predisposition for the onset of the disease. We have already previously discussed studies that propose that as many as 90% of diseases stem from emotional imbalances.

I would like to suggest, and have noted over many years, that what actually passes through families are particular emotional problems that create an environment for that specific malady. For example, hereditary self-rejection will give opportunity for autoimmune problems to proliferate in a family line. So, dealing with rejection which has led to self-rejection will remove the predisposition for further generations to suffer. I have observed other troubles such as bitterness and resentment in families that suffer from illnesses such as cancer and arthritis. For the glorious Church that will shine in these dark times, disease prevention may well be just as important as cure.

Epigenetics and secular science
Incidentally, modern secular science confirms the biblical generational principle. Most of that which the modern world is discovering relating to people can be found in your Bible which was written thousands of years ago by the creator of everything! It is already well documented that disease can be hereditary or generational. Epigenetics is an area of science that is stating that habits, behaviour and addictions, for example, are also transmitted through the family.

The following statement is quoted from an article on Epigenetics that I was sent. The passage is from a Neuropsychologist, where Dr. Timothy Jennings explains:

The choices we make – the foods that we eat, the things that we watch – can affect how DNA is expressed. When we have kids, we pass on the sequence to them. So, if we become addicted to stuff, we can pass along to our children gene instructions that make them more vulnerable to addictions. So, take pornography addiction, for instance, since it's the fastest growing epidemic in today's church.

According to a recent study, 68% of Christian men are addicted to porn. Most likely, they are unaware of the hereditary ramifications of viewing porn. It doesn't happen generally with one exposure to pornography. It's the repetitive volitional exposure to pornography that will cause this type of gene expression change to happen".
*Dr. Jennings has a U-Tube series explaining Neuroplasticity and Epigenetics

In practice, we have usually found that the parents of men addicted to porn have also had the problem. Christians are not exempt from these principles and temptations in the World, but we do have the option of freedom. This is just one example. We acknowledge that whether we are dealing with beliefs that need truth, or sin problems that need deliverance or other ministry, generational sources are something that we need to be aware of.

Conception
Our next source is at conception. We have just discussed how dispositions towards beliefs, physical predispositions, behaviour and even habits can pass to us, generationally and spiritually. This would pass to us at conception. It is well documented that the point of life beginning is as the sperm meets the egg and that there is at that moment a little *fireworks* display. For many Christians we would accept this to be the time where the human spirit and soul were placed within that first single fertilized cell. The scientists tell us that this flash of light is the moment when life begins.

We thank our mothers and fathers for joining with God in creation in providing our chemical bodies. But indeed, our spirits and souls are created by our Father in Heaven, who purposed us for Himself to spend eternity with Him. However, we are looking at the challenges we face that hinder our fruitfulness on the journey as we prepare for that time.

Transference at conception
In the following passage, King David ties his weakness and subsequent iniquity with Bathsheba to sinfulness that he received right at conception. Notably, in Psalm 51, verse six, he cites the solution and best defence against self-deception and sin as being truth in the inner parts, or heart as some translations render it.

Psalm 51:5-7, "⁵ *Surely I was sinful at birth, **sinful from the time my mother conceived me**. ⁶ Surely you desire **truth in the inner parts**; you teach me wisdom in the inmost place.⁷ Cleanse me with hyssop, and I will be clean; wash me, and I will be whiter than snow*" (NIV, Emphasis mine).

Many years ago, we were traveling interstate between cities. I was asked by a person that I knew if we would be prepared to minister to a relative of theirs as we passed through their city. On the way to the home of the subject I did a little research on the internet regarding their disease. They were suffering from an unusual heart disease, and according to the medical information that I read on the internet it began at *conception*. This amazed me that medical Etiology of the disease stated that it began at the time of a couple of cells receiving life. There is no heart, so how physically can heart disease begin here if you are basing your study on physiology and scientific evidence and not spiritual concepts?

It turned out that, as is the case with many forms of heart disease, fear was at the root. In this case, fear of death was the problem, which could indeed, be passed at conception. The Lord gave the person a picture which they reported as resolving the fear that was received at conception.

As a source, I will not spend much time on conception as it is relatively unusual for a belief to be birthed right in that moment. However, it is good to be aware of the possibility. None of these sources of beginnings are places that you deliberately look for or suggest. It will usually come from the person that you are working with.

Let me offer this story to illustrate what I am saying. Please note again that it is a fairly rare occurrence, which has presented on a few occasions in more than 20 years of facilitating this kind of ministry. I would hate to spark off a group of people targeting ministry to *conception* as Christians tend to do.

Important note:
People seem to love; 'this is how you do it' models. This is the exact opposite of how this ministry works. We are not directive at all as

to where the ministry should go. But as we explore what people are 'feeling and believing,' as the beginning point, with the direction of the Holy Spirit we *discover* the source.

A young lady was presenting with a feeling of defilement and a sense of being unclean. As we asked her questions and explored her history, we could find no event that would cause her to feel that way. An impression came into her mind of her father forcing himself on her mother in rape. The source of the defilement and uncleanness having been revealed she was subsequently set completely free. As I have stated, this is a very rare and unusual case, and would certainly discourage anyone from suggesting this as a source to anybody that you are helping. If it is something that you need to know, the Holy Spirit will reveal it most likely to the person.

Prenatal, 'before birth'
I have digressed a little here and there but we are looking to find the beliefs that we hold in our hearts that are not God's truth or perspective. In the case of taking in beliefs *prenatal* or while we are still in our mother's womb, we need to realize that these beliefs were initially feelings. Later, when we have words, we can describe the feelings with words. The words are a verbal explanatory version of the feelings or emotions and are one and the same. There is a great deal of science and evidence that indeed a child is impacted by that which both the mother and father are thinking and doing whilst the child is still in the womb [1].

We see instances in the Bible, such as John the Baptist, leaping in the womb when Mary was visiting, carrying the unborn Jesus.

Luke 1:41 says, *"And it happened, when Elizabeth heard the greeting of Mary, that the babe leaped in her womb; and Elizabeth was filled with the Holy Spirit"* (NKJV).

This is an area that you may commonly find yourself ministering in. Again, it is vital that you do not suggest this as the source. When you have exhausted all other possibilities of where beliefs may have begun, and there are no memories then this is a *possible* source.

---

[1] For further study: The Secret Life of the Unborn Child by Thomas Verny M.D. with John Kelly.

Note:
Many people who do not immediately have memories may have suppressed them over time because they are too painful or fearful. There are other reasons for not immediately being able to access memory which we will discuss in a later chapter.

A feeling of not being wanted in a prenatal setting may later be described in words as the belief that no one wants you or perhaps that you are unacceptable. Put simply, rejection is non-acceptance. I have noted, over the years, some predictable beliefs emerging when a child is not accepted when they are known by the parents to be present: 'I don't belong, I am an intruder, I shouldn't be here, I am not wanted, I am not loved...'

There of course can be other reasons coming from memories and events that can cause you to hold those same beliefs. I reiterate that it is vital to not try to take people to a source that you believe may be the root. Just begin with the presenting problem and work backwards into their inner reality.

For example, we have all seen people who come into church, are warmly accepted, loved and valued. Eventually they find a reason to move on, and so they go to many churches, finally, sadly often leaving church altogether. Many times, the reason is, that no matter how much love that they receive, if they hold a belief in their hearts that they *do not belong, are not an accepted part of the group, not really loved, wanted or valued*, they will eventually leave.

All of these beliefs promote anxiety for them in the form of fear of rejection. Once having been rejected, we fear it happening again. This is the most common kind of fear and anxiety, fear of man.

Other kinds of beliefs from prenatal influences
It is very much the case that we can receive any kind of belief that the mother is feeling. If a father has left the mother because he found out that she was pregnant, she will most likely feel she is not important or valued. The child may grow up believing that men will not be there for them and that they do not value you or treat you as important or valuable. This is likely to be a possible root to behaviour such as extreme self-importance and is behind issues

such as narcissistic attitudes. There can, of course, be other events in childhood where these same beliefs have taken hold. A mother, who already has small children and is struggling to manage in some way, may produce a child who has imbibed the mothers' anxious feelings and goes through life stressed from a belief that they will not be able to cope.

An example of how specific situations produce matching beliefs
I teach on prenatal beginnings in our School of Healing and Freedom, and a number of years ago there was a young lady in her mid-twenties attending the sessions. When I began explaining this area, she reported to me later that in her mind she thought to herself, *As if Steve!* The next morning, she was booked in for a ministry session and she was set free from some fears and different problems coming from her memories. Eventually we came to a belief that we discovered began when her mother found out that she was pregnant with her. The situation that she wanted help with was that she had always felt excessively responsible for her mother's life and happiness. Now in her mid-twenties their relationship was such that the daughter's role was that of mother, and the mother looked to the daughter to resolve her problems. The mother even rang up during the ministry session for advice.

As the young lady focused on the feeling of being responsible, and I asked some questions to refine the emotion and belief, the situation unfolded. She remembered her mother, who was 17 years old at the time of discovering the pregnancy, once saying to the unborn child something along the lines of, *you've ruined my life.* For mum, it was the end of being able to do whatever she wanted and she wasn't prepared. The child now believed that she was responsible for the mothers' happiness and it played out in life and their relationship. When God brought perspective, she was greatly relieved to be free of the burden, and promptly booked her mother in for a ministry session for her issues as well!

The point is that we can be very vulnerable to the thoughts and feelings of our parents in the prenatal setting. I could write for some time stories such as people with fear of water that were at Sea in storms in a prenatal event and numerous other situations that are the basis of a person's troubles.

People are going to receive freedom in different ways in their healing moments as God touches them and sets them free. I recall one lady suffering from prenatal rejection reporting something like a warm blue star touching her heart as she felt the pain emanating from her lack of acceptance.

Keeping it simple

Whether prenatal or from another source, you can make an educated guess as to what a person may have been thinking in a given situation or circumstance. As an example, it is common to find a child that has, for instance, been abandoned by the Father either before birth or in early childhood now holding a fear of abandonment. Beliefs such as, *there is no one there for me, there is no one there to protect or provide for me, men don't think I am important*, or other predictable beliefs are common. Once abandoned, insecurity will be a large part of their life, and having been abandoned then the fear of it happening again will be a prominent anxiety. People with these kinds of wounds will typically be controlling and possessive around relationships, often needing constant reassurance that those around them will be there for them. So, it begins in the mind with a fear of abandonment belief such as, *I could be left alone*, and ends in the body with physical problems such as Asthma.

Adopted children may have beliefs such as *where is everybody (familiar) gone? There is no one there for me.*' (That should be there). This can create a considerable amount of fear, anxiety, and even depression.

Helping locate a person close to their beliefs

So as ministers, in our efforts to help we can look at a situation or circumstances, make an educated guess and propose what might be believed, and offer it as a suggestion. This could come out in a statement from you, for instance in a situation where it is known that parents decided not to keep you, as, *So, do you feel like you are not wanted?* People actually know what they feel if they are honest. They will either say *yes I do, no, not really*, or *that's close, but it is more like this or this!* You have simply landed them near their belief. Before you invite the Lord to bring truth there, you might ask a further question such as; *do you feel that there is any reason that you were not wanted?* They may reply that they just feel like they were not wanted, and that is the belief that they hold, or they may respond with something along the lines of *I feel as though I was not wanted because I was in the way,* or some other kind of qualifying belief.

Note:
If a child is rejected pre-birth, or even after birth and they are feeling not wanted, then even though the parents might change their mind and accept the child later, or perhaps decide to stay together, the child will still have already received the rejection in that moment of emotional breach.

Whatever the source, the thoughts and beliefs that have been encoded in the heart will match that which you would reasonably expect to be taken in given the content of the event.

Note regarding suggesting possible beliefs
Some ministries doing this kind of work would never suggest a possible belief. Their guidelines could be something such as that the person must discover the belief themselves. I could never see any practical reason for this. People come to you to help them identify whatever it is that they believe is causing their problem. Basing your suggestions on what you would expect could be reasonably taken in as a belief can make a session dramatically shorter, which leaves you more time to minister into other areas. I have never seen anyone agree with a suggested belief to please me. They either say, *yes exactly, almost, but it's more like this, or, no, that is not it.*

The more ministry experience that you have, the more discernment and skill you have at helping identify beliefs. Of course, it is not a technique or method that has to be followed. The same results are achieved simply by asking questions. Suggesting belief options is simply a tool that may be appropriate in some situations. It may prove to be helpful with, for example, some subjects who don't quite understand what it is that you are looking for.

Gender confusion with prenatal influences as one potential source
Many times, I have found people who feel that they should have been the opposite gender. This often stems from people wanting the child to be born a particular sex. A few years ago, when I was teaching Pastors on this in Africa, one of the hosts took the platform after I had finished the session. He bravely proclaimed that when his

daughter was in his wife's womb, and given that they had wanted a boy, he prayed and prophesied over the child that it would be a male. Now, he confessed, as a grown-up girl, when he leaves the house she puts on his clothes. It really is best to leave the selection to the creator.

At times I have ministered to some farmer's daughters who illustrate this affect. Their hair is cut like men's hair, they wear men's overalls, and they can often outwork the men on the farm. It is not uncommon for them to also exhibit lesbian tendencies. The farmers have wanted boys to help with the farm work and so these girls have felt from before birth which position in the family that they should fulfil. Remember, as a principle, *as a person thinks in their heart so are they!* (Proverbs 23:7). These girls think in their *hearts* that they should be boys. That is how they are in terms of their gender orientation and behaviour. This then becomes the basis of their identity. In the same way I have ministered to men who believed that they should be girls and have various predictable distortions of their personality.

Note:
There are other reasons for gender disorientation and preference.

A final note in relation to prenatal ministry if it presents as the source

Spiritually, God intended for us to be accepted, valued, received and loved right from our very beginnings. A rejective spirit is from another kingdom which is not the kingdom of God. In the event that our commencement to life and relationships was under rejection there is often a spirit there which also needs to be dealt with. Once the person is connected to the feelings and beliefs, postured to receive from God in whatever way He chooses to touch them, simply tell the spirit of rejection, fear or whatever else to go. Most times this is not a dramatic deliverance. For example, the person may suddenly have some emotion as the spirit leaves, cough as it comes out on the breath or exhibit involuntary deepened breathing. Quite often you will not see much happen but the person will simply report feeling lighter.

Am I 'qualified' to minister healing or freedom?

You do not need to have some big ministry to do this, as it is firstly, the work of the Holy Spirit, the finger of God. It is in the name of

Jesus Christ, not your name that you are commanding it to go. Remember redemption! Regardless of how you see yourself at the moment, the Father sees you as perfect, (Hebrews 10:14), seated in the heavenlies with Christ (Ephesians 2:6). Positionally, over all of the works of the enemy, in Christ, with authority over all of the power of the enemy (Luke 10:19). This is regardless of whether or not you are a brand-new Christian or having a good or bad day!

He made us and anointed us with the Holy Spirit so that we could do these good things! We just need the heart of God in wanting to see people helped by receiving His provisions. It is not about personal perfection or being good enough in our own eyes. This ability to have the Holy Spirit work through you, as you are, is the grace of God. He surely smiles and is pleased when we have enough faith to trust Him at His word.

Ephesians 2: 8-10, " *8 God saved you by his special favor when you believed. And you can't take credit for this; it is a gift from God. 9Salvation is not a reward for the good things we have done, so none of us can boast about it. 10 For we are God's masterpiece. He has created us anew in Christ Jesus, **so that we can do the good things he planned for us long ago**"* (NLT, Emphasis mine).

Peter had to realize his own human weaknesses, and all of God's supply and provision, before he was suitable to humbly serve God. Peter denied Jesus proving his humanity. In spite of this failure, Jesus' next instructions to him were to go and feed His sheep. Now aware that he was to work in the grace of God's provisions, the power of the Holy Spirit and the name of Jesus, he was ready to serve. He now was able to make the following statements which we should all humbly identify with:

Acts 3:12 "So when Peter saw it, he responded to the people: "Men of Israel, why do you marvel at this? Or why look so intently at us, as though by **our own power or godliness** we had made this man walk"?

Acts 3:16 "And His name, **through faith in His name**, has made this man strong, whom you see and know. Yes, **the faith which comes through Him** has given him this perfect soundness in the presence of you all" (NKJV, Emphasis mine).

Later we see this principle of total reliance on God and His righteousness was acknowledged by the Apostle Paul. Along with Peter, a key to his success was the knowledge of his own imperfect human nature. As with us, he was still undergoing the process of sanctification.

Acts 14:3, "*Therefore they stayed there a long time, speaking boldly in the Lord, who was bearing witness to the word of His grace, granting signs and wonders to be done by their hands.*"

Acts 14:15b, "*We also are men with **the same nature as you**"* (NKJV, Emphasis mine).

They acknowledged willingly, that they had the same nature as these men. In the Greek language, the word translated nature means similarly *affected, like passions*. They were pointing out that they were aware of their human weaknesses and propensities, and without the Grace of God and the works of the Holy Spirit, these things would not be happening.

The point that I am making is that you don't step back from taking authority over an evil spirit because you are not perfect in your own eyes. That is the best place to be! His grace is sufficient for you. You are, through Jesus, perfect in God's eyes and that is all that matters. In the unlikely event that you are actually perfect in all of your ways, then you no longer need Jesus to make grace available to you. However, if that is the case, you most likely are in deception and have some serious pride issues which, incidentally, seem to be on the top of the list of things that God does not like!

A key to all kinds of ministry is to base your worthiness and consequent authority to minister, in the name of Jesus, on the completed work of redemption, as opposed to where you are up to in the ongoing work of sanctification. It is also wise to base your own worthiness in qualifying for any kind of healing or freedom, on the redemptive work of Jesus rather than where you have come to in your own version of being good enough. God very pointedly marks out that our own efforts at righteousness, as opposed to His provision through Jesus falls along way short.

Isaiah 64:6, "**All** of us have become like one who is unclean, and all our righteous acts are like filthy rags; we all shrivel up like a leaf, and like the wind our sins sweep us away" (NIV, Emphasis mine).

Romans 3:10 As it is written: "There is **no one righteous**, not even one" (NIV, Emphasis mine).

God Himself not only heals our diseases, He deals with the reason for the disease to begin with. I have never seen God not heal or free a person physically, emotionally or spiritually if they receive from Him with a simple faith. This includes people with some fairly unsanctified behaviour and attitudes at times.

Psalm 103:2-4, " ² *Praise the LORD, O my soul, and forget not all his benefits,* ³ *who forgives **all** your sins and heals **all** your diseases,* ⁴ *who **redeems your life** from the pit and crowns you with love and compassion* (NIV, Emphasis mine).

Addressing the evil spirit
Most times, if you have the person connected to their feelings and beliefs, and you address a spirit as we have said, you may see a sudden release of emotion, or they may simply report that they feel lighter or free. They may report that, at the moment that you told the spirit to go, God communicated with them in some way. It really doesn't matter whether you address the spirit in a whisper or a yell. It is not volume or some kind of show that releases the person, it is the place of authority that God has given that matters. Equally important is the permission of the person and their desire for you to address the spirit. It is largely a matter of exposing the spirit and its hold that makes the ministry effective.

I know, in different nations across the world, a number of little, very old ladies, who are very adept at casting out demons without changing the tone of their voices. So physical size, personality, emotional intensity or strength really are not relevant; it is really about understanding the authority that you have in the name of Jesus.

The example of the Canaanite woman, in Matthew chapter 15, is an excellent illustration of spiritual authority. The woman came with a presenting problem of a demon troubling her daughter. Jesus is not recorded as saying or praying anything regarding the demon or going to the lady's house. He simply said that as a response to the woman's faith that her child would be set free. There is no mention of a manifestation. Notably the story describes the result of the child being set free as healing. Other times we see demons come out just in the presence of Jesus or later the Apostles in the book of Acts.

Matthew 15:22, "*A Gentile woman who lived there came to him, pleading, "Have mercy on me, O Lord, Son of David! For my daughter has a demon in her, and it is severely tormenting her."*

Matthew 15:28, "*Woman," Jesus said to her, "your faith is great. Your request is granted." And her daughter was instantly healed*" (NLT, Emphasis mine).

Demonic amplification

Demonic dynamics will be discussed in more detail in later chapters. I want to point out that, the belief that matches the emotional breach is often the entry point for a demon stronghold. Dealing with the beliefs that give ground to the spirit is far more important than the spirit itself.

If you put your favourite songs through an amplifier, it is the same music, but now it has power. Evil spirits or demons, as we also know them, work in much the same way. You can have an emotional problem without having a spirit attached, which is going to be the case in most *Truth Encounters* sessions. You can hold the same belief, but the pain or response is now magnified by a demonic entity. This is why I believe people will often report some measure of emotional release or freedom in a prayer line, at a healing meeting or church service. The presence of the Holy Spirit has caused the evil spirit to move off.

Prior to our working in *Truth Encounters* we would cast out demons. Some people would report a measure of improvement, and others would be back in the same condition a week later. The problem was that we drove the rats away but didn't clean up the rubbish, being the negative beliefs causing the brokenness, pain or anxiety.

I am often in churches where the ministers proclaim that God is going to move and heal everyone's hurts and issues in the service. I have not yet seen this happen, although God can do absolutely anything so it is possible. The only predictable way that I have ever seen God completely freeing people from heart-based beliefs is through some kind of *Truth Encounter*.

Healed of Anorexia Nervosa
A number of years ago I was attending a healing meeting and I saw a man there with his wife and daughter whom I had seen in other healing meetings in another state. He also recognized me so we were chatting together. As we went along, he reported that he was there because his daughter had anorexia nervosa and had been hospitalized in a critical condition, as I recall more than once. I could see the desperation in his eyes and encouraged him to have faith and expect a breakthrough. I realized that he had brought her to a number of healing meetings with no result in the past.

My experience told me that people may get some partial help through deliverance in a prayer line, but that usually they are freed by dealing with the beliefs. Feeling that I should offer some help, I hesitantly said something along the lines of: *This is an excellent ministry, so there is every chance for her healing this weekend! But, if you don't get the breakthroughs that you are looking for, we see God bringing healing to these kinds of complaints in other ways.* And I gave him my card.

A month or two later I received an email reporting that she had been in hospital again and could we help. When we were near their town we dropped in and did a session with their daughter at their local church. We then headed off to minister somewhere else and heard nothing further. A year or so later we were in a meeting in their state and after the service the glowing mother came up to me and reported that from the time of her session, the daughter had simply improved and put on weight returning to health.

God can do anything, but personally I have not seen complete emotional healing in a normal prayer line. We do at times minister a *Truth encounter* in prayer lines but only on rare occasions, or if it has just been taught and people are aware of the source of their issues.

Important Note:
I never think about evil spirits when I am ministering in a *Truth Encounter*. I am focused purely on finding the beliefs. If there is one present, and you understand demonic dynamics, you will become aware that it is involved. Don't go looking for spirits. Most times with *Truth Encounters*, if there is a spirit implicated it will leave when the beliefs are resolved and you may not even be aware that there was one actively working [2]. This is because the spirit is usually involved in the sinful responses or reactions to the hurtful belief. Once the hurt is resolved they no longer need or want to respond in this way. So, you can see that the spirit has a hold because of their wilful cooperation. In a very practical way, the truth has made them free.

Examples of this could be issues such as; bitterness, unforgiveness, rebellion, pride, self-pity, anger, control, fear and so on. Most of the time these issues are present without any obvious demonic stronghold or amplification. Both you and the person being ministered to may never even become aware of the demonic presence that was possibly involved at some level. For more information on spiritual issues see section 3 on dealing with demonic influences.

---

[2] The depth of the pain can also have a bearing on the strength of a spirit and its power and influence in the host person.

CHAPTER 15
Memory

Most of the time we are helping people, and indeed the majority of their problems, are going to be found in beliefs learnt or interpreted as conclusions about their identity or the situation found in their memories. We will therefore examine how these beliefs may be deposited in the heart.

Some people question whether or not accessing memory in a ministry setting is a valid activity. If I asked most people what John 3:16 says, they would quickly respond; 'God so loved the World....' How do they know this? They remember it. How to find your way home, sit on a chair, speak, or do anything at all, is based on learning and remembering. Memory is therefore related to every single action that we perform, including breathing.

Some people put up questions such as why do we have to look back? They quote the Apostle Paul, who urges us to forget the things which are behind. In the following passage and its preceding verses, you will see that he is not talking about ignoring life-shaping memories. He is in fact talking about forgetting his achievements as a Pharisee which he now counts as *rubbish*.

Philippians 3:13-14, *"[13] Brethren, I do not count myself to have apprehended; but one thing I do, forgetting those things which are behind and reaching forward to those things which are ahead. [14] I press toward the goal for the prize of the upward call of God in Christ Jesus"* (NKJV).

Others comment that you shouldn't spend your whole life looking into the past. I agree that we should be moving on and working for the Gospel. But we also set aside specific times where we deliberately deal with issues from our past. I recently heard a comparison between a rowing boat and a canoe or Kayak race. In a rowing boat you are moving forward but looking back all the time. Whereas, in a canoe or Kayak you are looking at where you are going and moving forward. On occasions, however, even in a Kayak it is good to look back and see if anything from behind needs to be considered and dealt with. Checking what is going on behind out of sight that might affect the outcome of your race?

In terms of negative beliefs and emotions, it is a critical part of the healing process. The initial memory where a belief is taken in, is the place with the most detail for accurately examining and identifying the conclusion and consequent belief from the circumstances taken to heart.

It is good to note that memory does not simply relate to the past, it also has implications for the future. For example, if someone has had an event where they were perhaps publicly embarrassed, they will now be on the lookout for potential places or situations where this could happen again. This will then be a source of low-grade anxiety and will often be present in gatherings. The long-term effects of this will have an outworking in the physical body as being the end of the line for the sub-surface thought.

The scientists tell us that a small almond shaped section of nervous tissue in the brain named the *Amygdala* is responsible for memory and emotions. It is considered by some to be the fear centre. When something significant such as embarrassment occurs, the Amygdala is activated, and its response could be something such as; *That wasn't good; I better make a good memory of that so that I can make sure that it doesn't happen again!* From the initial event, memory projects the new belief about possible repeat situations out into the future to try to prevent a repeat occurrence.

All fears or responses to particular stressors have their beginnings in memory of some kind. The possible exception to this may be a fear that has passed through the generation line.

Critical events
The first time that we do anything is a significant moment in terms of encoding information about how we perceive that activity. Our early impressions of how we perform in areas such as the school environment for example, are a common place of memory where people arrive in a session. How our parents and teachers regarded and assessed our efforts will affect the way in which we view our person and ability to perform and meet requirements. We could perhaps be compared to a sibling who is academically interested

and gifted and come away with some kind of inferiority belief or low self-image. Typically, these would be unconscious inner thoughts such as; *I am not as good as others. I'm dumb, a loser, useless, not like other people, a failure*, etc. etc.

This certainly has impact when we are deciding about our identity as a child, and while our brain is plastic and impressionable. Later in life we will use those beliefs to interpret other critical first-time events such as sexuality. Usually if the initial experience is not positive, they will see those activities through the filter of their existing self-image beliefs, having already learnt that they are *inferior or cannot perform as others can*. They will use these pre-existing beliefs to reach a conclusion about whether or not the activity is positive and reinforcing or yet another place for anxiety.

Note:
In much the same way as parents and teachers should remove pressure and help a child see their academic endeavours in a positive light, the church should help their newly-weds with realistic expectations to help them to qualify their performance in the learning process of areas such as sexuality and relationships. This would hold true for other significant first-time events such as speaking or sharing in a Church service.

Traumas and Episodes
A number of years ago we were conducting our healing school and a Chinese lady came into the session with her husband. All the way through the teaching she would cough every few seconds, not being deliberately disruptive, just unable to prevent it. The next day she made an appointment to be on the ministry list to receive some help. As we interviewed her it came to light that she had been in an accident crushing her chest, and this was the beginning point for her coughing. She was a very brave lady and connected with the fear belief proceeding from the trauma, which was as I recall; *I am going to die.*

As she remembered the event and connected with the belief and feeling, we invited the Lord to bring His truth. In this instance, because she was connected with the event, a spirit of fear of death was exposed and manifested, and then came out. At the same time God communicated to her regarding the trauma belief. She was free and sat quietly throughout the day, finally testifying to her healing in the evening service. She was healed and freed from some other problems, and as a result, was so pleased that she translated all of the considerable amount of school notes into Chinese for use in her own nation.

Notes:
1. It is unlikely that if we had gone after the spirit of fear that we would have had the same success in seeing her set free from it. Identifying and feeling the belief which the spirit rode in on at the point of weakness exposed it, and brought it into the open with nowhere to hide. Dealing with the belief closed the emotional breach that gave it place.

2. We are not hunting for demons, even in traumatic situations, we are looking for the beliefs encoded as that is where the problem really lies. If there is some evidence of demonic replay, stronghold or amplification then simply tell it to go. I usually do this while I have the person focus on the beliefs producing the feelings. This way the spirit is exposed. The same can be applied to dealing with areas such as lust problems. Being exposed to pornography for example can be a type of trauma which is deeply encoded in the memories. If there is a lustful spirit there then having the person think the thoughts from the trauma can in some cases cause the demon to be brought to the surface because you have connected with that which it holds!

3. Let me reiterate here, don't go looking for demons, but be aware that they may be present particularly in regards to trauma. Most *Truth Encounters* you will not even give demons a thought. (More on Spiritual dynamics in Section three).

Episodes

By *episodes*, I am referring to individual events where beliefs were the conclusions arrived at in that critical moment. For example, sexual or physical abuse which are usually extremely traumatic in nature. Your parents, forgetting to pick you up for school, might be a one-time episode where you conclude that you're *not important, and really don't matter*. But it may not be traumatic, because even though you are feeling hurt because of the omission, you are having a great time with the other kids in the playground.

Sexual abuse

To be abused sexually is a traumatic episode which can affect many areas of the personality. From the damage and brokenness involved, there emanates rejection, fear, confusion, degradation and low self-image. This is a significant area, when you consider that indications in the western world are that, as many as minimally fifty percent of women have had some form of inappropriate sexual behaviour acted out on them. This could range from being touched by a friend of the family or relative right through to penetrative sex with a small child. Having ministered to a great many of these victims, I can offer hope that God will faithfully set you free. I also offer a list of possible beliefs that are commonly present with people who have been offended against in this way.

Inferiority

I am dirty, unclean, not like other people, ruined, a nothing, and I'm bad.

Confusion

I am overwhelmed, and don't know or understand what is happening.

Guilt

Somehow this is my fault. I have done this. At times children will get attention, value and importance, at a neighbours' house when they have been receiving none at home. This may include sexual behaviour. The guilt is too much to bear because they know that at some level that they wanted to be there. On occasions I have ministered to people who have felt guilty because they have felt physical pleasure in the act. Nerve endings are nerve endings; they do not discriminate between whether an event is appropriate or not, they simply report sensations. So, if they felt pleasure then it was not their fault either, but this is something that they need perspective from the Lord on. More often abused people would report pain.

Fear

This can be in the form of being overwhelmed physically and emotionally and not understanding what is happening. Beliefs such as; *I cannot cope, it is too much to bear, I am trapped, overpowered, there is nobody here to protect me,* may also be present. Further, fear from threats from the perpetrator over being harmed if they tell anyone, or being afraid to tell parents because it is a relative or even that they expect punishment from their harsh family may also be present.

If the abuse continues, with subsequent events, usually these later times are interpreted through whatever beliefs are already held from the initial episode. This could be the person believing that it is happening again because; they are bad, dirty, naughty or some other belief that *they* already hold as being true about themselves.

Some of the sad outcomes from sexual abuse are that once a person has concluded at heart level that they are bad or dirty, then why even try to be good; after all they are ruined and spoilt anyway. The result of this kind of inner dialogue can be a promiscuous lifestyle. Perhaps they have learnt that sexual acts give you favour, *love* or acceptance from men.

The exact opposite of promiscuity is the issue that you most commonly deal with, and that is sexual dysfunction. The act of sex by association connects you with all of the fears, feelings of sex as being dirty, guilt and defilement. Enjoyment and participation of sex is no longer an option for you. This can be a great barrier to having a wholesome, complete and intimate relationship with your spouse. Sadly, in this age a high percentage of males have also been abused.

I ministered to a man some time ago who reported that before he and his wife were married, they had had a very active sex life. (I am not making comments on the appropriateness of this behaviour here). After they were married, she shut down and the sex life that they had enjoyed ended. Once I had ascertained that she had been abused as a child, I explained to him that most probably before they were married, she felt as though she was in control and could walk away at any time. After they were married, she would have unconsciously been feeling as though she didn't have a choice any more, wasn't in control, and now she had to have sex. Possibly she also felt that she was trapped and couldn't get away. These were all unconscious thoughts that she had learnt in the abusive episode. Unintentionally her inner beliefs were now being triggered and her emotional priorities dictated her behaviour. Whatever the inner thinking, God has a greater truth to set you free.

Repetitive themes

God Himself encouraged repetition as a means of making our beliefs permanent memory, or our *default position*. For example, we recall Joshua being told five times to be strong and courageous. In other words, meditate on your responses until they are an automatic neural pathway. God is saying here that you need to set up a *shortcut* to how to react when you are under attack. Then, you no longer need to think it through, it is already decided who you are and how you are and for that matter how God views you. Repetitive themes from childhood, when our brains are *plastic*, malleable, and particularly impressionable, become long term beliefs that we hold.

Deuteronomy 6: 6-9, "*6 And these words which I command you today shall be in your heart." 7 "You shall teach them diligently to your children, and shall talk of them when you sit in your house, when you walk by the way, when you lie down, and when you rise up." 8 "You shall bind them as a sign on your hand, and they shall be as frontlets between your eyes." 9 "You shall write them on the doorposts of your house and on your gates"* (NKJV, Emphasis mine).

God is instructing Israel to have repetitive exposure to His commands so that they become heart beliefs and permanent pathways. Someone once said to me; *isn't filling up with scripture like brainwashing!?* I am not sure about you but by the time I began walking seriously with the Lord my brains needed washing! In any case I would also like to highlight from the passage, the command to *diligently* teach them to the children. God the creator of our beings knew how important it is for our children to receive His word in that critical time of plasticity when we are deciding about life. Prevention, and being able to walk with God minimizing areas of serving the enemy, leaves us less open to being hurt, and in a much better place to be fruitful. However, even if we are incorrectly programmed God is always holding out His hand offering healing and help.

Repetition in Modern life

For many people the very important pre-adolescent time is a period where they are being told or shown that nothing that they are doing is good enough. We have educational systems which cater for people whose minds think along particular lines. Most likely, very similar to the academics and educators who prepared the system. History is littered with billionaires, inventors, entrepreneurs and successful people who did not function well at, or even complete, school.

For many people, school for example, is a place where they can be repeatedly confronted with learning that they are second rate or inferior. Families that have high demands on performance or perfection and don't offer love, encouragement and acceptance are environments of repetitive reinforcement of this inadequacy. I remember my son when he was first learning to ride a bike. He wobbled around the front yard taking out the new tree that my wife had planted. He then disappeared down the sideway from where an enormous crash emanated. When I went around to find out if he was alright, he had ridden into the BBQ knocking it into the tin shed. He made some kind of statement such as; *I can't do it, I suck! My response to him was something along the lines of; you're doing great, it took me more goes than that to get as far as you did! Really?* he said looking encouraged. What just happened? I guarded his heart by helping him interpret the situation in a positive light.

Note:
Before you feel that you have failed on your own parenting journey, I was not always so impressive with my parenting skills; we all have to learn.

The point is that if we are always encouraging, always finding the positives, then we are keeping their heart self-beliefs in God's order. As the Apostle Paul put it:

2 Corinthians 10:8, "... *for even if I boast somewhat freely about the authority the Lord gave us for building you up rather than pulling you down, I will not be ashamed of it ...*" (NIV, Emphasis mine).

Many people have only ever experienced criticism and disapproval, being programmed over and over again with their shortcomings and failings. Those who are around my age or older grew up in *the little children should be seen and not heard* generation. The implication of this statement is that you are some kind of second-class citizen as a child, not significant, valuable or important. And that is exactly what a great many people believe inside, that they simply don't matter, or that they are a nuisance, in the way, unacceptable or feel as though they are *a nothing*. Those who were meant to be guarding their hearts were unwittingly programming them through repetitive reinforcement that in some way they are not good enough.

In defence of all parents I would like to add that most fathers and mothers love their children. They would not deliberately hurt their families and would certainly have done things differently if they understood the ramifications. In some measure the church is responsible for having failed to teach its members how to protect their children in this vital area. In any case, most are likely parenting out of that which they received themselves, and the modelling that has passed through the generation lines.

Today, most children receive their training from media, much of which is run by people from the *children should be seen and not heard* generation and is slanted towards *my rights* generation which is a knee jerk reaction to being made to feel second rate. It is not too surprising to see this response from children of that era, leading to giving children full rights and decision-making authority long before they have the knowledge and wisdom to cope with running their own lives.

Possibly, an inner decision to not put that inferiority onto their children came as a result. Consequently, many modern children grow up under the belief that they are special. They are special to God, but in life they are no more special than anyone else, and when they grow up it is often a shock for them to find this out. We, as the Church have to take responsibility for equipping our people in how to Biblically train our children and bring them up in the counsel of the Lord.

Upgrade information
We don't want to confuse the healing of our heart beliefs with the renewing of our minds. There are many things that we learn through life that are not deeply recorded. We are talking here about areas such as identity beliefs. This is for God to free us from. But if we simply have wrong beliefs about how to do life then receiving improved information will renew our minds.

Let me say here that most of the changes in how we live and see things come to us through reading our Bibles or hearing the word taught. If this were not so, then why would we even bother to preach and teach. All that we are talking about here relates to areas and issues that we cannot overcome through better information. If we read in the Bible that we should build each other up and not judge each other, we might think; *well that is a better way of living than that which I am doing now!* And having made the decision we become a hearer and doer of the Word.

There is a great old story of a lady who was cooking a roast. Her friend was watching her and asked her; *why do you cut the roast in half before you put it in the oven?* The lady replied; *I actually don't know, my mother always did it that way so I will have to ask her!* When the question was presented to the mother her response was; *Oh, I only have a small oven, so I have to cut it in half, but you have a big oven and that is not necessary for you!*

The lady just received better information on how to do life. To keep this ministry in balance and perspective, there is still a preeminent place for Biblical advice (Counselling) and Bible teaching. In fact, on many occasions as we go along with the healing ministry there is a concurrent thread of teaching running through the sessions. I have unfortunately known of people who become proficient in the *Truth Encounters* ministry who have, as a result, felt that they are qualified to give advice on, for example, relationships. Some of them do not have sound Biblical knowledge and consequently their own relationships are not in order. This is something that Pastors who allow groups to minister under the covering of their church may need to take note of. Beware that a person who is equipped and now helping and seeing people set free is not going beyond the guidelines that you allow for the ministry.

CHAPTER 16
Types of Beliefs

Other ministries use different names for identifying types of beliefs. Over 20 years of working in this area we have found that they commonly fall into one of the following categories. It helps to know what type of belief you are dealing with because you then understand the kind of circumstances in a memory that you are looking for.

Identity beliefs – about self

Identity beliefs relate to that which you perceive about who you are and how you are. Rather than a lengthy discourse let me suggest some common beliefs reflecting how one's identity is seen:

"I'm not loveable, I'm unacceptable, not enough, less than others, stupid, a nothing, dumb, ugly, a failure, a loser, useless, weak, I don't matter, am not important" and so on. Notice that they are all beliefs relating to your identity, about 'self'.

These types of *heart* beliefs are at the root of many anxieties. Unconsciously you are worried about people discovering your shortcomings or reinforcing them. When I am preparing people for ministry, I often explain identity beliefs to people using a story which I have constructed but is based on stories that I have heard over and over again.

Sample story

Imagine someone who has come to you is reporting how much anxiety they are going through. How I would deal with it may run something like this;

Fred: I have a terrible problem with anxiety.
Me: Can you give me an example of how it affects you?
Fred: I was at work the other day and heard the main door behind me open; I had an anxiety attack and reached for my pills.
Me: If you stop and think about the situation for a moment, what was it that you were worried about when you heard the door open?"

Fred: Thoughtful pause; Mmmmmm...I was nervous that it may have been the boss.

Me: And if it was, what are you worried about happening?

Fred: He may have come over and looked at my work!

Me: And if he did, what do you think could happen?

Fred: He might tell me that it was no good.

Me: I am sure that that is not a good feeling. I want you to close your eyes and feel what it is like for him to tell you that your work is not good enough and let your mind connect you with other historical places where you have felt just like that.

Fred: Pause; I have just remembered that when I was in kindergarten, I was doing a painting with some other kids and the teacher was coming along looking at everyone's work. The first person was Mary and the teacher said that Mary's painting was so creative, and then Johnnie's was so neat and all in the lines. When she saw mine, she said, it was the biggest unrecognizable mess that she had ever seen in her life!

Me: As you look at that criticism and rejection, I want you to look for the conclusion and belief about yourself that you came to.

Fred: With some emotion; I'm useless, not as good as others.

Me: Let's ask the Lord what He considers to be true about you being useless and inferior. Just concentrate on those beliefs and feelings and listen.

Fred: Pause; He said, why would He have called and chosen me if I was useless. He said that all of His children are created equal, they have different gifts but none are better than another. I have just remembered that I was the best reader in the group!

Me: So how do you feel about people discovering that you are useless and not as good as them now?

Fred: Honestly, I feel that I am fine just as I am. And I am just the same as everyone else, the same only different, different in a good way, unique!

Identity beliefs also have a bearing on our relationships and how we respond, react to, and deal with others. They also reflect on how we relate to ourselves, and ultimately God. Truly, *as a man thinks in his heart, so is he*, in terms of how he reacts to others, and also how he sees himself.

Proverbs 23:7, *"For as he thinks in his heart, so is he"* (NKJV).

Let us propose that a person thinks that they are not good enough because they do not do things well enough. By now we know that this is a belief that was learnt in an event earlier in life. As a result, if that person feels, whether it is true or just a perception, that you are criticizing something that they are doing then you can expect some kind of angry response. They are angry at you for making them feel that which they already unconsciously believe, but they are also angry at themselves for not being able to do things well enough. Whenever negative emotions are present, they may be directed outwardly as a reaction, but they also exist inwardly connected to an area of hurt as well. So, this person might struggle to forgive you for how you are making them feel, but they probably haven't any forgiveness for themselves either for being the person who you can find fault with, because of their perceived imperfections and shortcomings.

This will also reflect in your relationship to God. You will be a double minded man. In your human spirit, which is now one with the Holy Spirit, you know that you are loved and accepted. But in your heart, you believe that you are not good enough because you cannot do things well enough. Therefore, how could God consider you as good enough, when you don't believe that you are yourself at heart level!

James 1:6, *"But let him ask in faith, with no doubting, for he who doubts is like a wave of the sea driven and tossed by the wind. 7 For let not that man suppose that he will receive anything from the Lord; 8 he is a double-minded man, unstable in all his ways"* (NKJV).

Sometimes we believe in God's goodness mentally, but the lack of faith in our hearts is because of our doubts about our worthiness to receive. Jesus pointed out that we can have whatever we believe in our hearts, not our heads. So, for faith to flow we have to believe that God is greater than our hearts. We need to receive His truth about our value and worth.

Mark 11:22-23, *"²²So Jesus answered and said to them, "Have faith in God." ²³"For assuredly, I say to you, whoever says to this mountain, 'Be removed and be cast into the sea,' and does not doubt in his heart, but believes that those things he says will be done, he will have whatever he says"* (NKJV, Emphasis mine).

We had not been involved in this ministry all that long, when one day I noticed my wife getting a bit agitated as I was wiping down the kitchen bench. I commented to her that I could see that me doing this was making her angry. After a short time, we identified that to her it seemed as if I was implying that she was not doing a good enough job, that she was an untidy person. After a short period of ministry into the memory where she had first learned this, and truth from the Lord, her whole attitude changed. Now instead of being upset, she felt it could be a good idea while I was helping to sweep the floor and put out the rubbish as well.

Situational beliefs

As the name suggests, these are beliefs which have come out of a situation and may or may not relate to your identity. Phobic beliefs fall under this category. An example of this type of belief might be something such as having panic attacks in small spaces where you feel captive, such as an elevator. As you focus on the feeling you might, for example, identify that the anxiety about small spaces might be that you will not be able to breath. As your mind does a data match with other places holding those feelings you remember as a small boy playing football at school. You managed to get hold of the ball and five or six boys jumped on you and held you down. In that moment you were crushed, trapped and struggled to breathe. As you focus on the situation, we ask you what will happen if you can't get away and breathe. The response is; "I can't breathe, I am going to die!"

There is nothing here relating to identity, it is all to do with the situation. As we have the person embrace the fear feeling and the belief that they are trapped, can't get away, and are going to die because they cannot breathe, we ask God for His truth. Which could simply be words, or a realization that they did not die, or some other communication that sets them free?

Story

Some time ago I was waiting with our lady bank manager in her office for some other staff to come in to work out a financial proposition that we were putting together for a church development. While we were waiting, we were casually chatting and she made the comment; *I see that you travel overseas quite a lot*. I affirmed her statement, and she went on to say that she would love to be able to travel but she has a fear of flying. I said to her that our ministry experience is that often when people are afraid to fly that it usually began with a traumatic memory along the lines of perhaps a child being in a swimming pool and getting out over their heads. They can no longer touch the sides and they cannot swim. They feel like they are out of control and are going to die. When they go on an airplane their mind automatically makes the connection. *You are not in control, can't touch the bottom, there is nothing solid beneath you and therefore you could die!*

She looked at me in amazement and said; *I just remembered when I was a small girl, I lived in the country and was in the local swimming pool. I went out too far into the deep end and thought that I was going to die!*

The point is, it is a belief from a situation, nothing to do with identity. These are just simple terms we use to differentiate between types of beliefs. Incidentally, there can be many other situations that can produce a fear of flying. I recently encountered a lady with three different reasons from three individual memories that caused her to be afraid of flying.

A few years ago, my wife ministered to a lady who had a fear of flying. Her husband was very frustrated because they were getting older and he was eager to go adventuring. She received ministry for this fear and some other issues and then they went home. We did not see them again for a number of years, but eventually we ran across them again. I remembered her fear of flying and enquired about how she was going with it. She responded excitedly that they had now been around the world several times.

Objection beliefs
These are beliefs where for some reason there is an objection held that stops the person from proceeding to the memory or receiving from the Lord. An example of this could be something as simple as somebody believing that they are doing the wrong thing if they allow the possibility that their parents were anything less than perfect. Before they will go to places where, perhaps their identity was damaged, you will need to find out and deal with why they think that being real about their parents is doing the wrong thing. You are not seeking to dishonour them, rather find the source of your own problems.

At other times people will come into a session and you can observe that they are very tense. Sometimes I will simply suggest something along the lines of; *do you believe that you won't be able to do this ministry?* or *Are you afraid that I will be disappointed if you cannot do this?* They often look a bit surprised but respond with a ready; *Yes! How did you know?*

We need to deal with the fear of failure memory first. This may be a place where they may have disappointed someone by not being able to do what was expected, or perhaps a place where everyone else could achieve and they could not, or something similar.

I recall one man being hesitant to let himself connect with his memory. I asked him what he believed that made him object to seeing the content of his historical event. He reported that he was afraid. I requested that he focus on the fear and identify and clarify exactly what it was that produced the anxiety. He told me that he was afraid that he would be out of control, which was clearly to do with what was going on in the memory. I asked him to focus on the belief and invited the Lord to bring His perspective. The man sat quietly for a moment and then opened his eyes and looked up at the same time making the statement; *I **am** out of control!*

This communication from the Lord meant something to the man in his inner parts. It was good truth as we all have very limited control over the World we live in, even the actions of those close to us. We never really know if an aircraft is about to come through our roof or the stock market may have just crashed and we have missed the news! The truth is that we are all largely not in control, but God is, and He is able to protect us. This resolved the resistance issue and the man proceeded into his memory for freedom.

Perhaps a final story in order to illustrate another way that *objection beliefs* may present and impact the ministry time. First, I note that you do not need to look for these; you will simply observe that they are present. And secondly, you will not run across them in every session, they will be involved occasionally.

Objections to letting God speak to you
Periodically you will encounter people who hold beliefs that prevent them from receiving from God. These could be simple thoughts such as; *I'm not worth His time, of course He will free others, but He*

doesn't care about me, and everyone else can do it, (hear from God) but I won't be able to!

These beliefs have been learnt in specific memories that are best dealt with first. You may recognize that there is some kind of blockage to them hearing from God, and this is probably the main cause. Still other people hold beliefs that God does not interact with people today, or at times we run across those who have been trained in another ministry model and refuse to listen for God's voice because; *this is not the way we do it!*

Story
A number of years ago, we were ministering to an attractive young lady who was needlessly jealous of other women. She was successfully ministered to and received freedom in other areas but her jealousy problem remained. It caused major problems in her relationship with her fiancée who could not even watch the news on television because there might be a pretty weather girl. If there was a magazine around with a girl on the cover it was quickly put away. If they were at church, he was watched constantly in case he looked at another girl. If she even thought that he may have noticed another girl, real or imagined she flew into a rage. As a perceived solution to her jealousy she had become very controlling in her relationship.

We identified the source as being a time where, as a small girl of around 3 or 4 years old, the family would receive visits from a friend who was a handsome young man. He would fool around playfully with the little girl and gave her attention which made her feel special and loved. She concluded that this special affection and attention was only for her. One day the young man brought his girlfriend along with him. The family had known that he had a girlfriend but the little girl did not. For her, this was an intensely traumatic moment. She was devastated that someone else clearly had a greater measure of the attention and affection of the young man. She was overcome with jealousy. We could summarize jealousy as; *you have what I would like to have.* She also felt incredibly inferior. Here was a mature adult girl with modern clothes and a fully-grown shapely figure. She concluded along the lines that, she was; *Not enough, and could not be what she needed to be. The other girls were better.*

Later, as an attractive adult woman herself, this thinking was unreasonable. She continued to fear losing her male partner and to be jealous of other girls who could take him away because, unconsciously in her heart, she was afraid that he would see another girl who was more, and prefer her. This for her was a logical inner conclusion which matched her historical event. Having identified and confirmed these beliefs with her we invited God to communicate the truth to her to set her free.

In other things that we had dealt with her she had no problem in hearing from God and receiving her healing, but this was different. So up to this point we can see that she didn't have an issue with going to the original memory or accepting her beliefs. Now, however, she held an *objection* to having God speak to her and receive freedom from her jealousy and resultant ungodly control.

We eventually worked out that she believed that if she let go of the control through healing, then her fiancée would go ahead and prefer another girl. So, for her, the jealousy was tied in with what she perceived to be true, and control over the situation that she was insecure about, was her solution to the problem. She simply did not want to be free because she felt that staying in control was going to protect her from losing her man. Sometime later when she realized that she would lose her man anyway because of her jealousy and control, she committed her will to the process. She then received truth about her beliefs and was delivered of the spirit holding the jealousy and controlling behaviour.

I want to point out that the spirit was not the problem, her will was the issue. The spirit had come in on the sins of jealousy and control, beginning with the emotional breach that was created with the shock of discovering the adult girlfriend. She was deceived unwittingly into believing that controlling her male boyfriends was the solution to the perceived situation. This opened her to cooperating and participating with a sinful attitude inspired by an unholy spirit.

As long as she believed that the control served a purpose for her, the spirit had ground to magnify, amplify and hold her bound. As the spirit worked through her it also held the fiancée in bondage, not being free to relate with females in a normal way or even watch television. Simply trying to cast out the spirit without identifying the belief that gave it place is normally a fruitless exercise. In a sense she held the spirit to herself believing that it was serving a purpose for her. Of course, she was unaware of the spiritual element of what was happening. Once she permitted herself to be freed of the beliefs behind the jealousy there was no need for the *protection* afforded by the controlling attitudes.

The same is true with deliverance from all sin-based issues. Until you are wilfully convinced that you need to fall out of agreement with the sin, then you will most probably stay in bondage. It is vitally important therefore, to understand that genuine repentance is the basis of deliverance. Repentance in the Greek language means; *change your thinking, reconsider your ways.* Often, we are unwilling or unable to do that until we discover what it actually is that we are thinking in the heart that puts us in a place of harbouring or hosting ungodly actions that give place to the devil. Hence, this is one application of the verse; *you shall know the truth and the truth shall make you free.*

2 Timothy 2:25, *"In meekness instructing those **that oppose themselves**; if God perhaps will **give them repentance** to the acknowledging of the truth, 26 And that they may recover themselves out of the snare of the devil, who are taken captive by him at his will"* (KJV, Emphasis mine).

Note:
The word of God teaches us what sin is so that we will know what manner or type of spirit we are cooperating with.

Luke 9:55, *"But He turned and rebuked them, and said, "You do not know what manner of spirit you are of"* (NKJV).

Note:
Not all controlling behaviour or jealousy has a spirit resident inside the person. It is still cooperating with an unholy spiritual influence even if it is weaker and from outside the host person.

However, if as in this case there is a blockage, or there is an unusually strong resistance to ministry, you may find that a spirit on the inside is the cause. It is more attached to the responses or solutions to the hurt rather than the pain itself. Chasing the spirit will not bring the freedom; dealing with the hurt that produces the need for the ungodly reactions and activities, which sometimes opens the door to an evil spirit, is the most important focus. Once the truth is received, freeing the person from the troubling belief, then the spirit may manifest, or simply leave once the reason for its presence, is removed.

Going to the deep place where the belief resides

This ministry can be carried out anywhere and at any time. For the best possible results, I find that a quiet room, in preferably a one on one situation affords the person receiving ministry the best possible opportunity to concentrate without distraction. I do remember situations such as ministering to a man who was suicidal on the side of a very busy street. There were noisy cars and motorbikes' roaring past, but the man seemed to be unaffected, and to my amazement, was able to focus on the source of his pain and receive his freedom.

Normally we try to have a quiet room. Having heard their story and made a few notes about areas that may need ministry I encourage them to go to what I call, *periscope depth*. In other words, close their eyes, shut out the outer world and concentrate on the inner deeper place of the heart.

Beliefs, feelings and memories

At times, as you hear the story and the presenting problems, you will note statements that reflect inner beliefs. At other times, some emotion will come up, but it does not seem to be at that time connected to the belief. I liken this to those multi story concrete car parks that are in many cities today. Each level has a number which is usually painted on the various doors to the stairs and exits on that level. It is almost as if, from this door over here, you hear a belief statement that does not hold feelings. But from another door over there proceeds some emotion. They do not seem to be connected here on level 5, but as you ask questions and embrace the thoughts and feelings eventually you end up in the basement, at the initial memory where the first-time belief was taken to heart. So, the basement holds the circumstances in the memory which produced the conclusion, which became a permanent belief that produces and matches the emotions.

Secondary memories holding the same beliefs

Often people will not go directly to the first memory where the belief was interpreted and encoded. For example, someone who believes that they are not as good as other people may have memories later in life or even recently that seemed to confirm this thinking. This could be a marriage break up or failure to perform in secondary school. You could be stopping off here to connect more intensely with the emotions or to refine the belief. Ultimately, as we have previously stated, their identity beliefs will have begun before the age of 10 years old.

For many years, we fostered both long term and short-term children, so we can confirm from experience that what both the Bible and science say about this being the critical formative age is true. Into your family come children who are *pre-packaged* with their inner thinking about themselves and life. The same can be said about everyone who walks through the door of your church. *Something happened* that they most likely didn't ask for; they are clothed by life. Our mission is to be equipped to help them, offering God's answers and provision.

Very commonly, the beginning point for a ministry session is the report of the subject, having been triggered in a relationship or particular situation. In the event that the emotion from the belief is strong in the current relationship, but not so strong in the initial memory, you can have the person switch backwards and forwards from the strong feelings from the present time to the event held in memory state. This will help to identify and accept the accuracy of the thoughts and feelings from the source.

Interpreting other people's lives through our own beliefs

We have already highlighted that our lives, behaviour and responses are shaped by what we believe in our heart. It also affects how we perceive the situations of other people, and indeed how we see life.

Proverbs 4:23, *"Above all else, guard your heart, for it affects everything you do"* (NLT, Emphasis mine).

A person who grew up in poverty will be able to empathize with poorer people in the World. A Pastor who grew up being treated as though he was not important or significant, will not let anyone out of the door on Sunday, until they have been greeted and made to feel that they are valuable.

What we believe about ourselves and life is projected onto others even if they do not hold the same beliefs. We expect that they would feel the same as us. Someone who grew up with injustice will consider it vital to stand up for those who are oppressed.

On a number of occasions, I have had mothers come to me in a very distraught condition because their daughters are going through a marriage break up. When I suggest that these situations are probably stirring up beliefs within them, I usually receive a response along the lines of; *shouldn't a mother be feeling this for their child?* Yes, they should, but I encourage them to take the opportunity to investigate and see if any of the feelings that are present are connected to their own experiences. Usually once we have worked through all of the emotions that the situation has provoked in them, they are only left with a mental sympathy for their child's circumstances. In other words, *all* the feelings that they were experiencing were tied to interpreting what their daughters should be going through by their own inner beliefs. The daughters probably have their own historically based reactions to the situation.

Common beliefs, different personalities
After a period of time doing this ministry, you begin to find repetitively that there are some very common beliefs that you deal with over and over again. What does change is the differing personalities of the people that you are working with. Some people are very emotional while others have little emotion and are largely cognitively mind-based people.

I have seen at times that some *brands* of inner healing seem to think that if you cry you are being touched by the Holy Spirit and being healed. In much the same manner people can think that a person crying in the church service is being healed by the Holy Spirit. That is possible, but I think that most times the presence of the Spirit may be softening emotions. We tend to bless the emotion and pray something such as; *more Lord, bless them more, heal them Lord.* If we asked them a few questions we may find that, for example, it was that song about the Father that moved them, because their father left when they were a child, or something similar.

The key to the healing is identifying the belief, not the degree of the emotion. Someone who experiences feelings intensely may struggle with emotions daily. A more stoic person may simply get on with life but have issues, such as anxiety, or belief-based behaviour such as the need to succeed, be regarded, or be right. The emotional person may have a dramatic time in the ministry session and express a great sense of relief and freedom.

The more cognitive person may only feel enough to identify and resolve the belief. They may not report much more than that the belief no longer feels true. Just because they lack the euphoria does not mean that they are not free. They are more likely to experience what has happened in terms of how they see life, their sense of peace and wellbeing, and notice that old responses and reactions have disappeared when certain stressors are present.

Ways in which we remember

1. *Emotionally:*
Fear, anxiety, rejection, grief, unworthiness etc. We access memory by connecting with the initial places that hold these feelings.

2. *Pictures:*
Memory events from very early life may just be a vague impression rather than a clear picture. Some people have incredibly vivid memories with amazing recall of detail. This can relate to the level of trauma and corresponding strength of the picture. Some people can have memory pictures that are not connected to emotions. They may have pushed the emotions down because they are too frightening or painful to look at.

One lady I was working with told me the story of having to get her own birthday cake as a child because her birthday had been forgotten. She was laughing about it as though it were a funny story. The emotions did not match the situation. She should have been feeling hurt and sad. It is necessary to accept the true feelings in the memory to identify that which you have believed.

3. *The body:*
(Somatic) headache, stress, breathing, tension, stress, muscles, nausea, aches and pains, etc. Have you ever had that sick, dread

feeling in the pit of your stomach? This is a probably body memory connecting you to a belief learnt in a previous situation. In a ministry setting you would have the person focus on this feeling and look for other places where they may have felt the same.

4. Senses:
Smells, sounds, taste, and touch etc. A commonly used example of this is music from your past which may make you feel happy or sad. The song is associated with a time in your life which may have been positive or negative. It may relate to bringing you to a visual event that contains something significant. Some people do not like to be touched or hugged. It connects them to times where touch may have meant something negative. You can have them focus on the thought of being touched and this will often bring a memory to them which contained these feelings.

5. Words:
Some phrases or unkind nicknames may be joined to unpleasant memories that are to do with the shaping of heart beliefs.

Sample questions
As you begin to work in this ministry, or even examine your own thoughts, you will find that there are only a certain number of questions available to use and I suggest some here. You can of course be creative and come up with your own.
"What will happen if ... ?" (e.g. ...'you have to fly overseas').

Note:
We call fear the **what if spirit!** so **what will happen if?** is a good basic question for fear, anxiety, stress or insecurity.

"How does it feel to think that ...?"	(e.g. ...'there is nobody to protect you').
"How does this make you feel ... ?"	(e.g. ...'to think that you don't matter').
"Why do you think ... ?"	(e.g. ...'no one cares about you').
"What does this mean about you ... ?"	(e.g. ...'that everyone else is able to succeed').
"What does it make you ... ?"	(e.g. ...'if you are the person who is ignored').

Chapter 16: Types of Beliefs

"What do you believe is true about you ... ? (e.g.... if someone has perhaps, learnt that they are stupid in an event).

Typical belief samples

Fear:	"This or that could happen!"
Anger:	"They don't care about me!" "This is not how things should be!"
Rejection:	"Nobody wants me, I don't belong, am not a part of this."
Stress:	"I can't cope!" "It's hopeless." (Depression)
Sadness:	"I am not loved."
Rebellion:	"It's not fair!"
Performance anxiety / inferiority:	"I cannot do what others can do."
Insecurity:	"People aren't doing what they should be doing."
Bitterness /resentment:	"I will not forgive them for what they have done" or at times, "what they have not done that they should have!"

All of these kinds of perceived beliefs affect relationships and often produce sin responses and reactions.

The demeanour of the minister

If you are going to be effective in this ministry you will need to become a good listener. Slow to speak and quick to listen is great wisdom. You hear what a person is saying to gather information and note cues that may point to beliefs. In addition, you are looking to God for prompts, inspiration and information. I have already discussed the car park analogy. Occasionally, once you gain some experience, it may be obvious to you what a person believes. However, if you suggest it, they may well deny it. It will not be until you arrive in the *basement* that the belief is alive and significant to them.

If you are not yet mature as a Christian, or indeed free from your own issues, you may have a need or tendency to be vocal about all that you know and think. This may not inspire the vital trust that is needed for a person to share their most intimate details. The need for confidentiality is absolutely critical. I have shared a number of testimonies and stories in this publication. If I think that a story might be helpful in the teaching and training environment, I will ask permission to share it. Without a person's consent I do not talk about details of anyone's ministry time. It is something personal between them and God. People coming for help will usually sense whether or not it is safe to open up the areas that their lives are built on with you.

Positioning

The most important area of any healing or freedom ministry is to have the person aligned to receive from the Lord. Jesus taught about the Kingdom of God before He ministered. It is vitally important that people understand what the issue is, and what God offers in terms of resolving your problem. Therefore, explaining or teaching about the ministry is key. This can come in the form of your own explanations, a work up book, video or audio teaching.

In an environment, such as attendees of our healing school, people who want ministry already know what to expect and how it works. In other settings, where possible, to be thorough and most effective, we will do a work up session first where we explain and teach about the ministry. We have found that God will not usually override a person's free will and choice. Consequently, He will only do for people that which they want and choose. This can be frustrating for some new ministers. They can see the answer to the problems and try to push people to deal with their issues. Jesus only ministered to those who came to Him. Given that He was preaching repentance, and many did not want to reconsider their ways or change their thinking about their lifestyles, many did not come. Our job is to teach what God has made available as best we can, and then be equipped to serve Him in helping those who come.

Being ready

Most people who have been through teaching on the subject or a workup session now see their problem and come to receive their freedom. Once in a while, I have someone who does the workup and, even though they now see the source of the issues, they feel that it is not something that they want to do. A small percentage never return, but many times they will return, weeks months or even years later, desperate, reporting that they are now ready to do whatever is necessary to be set free. I have come to realize that although we finish work for the day, the Holy Spirit goes home with them, and never ceases to work with and encourage them.

Common reasons why people may not come for ministry
1. Ignorance
They simply do not know about this opportunity for freedom or they have received a distorted picture of it from some source.

2. Alignment
It does not fit into their theological or ministry method framework.

3. Pride
Pride is the most common reason. Many people are full of their own opinions and views. Having some knowledge, they become *puffed up*. They want to fix the problem themselves without help from others, working it out in their own minds. Remember the Pharisees who considered themselves above the common sinners. Jesus at one time rebuked them for searching the scriptures because they thought that the written word alone would provide eternal life.

Pride says, *I will fix me!* in a sense, following on from the temptation in the garden to be *as or like God!* Pride wants to set up a monument to self to bow down to and be, in a way, your own god. Jesus pointed out that the scriptures actually do not fix you without Him, the word made flesh. He is the person whom the Holy Spirit can work through and meet your needs. The principle is the same for receiving the promise of eternal life, and also receiving other provisions that come through Jesus.

John 5:39-40, "[39] *You diligently study the Scriptures because you think that by them you possess eternal life. These are the Scriptures that testify about me,* [40] *yet you refuse to come to me to have life"* (NIV).

The beginnings or ground that gives place to pride is found in inferiority and low self-image. Pride, or making yourself above others, in your own thinking is the devil's solution for the perceived weakness that you hold about yourself at heart level.

Proud people are probably the ones who stay away from receiving help more than any others. Their behaviour, or how they appear, is often the exact opposite of a person's inner belief. For example, a person who walks around appearing self-important and superior almost certainly believes in their hearts that they are not important and are inferior. Now, the only viewpoint that holds any importance for them is their own. They will have the attitude that you better listen to them and often hold the floor in conversations. King Solomon was not kind in his appraisal of these hurting people in many of his writings.

Proverbs 26:12, *"Do you see a man wise in his own eyes? There is more hope for a fool than for him"* (NIV).

For a proud person to admit to any kind of weakness or imperfection strikes at the core of their sense of inferiority. And after all, what could anybody possibly know that they do not! The result is that many with pride issues avoid ministry. There can at times be an evil spirit involved in the resistance to help. Even if there is not a demon on the inside, pride certainly proceeds from spiritual influences even from the outside.

A while ago we had a new lady coming to our church who asked me if she could come for some help with her problems. She asked me if I could make sure that I don't tell the other leaders that she was coming. I replied with something like, *Sure, no problem. But I don't think that they would pay much attention, as many of the congregation comes for sessions and most of the leaders receive ministry themselves!* This seemed to put her at ease. The point is, isn't this what normal church life should look like anyway?

4. Control
We have already discussed that many people want to be in absolute control of their lives. For some of these persons, to be able to trust another, with the deep things of their lives is very difficult.

5. Fear
There are those who are simply too afraid of what might happen, what you might think about them, or what they may have to face to consider opening up for help.

6. Denial
Some people simply will not accept they have problems, or they may have a part in faulty relationships. These people expect that their

own emotional well-being would be fine if everyone around them did what they think they should be doing. This is called *projection*, where you deny your issues and blame shift your situation, feelings and responses onto everyone else. It is not surprising that we see the first instance of not taking responsibility for our own behaviour right back at mankind's beginnings in Genesis.

Genesis 3:11-12, "*[11] And he said, "Who told you that you were naked? Have you eaten from the tree that I commanded you not to eat from?" [12] The man said, "The woman you put here with me--she gave me some fruit from the tree, and I ate it"* (NIV).

Why do we need help?
Some people ask why they need to sit down with someone to do this ministry. Let me offer a couple of reasons.

1. If you don't commit to some kind of appointment then you will probably never get around to it. I used to say to people that it is a bit like going to the dentist, we put it off as long as we can. (Around 15 years ago I read of someone else making almost the exact same comparison).

2. To begin with, you most probably don't have the skills to find your beliefs, and you may find it hard to connect to deep painful events without experienced support. Eventually it may be possible to minister to yourself as it is a very simple process.

3. Discernment. If you've ever played the game of golf you will know that everyone will tell you how to improve and what you are doing wrong. Even bad golfers will give you advice, sometimes bad advice. The point is that they can see that you are doing something wrong. You cannot see your own swing, because you are in it. But they may not know what they are looking at.

Discernment in its simplest form, is being able to understand what you are seeing or looking at. It's a good idea to get your advice from a Golf pro whose own game is working well, rather than a *hacker* who is struggling with his handicap. Clearly the same is true in ministry; don't take advice from just any well-meaning Christian, it is worth checking the life and experience of the person that you are seeking help from.

Shopping lists

By the time a person has listened to teaching on *Truth Encounters* or has done a work up session, they should have a basic understanding of the ministry process. Many by now may have noteworthy memories coming to them. Anything that is a memory is significant or it would not be remembered to begin with. Few people can remember what they had for breakfast on a particular day 2 years ago; let alone many years ago because it really is not important.

We now ask the person to begin to put on their *shopping list* the areas that they may suffer with and are looking for freedom in. This can be known problems, such as never feeling that they are worth anything, or perhaps a fear of storms, or it can be a set of reactions that they have to specific situations.

A reaction example:

This may be something along the lines of; *I get very, very angry when my husband leaves his clothes on the floor*. This could come from some kind of belief such as, *nobody cares about me, and what I want*. A self-belief may be holding hurt behind that thinking, along the lines of; *I'm a nothing, I just don't matter*. The *I'm a nothing* is going to be the identity belief that holds the emotional pain. The anger is not the problem but is a predictable response to being made to feel like this.

Their *shopping list* may contain a list of issues that they are aware of, and also a number of trigger circumstances. We encourage them to simply write down any situations that produce negative emotions. Anything that makes them feel angry, sad, fearful, indignant, rejected, inferior, unimportant and so on. A *shopping list* could look something like;

I just never feel worthy of being noticed. (Looking for historical match).

My husband always seems uninterested in what I want....! etc. etc.

Some new ministers get nervous that they won't know what to do. As long as you remember that you are looking for the beliefs that produce the feelings, you are on the right track. We are not trying to give you methods, but rather principles. I am quite sure that my wife ministers very differently to me, but we are both looking for the same thing.

The people already have the problems so you don't have to find any. In addition, God has the answer for them already. Your job is only to help them find that which they believe in their hearts, then open it up to God to provide His truth. You can only minister to whatever they come in with for help. You may discern other issues, but if they do not want assistance in those areas, then you acknowledge their choices.

We can summarize the areas of responsibility along these lines;

Our part:
- To teach or instruct them in understanding the ministry.
- To help them identify and clarify the beliefs in their hearts.

The person's part:
- To be willing to seek out and note their issues.
- To be prepared to embrace and accept their beliefs, emotions and memories.

The Holy Spirit's part:
- To guide and inspire the minister and person in the session.
- To reveal God's truth and bring freedom.

Ways that God may communicate with people
An old saying says that *God talks how you listen.* He made your brain and soul exactly how He intended it to be. Some people think in words, others in pictures or impressions; let me offer some of the common ways that God might communicate truth to you.

1. In words:
I tend to think in words, so mostly when God uses my mind to communicate truth to me it comes in words. Interestingly I have noticed that as I have become more and more free that I also receive pictures and impressions at times either for myself or others. Some people get stuck here because they are waiting for flashes of light and a booming voice, or an audible word from outside your body. I explain it this way. My computer is set up with the fonts, letter styles, writing size and so on that I like. If I were to give it to you and ask you to write me a note, when you returned it to me, I might exclaim; *that is just my writing!* That's true; you just used my faculties or equipment to communicate your message to me.

In the ministry room, having identified the heart belief, I simply encourage people to let their minds go. When they hear something, occasionally people might explain that it just seemed like their own thoughts, but they heard this or that. We test and see whether or not it is God by looking at the old belief. Perhaps a person may have always thought that they were dumb. It felt true to them. Now they look for belief and cannot find it, or it is no longer true; it has always been true to them, but it is gone.

2. Pictures or impressions:

Many people think in pictures. I remember a man who was suffering from a rejection belief of some kind. When this man spent time with his own children, he would put his face up against their face as a sign of love and affection, indicating acceptance and connection. The man was focusing on his belief and feeling that he was rejected, and God gave him a picture, an impression of the Heavenly Father putting His face against the mans. Needless to say, he was deeply touched and moved. However God communicates to us, it is like a *prophetic now word* applied to our historical event.

In fact, I was ministering to a young man one day and as he embraced the heart belief that he held, the Holy Spirit took some words from a prophetic word that he had received a number of years earlier, and applied it to his belief, bringing healing. Why did it not bring healing before? The young man did not know what he believed in his heart up until this time when we exposed it. Then the Holy Spirit applied the words to the belief.

3. Scriptures:

Very often the Holy Spirit will use a scripture that people know well in their minds and apply it to issues in their hearts. By way of example, I was ministering to a lady recently and she was in a memory where she was struggling to keep up with the other children in being able to do her school work. As a result, she had come to a conclusion and belief that she still suffered with daily along the lines of; *I am dumb because I cannot do the schoolwork like the other kids.* As she concentrated on the school memory and felt the belief, the Lord put into her mind the book of Ecclesiastes: *Everything is meaningless!*

For her, this meant that the activity that she was basing her identity on really did not matter. This brought her freedom. If the reference that she was measuring herself against was meaningless then the conclusion that she arrived at had no basis and could not be true either. This was not a conscious act on her part to think differently, it was the result of the truth which the Holy Spirit communicated to her.

4. Realizations:

Several years ago, I ministered to a young man who came with the presenting problem of feeling as though he was responsible for everything that went wrong in his family life, his workplace, and even to some extent the world. As he connected with the feeling, we arrived at the place where he learnt a belief something like; *It's my fault if bad things happen.* As a small boy he was traveling in the back seat of the family car. They had an accident with another car as they entered an intersection. It was an emotionally traumatic event for the little boy. His father whipped around and said sharply, *have you got your seatbelt on?*

Now, it may seem ridiculous, but in that emotionally charged moment the boy thought; *This bad thing is my fault because I haven't gotten my seat belt on!* These thoughts are burned deeply into our brains in moments of crisis through an electro-chemical process known as protein synthesis.

As we explored the memory, he discovered that afterward it turned out that he did in fact have his belt on. He now realized that the truth was that it was not his fault at all. He had believed that it was because, after the moment of shock, it was too late to reinterpret the belief for him as a child after the emotional intensity subsided because the belief was in his heart. But now many years later the Holy Spirit reminded him of the complete picture and set him free.

Personally, I believe that one of the reasons that this ministry is so effective is that God dwells in eternity and not time (Isaiah 57:15). He is everywhere all of the time. He is already there ten years from now, and He is there in your memory, whether you knew of Him or not, as a child. So, we can identify your belief up here in time and counsel you about it with minimal change. But when He speaks into, and helps you reinterpret, your event with His truth He is actually there!

Another example of a realization could be a child coming into a room where mother and father are having a heated argument. In that moment the child believes that it is somehow their fault. Looking back and exploring the memory through the eyes of God they now realize, as they see more of the picture that was not as emotionally intense, that the parents were already fighting before they entered the room. So, how could it be their fault? God will at times bring freedom through realization. I have also seen at times people being set free at the moment where they realize why they believe what they believe, and where it came from, and for them that is the healing.

5. *Sensations, feelings, knowing:*
God is indeed very creative in how He communicates with us. Normally we do not know what He is going to do, or how He will do it. Sometimes He will give us insight into what He is about to say or do. I think in part this is on the job training for words of knowledge and learning to hear his voice for ourselves.

I recall one lady who had suffered severe physical abuse, and as she was accessing memories and beliefs, there was a light coming into the picture. When the light came in, she felt peaceful and calm, safe. I was frantically going through my theology to make sure that this was something Biblical. Remembering, Jesus, light of the world reassured me that this was something that God might do. The bottom line was that her fears were resolved.

Other people report simply feeling love. Still more, report that they just know that the beliefs they held are not true. I remember asking one lady after a session what she now thought of God. She thought about it for a moment, and then replied; *He's clever, He's very clever!* Amen. Our God is indeed very clever.

Wiring
Sometimes God will multitask and use the ministry room as a training ground for you or the recipient. Remember before David went up against Goliath, he found that God was with him in the private place, killing both lion and bear. He honed his skills as a shepherd boy before he was put into public ministry.

God is always about helping people, and He uses our time doing so to learn about Him and His goodness as we see His love, grace and ability to help His children. As we are faithful in little, it is a training ground for other things. Many times, as people hear from God in their healing moment, it becomes obvious for some of them, that God has put in them faculties such as receiving pictures easily. As they learn to understand what God is saying through the pictures and they reach out to Him for what He is communicating to them, they realize that they could reach out for something for others as well. So, ministry times can be a birthing place for prophetic ministries as they not only discover their gifting, but also get free enough and in the truth enough to use them. (That is in part, not having the words from God convoluted through their own soulish heart beliefs.)

Warning
Many ministries have gone off the rails and brought the ministry into disrepute by suggesting how God should communicate with them. For example, I have heard of people suggesting to picture Jesus in the memory. This is a recipe for disaster, licensing potential deception. I have had people report seeing Jesus in their memories perhaps two or three times in 20 years of ministering *Truth Encounters*. Even these were many years ago, and I cannot be sure that they had not been exposed to other ministries who practiced this and, as a consequence, thought that this was what was expected.

My wife has also been ministering this way for perhaps 10 or 12 years and has rarely seen it either. Our work is to simply help the person identify what it is that they believe, and then pass the ministry time over to the Holy Spirit to communicate truth as He sees fit. We are the assistants in the ministry, not the directors.

CHAPTER 17
Problem areas that you may periodically encounter

Conscious Objections
We have already discussed that some people will simply not want ministry for some reason; they might propose that they are a new creation so there is nothing left to do, and point to the finished work of the cross. If you cannot help them negotiate these conscious objections then you simply acknowledge their free will and choice. They may simply not agree with this form of ministry and either decide to resolve their problems themselves, or feel that another approach is better for them.

We can only teach about the ministry as best we can and testify to what we have seen and heard in terms of the results that we have experienced. Some ministers feel that now that they see the problems for what they are, and know the answer, that they need to push people to go to God for healing. God Himself does not force anyone to do anything; it is not in His nature. We see this in how Jesus dealt with the disciples recognizing their free will and choice.

John 6:66-67 says, " *[66]At this point many of his disciples turned away and deserted him. [67] Then Jesus turned to the Twelve and asked, "Are you going to leave, too?"* (NLT).

He could have proclaimed, *hey you guys, you can't go, I have invested a lot of time in you!* Instead, He enquired as to what they willed to do and which course of action that they had decided on.

Suppression
If you suppress something then you restrain, subdue, repress, or hold it back; like a sneeze, a cough or a yawn, at an inappropriate moment. When we are talking about suppressing memories, we are saying that you have chosen to not permit yourself to look at it for some reason. Perhaps it holds guilt, shame, rejection or some other unsavoury emotion in it. So, we restrain it from coming onto the screen of our minds, pushing it back, as a wilful act denying it, and eventually over time, we have repressed it to where we can no longer readily access it. The neural pathway that connected us to the

event has gone from a strong four lane highway with street lights to a broken-down potholed dirt track. It is now barely accessible, and we do not want to go to it in any case.

Usually if people have chosen to remember memories no more as an act of their will, then to see those pictures they now have to choose to see them again. They are still there, in storage, it is just that the connection to them has become weak. I have found that often when people now decide to explore those memories for healing that they come back a piece at a time. Just as they faded out as the connection became weak, now as they try to find them the pathway begins to strengthen.

I recall many young ladies who have pushed down abusive memories. When they have chosen to access the memories, they have come back as little snippets and pieces of pictures. As they have been able to accept each piece then another will emerge. Of course, it does not need to be an abusive situation, it could be something along the lines of denying that your father or mother did not love you. As a result, you push the place where you learnt this out of reach.

Dissociation

I have a wrist watch that has written on the back of it, Waterproof to 30 meters. I have often wondered what happens at 31 meters when the pressure becomes too great. Theoretically at least the outside circumstances become too great for it to deal with and it is overwhelmed, crushed, and broken.

Proverbs 18:14, *"A man's spirit sustains him in sickness, but a crushed spirit who can bear?"* (NIV).

Not being able to cope with, or bear a situation, can cause the mind to overload and disconnect from the event. Modern homes often have a circuit breaker on the electrical system in case the wiring is overloaded and damage might occur. If this looks like happening, it simply breaks the connection that allows the power to flow into the situation. Mentally we seem to have the same kind of protection in our wiring. If something is happening to us that we cannot bear, then the mind disconnects or dissociates from what is going on.

Over the years, I have found this to be a common phenomenon with traumas such as sexual abuse. If a twenty-year-old person was being sexually imposed on, in perhaps a rape or coercive sexual encounter, they nowadays, would normally have at least a basic understanding of the sexual act. If the same abuse is played out on, for example, a four-year-old, they have no understanding whatsoever of that which is going on. It is overwhelming and they cannot cope, so they disconnect from the event.

Often, they will project their minds onto some other activity to escape from the situation. After the event, the emotions and memories from the event remain compartmentalized and shut off because of the extreme feelings such as fear and powerlessness that they contain. There is usually some kind of belief objecting to connecting to the contents of the memory. This could be thoughts such as; *if I go there, I will not be able to cope, I will be out of control, I will die*, and so on. These need to be identified and resolved.

Story

A number of years ago, we were doing a school in another state, and there was in attendance, a young married man. From time to time his wife would appear for short periods of time but seemed unwilling to be very involved with the group. We were having a break and the Pastor asked if I would see the young lady and explain about the ministry. I agreed, and not knowing what her issue was, I went through how the *Truth Encounters* ministry worked. She thanked me and left. A little later the Pastor came back and informed me that she wanted ministry but did not have any memories relating to her problem.

Once we began the session, I found that her presenting symptom was that she was unable to have a sexual relationship with her husband because of the feelings that it produced in her. The emotions that she described were consistent with someone who had been abused. As she tried to connect the feelings with a historical event which matched that which she was experiencing, she reported that she had no memories whatsoever. I explained to her that there was some kind of belief that she had that prevented her from seeing what had happened to her, and that it had been an act of her will not to see the memories for that reason. I went on to encourage her that it will also be an act of her will to see why she objected to seeing her memory pictures.

After concentrating for a moment, she announced that it had been a member of family, a close relative who had done it. The perpetrator was considered to be an exemplary Christian and she believed that she could not possibly accept the event because of the closeness of the relative. She further believed that, because of their relationship to the father and mother, she could not tell her parents what had happened. This overload caused her to completely disconnect with the memory altogether. Once this was resolved, she was able to accept that which had happened to her and process the beliefs from the abuse and be healed.

A couple of years ago I was in that town again and she came over and greeted me. She had two small children in her arms and another holding her hand, so I am guessing that the original issue was resolved.

Before our children grew up, and as I would be driving them to school, they would often comment to each other, *Dad's dissociated!* They would see the glazed look and disconnection from the trip to school, as I was thinking in my mind through some ministry case or wrestling with understanding a scripture. The difference is that there was no reason for me to not reconnect with reality. For people who have suffered trauma and disconnected there is a reason.
The ministry in this situation is exactly the same. You just have to have their will aligned, and work through the objection belief before the healing can come. Usually, as with other beliefs, once the beliefs have been taken to heart in an abuse, these beliefs will now be associated with any later abuses and used to qualify these events as well. Other beliefs can of course be added from later times of offence if the circumstances or situation is different.

These memory bubbles, containing a younger version of you, hold reasons made by your will at the time as to why you do not want to see the event. It is valuable to remember that the current version of you is the *executive member of the board* if you like, and holds ultimate sway in exerting and committing your will.

Personas, masks and denial

The Pharisees and teachers of the law adopted a religious image which presented themselves as Holy men who were right with God. Many people who feel that they are not good enough as they are, will adopt some kind of mask or persona that they feel will make them acceptable.

We moved areas a lot when I was going through school, and I had to make new friends and fit into a new town environment many times. One of the ways that I found that made me accepted was to be the *funny guy*. For me this became my mask and you really could not get any deeper than jokes with me.

For some preachers, they don't feel that they are good enough just being themselves, and when they take to the platform you wonder who this new person is that you have not seen before. They are a mixture of their favourite speakers, which they know are accepted! For some people it is difficult at first for them to let you get behind their created image of themselves. You need patience and love to have them trust you sufficiently to take the mask off and own their inadequacies. These images often are not based on truth in regards to who they really are.

Denial and self-justification is also another possible hindrance to helping people receive ministry. If they feel that they have, for example, *every right to be angry!* Often, they will not be prepared to look at what it is in their lives that has been tapped into producing the response. Many people deny that they have any issues at all. It is everyone else that is at fault! As the saying goes; *everyone is messed up except for you and me, and now we mention it, I am not that sure about you!*

Is this counselling?

We do not consider this type of ministry to be counselling. We are not giving instructions regarding efforts that people should undertake to resolve their problems. We simply teach them about what God will do for them if they want to receive from Him. Then, if they choose to connect with the beginnings of their presenting issues, we assist them in defining that which they believe in their hearts. Rather than this being something that they can do, these sessions are all about letting God do what He promised to do in setting them free.

In the event that we do offer them some teaching in a session, we are simply forwarding the advice or counsel that the Bible gives us all. We are not telling them that they have to do this. We are simply helping them see how their lives could function better from a Biblical standpoint. As with all the instruction of scripture, it is entirely our choice as to whether or not we do it. Our work in the ministry room is to help them to receive from God in order for them to be able to live in God's order.

Is this psychology?
Physiology is the biological study of the living organisms of the body. Doctors understand the parts of the body and for the most part understand from these studies how the organs of the body function. They are not wrong about their observations and have some success in treating various maladies, and we are thankful to God for their efforts. We acknowledge of course that only the work of the Holy Spirit can bring miraculous, complete, and many times instant healing.

The New Testament is written in the Koine Greek language, and the word for soul is from the Bible; 'psuche.' In Latin the word for soul is; 'psyche,' which they identify as the identity or personality. Words such as psychology or psychiatry therefore refer to doctors who study and help people with the problems which relate to their souls.

The beginning of these studies historically points back to around 140 years ago. The Bible is the ultimate book explaining the activities of the soul pre-dating man's observations by a considerable amount of time. So, is what we are presenting: a study of the soul? Yes. Personally, I have never read a psychology book and simply began trying to help people by referencing the bible to find out how to do it. I had a break over Christmas in 2017 and the thought came into my mind to examine what they say that the unconscious or subconscious represents, and so I read a couple of internet articles on the subject.

The prefixes: un = not, and sub = under or below

The articles considered this as thought that is not conscious thought, or thought that is going on under the consciousness. From the various articles that I read, nobody seems to be able to clearly define which is which. In conclusion, what they noted that they are observing is the activities and issues presenting that are largely the same as that which the Bible says about the *heart*. Many of the things that they have learnt about the soul are not wrong; they are just limited without the Holy Spirit in terms of how they can resolve them. Just as with their observations of the body, they are limited with their treatments, so too are these *soul* doctors limited in that which they can offer. We appreciate their efforts and acknowledge that they bring some measure of help. The discovery and development of psychology was heralded as a great move forward for mankind's ability to heal himself, but if they had read a Bible, they would have found that the information in its fullness was there all along.

Very often people have come to us for help after many years of $200 a session visits to a psychologist. Dr. Jesus proceeds to consistently resolve their issues at no cost having already paid the price Himself. I am in no way trying to diminish the efforts or knowledge of these professionals; I am simply saying that God can do what they/we cannot.

Flow chart
The ministry process:
A person comes to you with a problem. This could be a mental, emotional, relational, addictive, spiritual, sexual or physical issue.
↓
They may have been *set off* or *triggered* by a life situation producing for example: anxiety, anger, sadness, bitterness, resentment, guilt, inferiority, rejection and so on.
↓
Your role is to help them focus on these feelings and reactions and to identify the **self**-beliefs which they believe at *heart* level, and which they may no longer immediately consciously access.
↓
The key components that you are trying to connect here are: The emotions, the **self**-beliefs producing the emotions, and the matching

memory pictures. (No pictures prenatal, perhaps a feeling or a sense of something)

↓

You have them focus on the presenting feelings and using questions help them to discover the **self**-beliefs producing the emotion, OR

↓

If they have a **self**-belief, such as, *I just never think that I am good enough*, have them connect with the feeling that should be associated with such a thought. (The emotion often comes up as the story is related or the memory is accessed and described.)

↓

Request that they let memories come to them or wilfully look for the memory picture, if they don't already have it, which contains the thoughts and feelings. (With some pictures that are remembered, it is not always immediately obvious as to why the beliefs have been interpreted here.)

↓

Having refined and identified the belief that was learnt, invite God to bring Truth. (You can be creative in how you request this to avoid being repetitive, but using phrases such as, *Lord, would you like to show Fred how you see this situation? Lord, would you touch Fred by revealing your Truth to replace what he perceives as the truth here? Lord, what would you like Fred to know about the belief that he holds?* and so on.)

Note:
How you address God in this setting is up to you. Some people just say; 'God can you please ...' others might invite Jesus to minister to the person. This is also Biblical as it is the Spirit of Christ who is communicating with them. Someone else might ask the Holy Spirit, or the Spirit of truth to free them with the truth. I often just say 'Lord,' but at times, mix it up a bit. I have never seen God hold back His blessing because we did not get the *method* exactly correct. If you really felt the need to be pernickety and be doctrinally accurate in regards to this, you could offer a prayer such as, *Father, in the name of Jesus, would you please bring your truth to 'Fred' through the Holy Spirit.* (And then seek ministry for your own fear of getting it wrong; cheeky grin!)

Chapter 17: Problem areas that you may periodically encounter

I offer this guideline as an example of how a ministry could flow, to help with what you are looking for, where you are looking, and how you look. In practice it all happens quite naturally and organically as you listen to a person's story and ask questions when appropriate. The Holy Spirit really will inspire your thoughts. When you first begin, feeling like you don't know what to do is a common, expected part of stepping into something new. You are beginning with far more information than I had. In the early days I would commence a session with someone, and if we seemed stuck or I did not know how to proceed I would announce that I felt it was a good place to finish for the day. Then I would go and pray and try to work out what I should do next.

Where to from here?
In the following section of this publication, I examine being able to discern or understand the types of beliefs that are producing specific feelings, attitudes or responses. At the end of each of these, I will attach scenarios of typical cases relating to those particular issues. In Section 4 we will examine the ways in which spiritual influences interact with, and are implicated in the beliefs. When are influences spiritual? Always. We are primarily spirit beings in a spiritually manipulated world. So, we are going to try and clarify how this affects us.

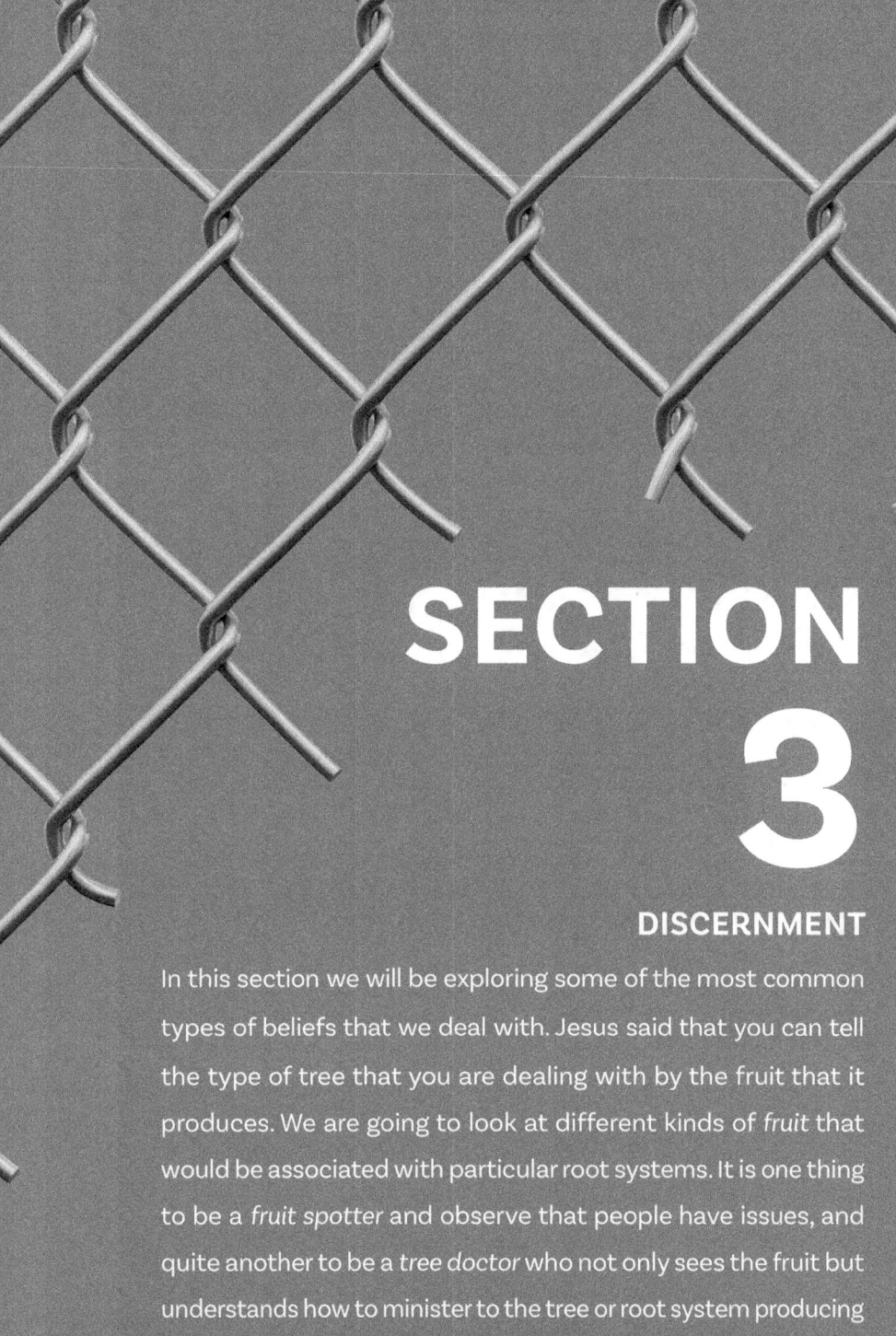

SECTION 3

DISCERNMENT

In this section we will be exploring some of the most common types of beliefs that we deal with. Jesus said that you can tell the type of tree that you are dealing with by the fruit that it produces. We are going to look at different kinds of *fruit* that would be associated with particular root systems. It is one thing to be a *fruit spotter* and observe that people have issues, and quite another to be a *tree doctor* who not only sees the fruit but understands how to minister to the tree or root system producing it. In this next section we provide an overview of these problems.

- Section 3: Discernment -

CHAPTER 18
Rejection

As we begin to look at the subject of rejection in brief, let us first define it and put it into perspective. Rejection is non-acceptance. The definition of rejection includes the following:

- to refuse to acknowledge or accept
- to forsake
- to refuse to have or use
- to cast or throw away as useless, worthless, or unsatisfactory
- to refuse to love
- to discard as unwanted or not filling requirements.

Many people hold heart beliefs that they are not wanted, don't belong, or perhaps that they are not loved or loveable. Still others feel as though they are worthless, not cared about, will never be good enough, or don't measure up to what is wanted. They feel that they fall short of the expectations of others. These beliefs all drop into the category of rejection, or not being accepted.

In the Garden of Eden mankind submitted to Satan and rejected God as Lord when they rebelled against His commands in regards to the tree of the knowledge of good and evil. Whatever kind of spirit that you participate with and submit to, you give authority to them over you in the area of your submission. Rejection was now a covering power that all future mankind was born under as a consequence of the fall.

I have previously pointed out that God never rejected humanity, rather we rejected Him. This was joining with Satan who had rejected God's Lordship in favour of *self-realization*. God is always redemptive and immediately He promised to repair the situation for His creation as we see in the following passage.

Genesis 3:15, *"And I will put enmity between you and the woman, and between your offspring and hers; he will crush your head, and you will strike his heel"* (NIV).

In this verse, God was informing Satan, the instigator of the rejection of God by man, that he was going to have his head crushed by a male offspring of woman. This is, of course, speaking of Jesus, who was going to suffer being struck on the heel. We need to point out here that the head represents authority, and correspondingly the feet step on, over or above their environment.

Jesus never lost authority. He only suffered in His heel as He crushed the head or authority of Satan as He walked through His mission. A part of this process was taking our rejection by being rejected Himself. He then dealt with the rebellious sin that put us under this power, in order for us to return to relationship with the Father.

Isaiah 53:3-4, " *³He was despised and rejected by men, a man of sorrows, and familiar with suffering. Like one from whom men hide their faces he was despised, and we esteemed him not. ⁴ Surely, he took up our infirmities and carried our sorrows, yet we considered him stricken by God, smitten by him, and afflicted"* (NIV).

I have never yet met a human being who did not have some evidence of the fruits of rejection in their lives. We were all born under this element of the fall. In my opinion, rejection is the *tap root* to most of our problems, and I consequently hold it up as being an area of prime importance. Not being received and accepted by another produces separation in relationships and cuts us off from love and nurture. This is true in terms of how we relate to God, but also how we receive others and even ourselves. If we don't believe that we are acceptable then we will struggle to receive love.

Without the assurance of love, we are going to have anxiety problems as is well evidenced in modern society. Articles vary slightly but figures generally indicate around one in ten Australians being on medication for anxiety and as many as one in five reporting that they suffer from it. These are the statistics for those who admit to having the problem. Statistics in the U.S.A. appear to be very similar.

1 John 4:18, *"There is no fear in love. But perfect love drives out fear, because fear has to do with punishment. The one who fears is not made perfect in love"* (NIV).

When we have our heart beliefs resolved, and also understand fully at a conscious level as well, that through redemption Christ dealt with our punishment and separation from the Father completely, we can then receive His love.

The potential damage of no acceptance

Around twenty years ago I heard a story from an English Bible teacher named Ruth Hawkey [3]. The account that she related helped me to fully understand the potential damage to humans who do not receive nurture in the form of love and acceptance.

The setting was an overloaded institution in Eastern Europe who had in their care 97 children between 3 months and 3 years old. Now remember that mankind's most basic need is to have love and acceptance communicated to them; connection. Because of the lack of staff, there was no time available for physical or emotional nurture. At 3 months there were signs of abnormality with the children losing their appetites, exhibiting poor sleep patterns and their eyes were becoming vacant and looking into space. At 5 months some were exhibiting serious deterioration. They were whimpering and their faces would become twisted and distorted if anyone approached them and tried to pick them up. Reportedly 27 died the first year with no physical reason; they were considered to have shrivelled up on the inside. 7 more died the second year and the survivors suffered with severe psychological disorders. There have been many such studies by people such as Rene A. Spitz that confirm the types of damage that these settings can produce.

We can testify to having seen many of these issues and manifestations present with very rejected children that we have fostered over the years. The point is that the result of not receiving love and acceptance from the parents, and subsequent lack of bonding and nurture can have pronounced effects on one's total person. These examples are of an extreme nature but they stand to illustrate that rejection has a profound impact; the only remaining question is to what degree it has touched us.

Possible beginning points for Rejection beliefs

We have previously discussed the resultant beliefs proceeding from the separation choices, decisions and situations leading to adoption and fostering.

---

3 Ruth Hawkey is the author of several publications relating to healing and freedom.

Parenting issues
Modelling
Many parents simply cannot communicate love and acceptance. This can stem from them never having had it modelled to them as to how to show the worth, value, love and acceptance that children need. It continues then as a generational cultural omission that leaves a breeding ground for children to come to their own conclusions regarding whether or not they are acceptable.

Empty 'love tanks'
Some parents have not received love and grace themselves so they are emotionally bankrupt and have nothing to give. They are themselves rejected and many of the efforts around their lives are in trying to meet the needs of their own wounded selves. Sadly, rejected people are most often rejective; *rejection rejects*.

Absentee
At times parents are absentees in their dealings with their families, and often at critical times where children are coming to conclusions about themselves. This can result from circumstances such as hospitalization, traveling for work, or even working long hours to provide for the family. They may also be physically present but emotionally unavailable. Perhaps they are addicted to drugs, alcohol, television, digital games and media in order to escape their own pain and consequent relational problems.

Physical bonding
It has been said that physical bonding and nurture is especially important from the mother who has been gifted to be relational and present, meeting the everyday needs of life. The fathers tend to be more task oriented looking to longer term provisions and developments for the family. He is more likely to be focused, for example, on building an outboard motor so that his family doesn't have to row the boat home. His tendency is to be a provider and problem solver. In the family dynamic, identity comes largely from his encouragement and approval.

Money
We live in a world that holds financial wealth at a premium. Often in the western world we will see parents substituting material giving for time, attention and genuine interest in a child. Somehow, we

have come to a place where we believe that if we have given them the latest media games to occupy them, this is love. Children know if you are just trying to get them out of the way. This is interpreted in their hearts with beliefs of unimportance, and lack of worthiness to be given time and relationship.

Other priorities
I once heard a story of a child attending a Pastors kids camp. She arrived wearing gaudy, out there, strikingly decorated clothing. She featured a big brightly coloured Mohawk down the middle of her head. I suggest that somewhere deep inside that person was a cry proceeding from their heart, possibly something along the lines of; *Would somebody please notice me, anyone, please!*
Being a Pastor I can empathize that it is all too easy to fall into being busy ministering to everyone else, preparing a message or studying the Bible. The truth is that children don't need a huge amount of time; you're not that much fun anyway because, after all, you are an adult. But they need a minute or two here and there to know that they are more important than whatever you are doing. I am sure that as the little children come to us, we, like Jesus, need to make time for them. I am convinced that God is more than pleased if you put your Bible down for a time so that they can understand how important they are.

Pastors are just an example; it could be any other activity, but the responsibility for modelling the heart of God should begin with us as parents. Parents have been given the responsibility to represent God in all aspects of His character. We have found that the *God picture* that most people hold is a projection off the parenting that they have received. If you never have time for them, they will expect that God is also too busy creating universes to listen to their needs. If you are often absentee, they won't even bother praying to God, because He is off somewhere sleeping on a cloud. If you don't take time correcting them and teaching them to respect authority and consequences for action, then they are likely to grow up without the fear of God and find themselves making choices that can eventually destroy or negatively impact their lives.

Conditional acceptance
A number of people hold rejection beliefs learnt through only receiving acceptance if they perform and meet the standards set

for them. These expectations could relate to behaviour, academic or other achievements. Fundamentally what is being projected onto them spiritually and emotionally is; *"If you don't measure up by doing this or that then you are not good enough, and therefore not acceptable!"*

Some parents have such high standards for their children that they create a breeding ground for performance anxiety and depression. If a child is only ever criticized and told that they are not enough, then the consequent belief will be that no matter how hard they try, they will never be able to be what they need to be for acceptance. This is an overwhelming belief that produces hopelessness and eventually depression. Inside the person, inevitably, the heavy load of never being able to meet expectations is too much and they become depressed. The devil offers them a way out and often times suicide is attempted. It is wonderful when people access a depression belief and God speaks something into their memory and you hear them report something like I'm ok! meaning, *I am ok as I am ... I can just be, I don't have to strive to be enough; I am enough because I am me!* Christian parents can be as guilty as anyone of metering out conditional acceptance based on performance. A fear that our children may not be good enough for God, leads us to impose all kinds of religious standards on them. In turn they grow up seeing God as a person who is watching to make sure that you get everything right. One mistake and He will punish you. God actually doesn't expect us to be perfect. He knows that we are created beings in a hostile fallen environment, complete with our old nature which has a tendency towards sin, a world full of temptations and a spiritual enemy who is constantly trying to deceive and gain sway over us. Sometimes we need to forgive ourselves for being merely created beings formed from dust, God has! And then we can extend this grace and understanding that we have received from Him by not demanding others and our children to meet our standards.

Psalm 103:10-14, "[10] *He has not punished us for all our sins, nor does he deal with us as we deserve.* [11] *For his unfailing love toward those who fear him is as great as the height of the heavens above the earth.* [12] *He has removed our rebellious acts as far away from us as the east is from the west.* [13] *The LORD is like a father to his children, tender and compassionate to those who fear him.* [14] *For* **he understands how weak we are; he knows we are only dust**" (NLT, Emphasis mine).

Some parents use their child's success as a part of their own value, to help shore up their own rejection and how they are perceived by society.

Inappropriate discipline
Excessive correction without love leaves a child to conclude that they don't matter; they are nothing, they simply live to fulfil all your wants and needs. If you have a genuine motivation towards the child, they understand this and will receive the discipline. If they feel that this is all about conforming their lives to you being pleased, and that you do not care about them or that which they want or need, that is, them, themselves, then this will read on their hearts as injustice, which will produce rebellion. The same is true of not taking time to discipline your child. They sense that you cannot be bothered and that therefore their lives are an inconvenience to you. You do not accept the responsibility for the outcome of their lives, and therefore they do not matter to you.

When our daughter was beginning to stand and wobble around the furniture at perhaps 10 months old, she would touch a pot plant or something and look around to see if this was ok or not. I would say, no. Then she would touch it again and look to see what would happen. I would get up and calmly go over and give her a gentle little smack on the hand. This only occurred a few times and at that early age she learnt that no didn't mean; maybe, or *If you try long enough you will get your way*, or *If you want to you can, because after all you have rights!* She learnt that no meant no. From then on there was no further need to test this because she already knew what would happen. No domestic violence and I never ever saw our children throw a tantrum, ever. Correction was done in love and as early as possible.

At the same time, we had a friend with a daughter the same age. This father's response to his daughters testing of boundaries was; *give them what they want and they will leave us alone!* Even small children understand this as that they are not worth the time.

There is an old jazz song that goes something like; *it ain't what you do, it's the way how you do it, that's what gets results!* This is profoundly true. If you discipline your child in anger with a statement such as; *You are really annoying **me**; now you are going to really cop it!* Who is it all about? You! It's about what you want, and how they need to be to be good enough for your love and acceptance.

The problem is that often parents don't take the time to disciple their children and eventually their behaviour becomes so unruly that the parents explode in anger and frustration. But if your child needs discipline and you calmly take them aside and give them a hug and say something like; *You know I love you so much, you are not a naughty child, you have done a naughty thing. We don't want you to grow up to have a sad life and get into trouble. So, I have to punish you.* Then having metered out appropriate justice where the punishment fits the crime you give them another big hug saying; *I don't like having to do that to you, but I love you so much that I needed to, and hope that we never need to do it again.* Who has this been about? Them! It has been about what they need and their good and they will receive it and even appreciate it. But when it is all about you, you can expect problems. It is the spirit that it is delivered in.

Feel free to disagree with me; this is my opinion and my experience. As a Pastor I have had young parents with babies ask about how to bring up their children. Using these kinds of principles, I have seen their children growing up happily, knowing the boundaries, well behaved, secure, and tantrum free. I recall one young couple who were continually receiving praise for their exemplary children.

I have already mentioned that we were in a foster care program for a number of years. Some of the children who came to us had been branded ADD. Using these kinds of principles, these children would calm right down when they came into our home. After a time, I began to interpret ADD in many cases as Appropriate Discipline Disorder. Many of these problems did not exist when the Bible was the basis of raising your children. We are in Africa doing ministry most years for, on most occasions, more than a month at a time. I have never yet seen a tantrum or a badly-behaved child. As the Africans are influenced increasingly by western values and humanistic approaches to parenting, it seems to be just a matter of time and they will have the same issues as we do. *It ain't what you do; it's the way how you do it, that's what gets results!*

Proverbs 22:6, *"Train up a child in the way he should go, and when he is old he will not depart from it."* (NKJV)
Proverbs 22:15, *"Foolishness is bound up in the heart of a child; The rod of correction will drive it far from him"*. (NKJV)

The Bible treats dealing with children, correcting them in love as a matter of prime importance. Clearly physical discipline is something only to be done where necessary, but if a child learns it early enough you can expect a good self-controlled life for them into the future. In much the same way as we do not consciously access heart beliefs that largely dictate our choices and behaviour, if we have grown up under discipline, we may no longer consciously know why we have a strong need to do what is right. It is in our programming.

When my children became adults, they have enjoyed playfully pushing the limits with me with teasing and so on. I still see in them a restraint as to how far they should go. They may not consciously remember exactly what will happen, but there remains a sense of consequence. Someone has said that respect comes before love. If they do not respect us who are meant to be representing all aspects of God to them, then in all probability, they will not have the necessary fear and awe of God that will protect them. If we do not love our children enough to correct them then they may well grow up lawless. This will inevitably leave them unable or not wanting to submit to the ultimate authority figure, God the Father.

Sadly, we see over and over in these times children from Christian families grow up and walk away from God because they only want their own way. The parents cannot understand what has happened. They have unwittingly brought them up in the ways of the World and not the ways of God. Often times they are afraid to discipline their children because of their own fear of rejection which tells them that they will be rejected if they bring correction.

Proverbs 23:13-14, *" [13] Do not withhold correction from a child, for if you beat him with a rod, he will not die. [14] You shall beat him with a rod, and deliver his soul from hell"* (NKJV).

2 Timothy 3:1-4, "*¹ But know this, that in the last days perilous times will come: ² For men will be lovers of themselves, lovers of money, boasters, proud, blasphemers,* **disobedient to parents***, unthankful, unholy, ³ unloving, unforgiving, slanderers, without self-control, brutal, despisers of good, ⁴ traitors, headstrong, haughty, lovers of pleasure rather than lovers of God"* (NKJV, Emphasis mine).

Rejection through Abuse

Verbal, emotional, mental, sexual and physical abuses are all strong sources of rejection. The *language of the spirit* or the attitude behind all of these is something along the lines of; *You don't matter, you are just rubbish that has to fit into what I want, you are nothing.* At heart level, matching beliefs are now held about your self-worth and acceptability. These acts destroy how you perceive yourself, your identity, value and importance.

CHAPTER 19
Results of rejection or non-acceptance

A love 'vacuum'

A person who has not experienced acceptance will often be, what is sometimes termed as, needy. In other words, they always need some kind of help, support or encouragement from others. Sometimes these people will suck the life out of those around them desperately trying to get you to meet the inner need they have. Very hurt people can have an emotional whirlpool that draws everyone and everything into it as a solution to their emptiness. This can include a propensity towards lusts, possessions, acknowledgement from achievements, possessiveness and jealousy around relationships. Problems such as hoarding can fit in here, where a person may feel that belongings connect them to a World where they feel unwanted.

These people will often crave acceptance from *parental figures* such as ministers, or will worship a sports hero or movie star. The person becomes the centre of their lives as a kind of replacement of the absent key figures of a father or mother. Many times, homosexual tendencies fit in here, with psychological studies reporting a high incidence of this behaviour being a response to not having received love and acceptance from a primary care giver in the critical early stages of life [4].

The need for acceptance and love can also be found as a strong motivator behind sex outside of marriage, adultery and even issues such as the epidemic of pornography. These illicit movies offer men the emotional stimulus of these supposedly accepting women being pleased with the efforts of the men portrayed in the pictures. Having dealt with many men with this addiction, I have come to the conclusion that porn for men is primarily about the acceptance and success in relationships that is craved. Clearly there is an additional highly exciting sexual stimulation component as a complication.

When men fear failure or rejection in relationships pornography is an easy option where there are no risks or needs to deal with working through harmonizing relationships. In a twisted kind of way often

---

[4] That is one of a number of reasons for these practices.

their emotional needs are met through seeing men received the way that they would like to be, and affirmed as they would like to be. Men with healthy emotional, relational and sexual relationships at home normally weather these worldly temptations effortlessly [5]. The truth is that nothing and no person can completely fill this belief-based love and acceptance vacuum. Only God can bring wholeness to these broken hearts with His truth and love.

Narcissistic behaviour
Narcissism is defined as an abnormal love and admiration for oneself. It is reasonably obvious that this is the person's solution to not being loved, regarded or treated as being important. From repeated dealings with *narcissistic behaviour* I have concluded that the underlying beliefs are normally something such as; "*I am not important and therefore not loved*".

Their countermeasure to this heart belief is that in their own eyes not only are they important, they are in fact the only person who is important, and they are indeed the most important of all people. This is in essence love of self based on self-promotion in their own eyes. This being the case, it is natural that what **they** think, want, and do is of the utmost importance. They have a tendency towards grandiosity and an inflated picture of their abilities and superiority as a human being. This by implication places everyone else as lemmings and lesser humanity. Because self is now firmly on the throne, they are prone to the whole self-syndrome. Self-consumed, self-centred, self-indulgent, self-justified, self-gratifying, self-important, self-protective, self-righteous, self-deceived and selfish, etc. etc.

In a Christian setting, unfortunately, these people believe for instance that they are going to be mightily used as prophets to the nations, or carry mighty anointing, are apostles and so on. Sadly, many are never used, because they cannot begin with small things or to serve under authority because it is beneath them. God Himself opposes the conformity to Satan's likeness in pride that has occurred in them through their broken heartedness.

It is very difficult for these people to admit weakness; (the deception is that the shortcomings that they are unaware that they carry are in fact only self-perceptions – and are not true anyway) they have

---

[5] There are other issues in play with addiction to pornography that often need to be dealt with.

built walls around the monument to self to protect the image of acceptability and importance from being attacked. Very often these people present as harsh or intense.

Perhaps the *my rights* attitude that we find in society today comes under this extreme focus on self. Possibly believing and fearing that nobody really considers that you are important, have worth, or deserve protection and provision, you then insist and demand that you are looked after.

Hermits and extroverts

Some people respond to rejection by hiding from people in order to avoid rejection. Even in company they present as withdrawn. In a sense they have accepted that they are unacceptable and not good enough and are therefore afraid to come out of their protective shell. Others will gravitate to wearing a *mask* and becoming, for example, the life of the party in order to be acceptable. When they go home, they are very often emotionally exhausted from the effort to rise up and be what they perceive is necessary to *be* wanted and accepted by people.

Others exhibit what is known as *harmonizing behaviour*. This usually occurs when they have learnt in childhood that they need to be whatever other people want them to be in order to receive acceptance. This means that they never really have their own identity and suppressing who they are to please others often leads to mental issues and maladies later in life. Some Christian commentators have suggested that problems such as Alzheimer's disease stems from these kinds of confusion about identity beliefs. I have witnessed that these components are certainly present on several occasions.

Loneliness

Another result of rejection is poor bonding and the inability to make close relationships. Beliefs such as, '*I am not wanted, don't belong, not worthy or worth acceptance, am not cared about*' and so on, presents a strong inner case for not receiving the affection of another, yourself, and even God. We all really do need to hear; '*This is my child, in whom I am well pleased*'. While we cannot accept ourselves, we will struggle to accept others as well. This makes healing and freedom in this area a vital part of returning to God's perfect order.

Matthew 19:19, *"You shall love your neighbor as yourself"* (NKJV).

Emotional immaturity

Some of us older folk who are *digital immigrants* find ourselves in a world where if you cannot get your smart phone to work you ask a 4-year-old to set it up for you. This might be an exaggeration, but often times by early teenage years, our children are very worldly wise on many fronts that we were never exposed to. Emotionally however, they have not developed. They have knowledge but it is not balanced with emotional maturity. Much of this can be laid at the feet of insufficient parenting and nurture. Modern society and living standards now, many times, requires both husband and wife in the workplace to sustain lifestyles.

Coupled with this is the phenomenon of children being overwhelmed with decisions that they are given and not yet equipped to make. In other words, they are made responsible for their lives before they have the knowledge and understanding to cope. I recall seeing a fast food advertisement where a very small child was having one choice after another fired at them. *Is it this kind of food time or this kind? Is it playing time or home time? and so it went. At this age it is possibly better to say; sit up here and eat your dinner. Go and play for ten minutes and then we are going home!* Parenting is a bit like having a length of rope. To begin with your child is completely under control and once they learn some self-control you slowly feed out more rope to them, letting them have more and more control, now a mix of self-control and your control. Finally, as they reach adulthood you throw them the last little bit of rope and they have full control, having gradually learnt self-control and taking responsibility for choices over time. Now your job as parent is finished in that area and you can take up your role as a support and friend. But if you give them all of the rope at the beginning they are out of control, not having matured in self-control and knowledge. More commonly trauma and abuses arrest the normal development of emotions as the wounded child distances themselves from harmful identity beliefs in order to cope with life.

Some people may come for ministry who still feel and behave like a child in some ways. Along with the beliefs about our identity and acceptability that is stored in your mind, is the, *how do I respond when I am hurt like this* information. This is why people at 40 years old or more can have an argument with their spouse and they both walk away and as they cool off, they are thinking; *that was childish, we behaved like 8-year old's!* In all probability, that was where you first took in the belief that you reacted to, and also the response which was now automatic.

Fear of rejection

Once a person has had the pain and negative experience of rejection, they will now be on watch to protect themselves from further rejection. Other fears such as fear of failure or fear of embarrassment, and so on, fall under this category. You must ask yourself, what will happen if you fail? In the past, most likely, you have learnt that this means you will not receive acceptance. Why did you feel embarrassed? Because you felt that something that you did or said was unacceptable!

'Fruit' or possible signs of a fear of rejection
Independence

If I am afraid that you might reject me, then an unconscious decision might be something such as, *I won't need you or your acceptance, and then I don't need to worry about you rejecting me! I will meet my own needs and be my own provision.*

Self-Pity

Feeling sorry for yourself could run closely with this kind of inner thinking. *Poor me, nobody cares about me. I feel sorry for me!* Inside we are singing that *somebody done somebody wrong song*. This nobody cares about me belief may at times also have an outward manifestation; *You must hear my story, how I have been wronged and then you should feel sorry for me too!'* It can lead to controlling behaviour and attitudes; *I must make people care about me, because nobody does!* This unconscious inner thinking stems from insecurity about being accepted and loved. The problem is, that if you make people care about you, do things for you and love you, is that you know inside that YOU made them do it, rendering it meaningless.

You can imagine if God pinned us to a wall poking us relentlessly in the chest with a giant finger saying; *Love me, you must love me!* In the end, for fear of being crushed, we would capitulate and acknowledge our love for Him. This would mean nothing to Him because He made us do it. And yet He extends free will and choice to mankind, which sadly we abuse. It is His, love, mercy and kindness that leads us to repentance, not His control. Where self-pity is, there is often times also resentment, bitterness, unforgiveness, and retaliation towards others and often self. Until healing comes to the broken heart it will be difficult to forgive. Once you have identified and resolved the belief/s producing the hurt, the person usually moves from; *It's all your fault for making me feel this way, to it's not your fault, you have your own issues to deal with.*

King David had it right when his spirit man was encouraging his soul that God had the answer to his pain and negativity.

Psalm 42:5-6&11, "*⁵Why am I discouraged? Why so sad? I will put my hope in God! I will praise him again - my Savior and ⁶my God! Now I am deeply discouraged, but I will remember your kindness. ¹¹ Why am I discouraged? Why so sad? I will put my hope in God! I will praise him again-- my Savior and my God!*" (NLT).

The late Noel Gibson wrote a number of excellent books on rejection in the 1990s. His wife Phyl gave us permission to reference his material after his death. He suggests some of the following, as symptoms that suggest the need for healing from rejection: In the brackets is my expansion.

1. Refusing comfort. (This could include throwing tantrums or sulking.)

2. Rejection of others. (If you reject someone first, if they reject you back then you can justify it to yourself – you feel that if you blow their candle out, then yours will burn more brightly!)

3. Signs of emotional hardness. (Harshness, criticism, judgment, the tongue.)

4. Scepticism, doubt, unbelief. (This stems from not being able to trust. Fearing people's motives towards you.)

5. Aggressive attitudes. (Feeling that aggression/anger, disapproval, in a verbal or physical form is the logical way to ward off further rejection.)

Chapter 19: Results of rejection or non-acceptance

6. Thoughts of revenge. (Retaliation of some kind coming from resentment to perceived hurt.)

7. Argumentativeness. (Point scoring and the need to win an argument and be right all of the time as a countermeasure to the low self-image coming from rejection - simply cannot agree or accept another's point of view.)

I recall working with a man many years ago, and no matter what you said or suggested his response was always; "*I know!*" One day he was driving a truck on a highway and I was the passenger. The traffic lights turned red and there was a police car pulling up at the lights coming the other way. I began to draw his attention to the lights, and that there was a vehicle stopping immediately in front of us. Before I could get more than a few words out he responded; *I know!* Referring to the fact that he had seen the police car, he had not however seen the vehicle in front and I will leave it to your imagination as to what happened next. Needless to say, it was an unpleasant experience stemming from the inability to believe that someone else may know something that you do not.

8. Stubbornness'/defiance. (People who feel that they have been wronged or aren't being accepted and dealt with fairly very often simply will not cooperate.)

When I was a little boy, I felt that I had been wronged with an event with my older brother. As a result, when I was punished for the crime without having, in my opinion, been properly heard I refused to cry or be penitent. As an extension to this we see rebellion, fighting and resistance to authority.

9. Burying emotions (Noel made this statement in one of his books which I took careful note of; *Some bury their emotions but tend the grave continually!*)

I took this to mean that while they do not permit themselves to feel the pain, there is a lot of time spent in making sure that the *body of rejection* is not forgotten. This could be in the form of self-pity, or resentment as to how they had been hurt and rejected.

10. Inner vows. (I thought I would add inner decisions to this list).

There is another reason why rejection beliefs and feelings can be buried or suppressed. For example, many times I find people who have closed down their emotions, using their capacity for self-control in an ungodly way on themselves. Often times this comes from a place in the childhood history such as being told that; *big boys or just boys don't cry.* Therefore, your acceptance becomes based on your not expressing emotion. Your conclusion and inner decision, or vow, is then something along the lines of; *If I am not accepted when I display emotion, then I will not have emotion!* Somebody has helped you misinterpret life and now you are bound by a belief in your heart that after a while you will not consciously be aware of. You require God's truth and perspective in this regard to be made free.

Note:
You never simply don't have emotions, even if you suppress them, they will often come out in your body as disease or your mind as mental illness. Jesus exhibited a full range of emotions in weeping, joy more than His companions, anger at times and so on because that is God's order. We deny our feelings at our own peril.

Self-rejection
This occurs when you accept rejection as being a correct assessment of your acceptability, worth and value. In a sense you continue to replay the rejection beliefs that you hold as now being your truth. In a ministry setting you will hear self-rejection statements overflowing from the heart out of the mouth. These will give you strong insights into the beliefs that people hold. It is extremely common for those who have rejection to also have fear of rejection and self-rejection issues. As they share their story or problem you may hear and note such statements as: *I'm just not good enough, I'm stupid, useless, a loser, hopeless, ugly, such an idiot, never do it right, am not as good as others,* and so on.

I was in the U.K. studying many years ago and befriended a very cultured Englishman named Charles. Towards the end of our studies he asked me a question. He enquired of me, *Are you always so sardonic?* I responded, *I don't know Charles, what on Earth does sardonic mean?* As I now understand it, it means laughingly mocking or being derisive, and in this context, he meant towards myself. In other words, I was making jokes at my own expense, kidding around about my shortcomings. It was however, reflective of some inner issues that I later had to deal with. At that time, I did however decide that if God had accepted me then He was more likely right than I was and so I needed to stop rejecting myself. That dealt with my mind in regards to the behaviour, later my heart was healed as well. This criticism of self, as an inward expression, will normally be accompanied outwardly by criticism of others because of the low self-image that it proceeds from.

False humility can probably come under this banner as well. With an attitude and presentation based around; *well I am just no one and nothing, I am not worth noticing, don't worry about me!* This is not humility, this is low self-image. You can, in fact, be quite confident but still be aware that in comparison to God you are just a created being. So, humility is actually a healthy perspective of your humanity. You have your God given strengths and weaknesses just like everyone else, you are neither greater, nor lesser, you are simply you!

Self-accusation, self-condemnation and self-bitterness
When self-rejection is extreme, it can at times extend to self-hatred because of your perceived unacceptability and inadequacy. Some Christian commentators consider this to be at the root of autoimmune disease. In the heart the belief is that you are not enough, a failure, not what you should be. This, through your shortcomings, makes you the enemy of your own acceptability. Your immune system then plays out its role of destroying the enemies of your wellbeing, which in this case has been inwardly decided to be you! Spiritually and emotionally you are now against yourself because of that which you believe about yourself in your heart.

The experts tell us that the immune system will then attack the weakest link in the chain, often being the organ that is most under load. This could be our stress system such as our thyroid or adrenal glands or other bodily organs. Commonly our pancreases are under such a load because of overeating which makes them the weakest link and we could develop diabetes. The bad diet then, is only creating an environment for the disease to prosper.

Why are many people very obese and have no diabetes and others only slightly overweight and contract the disease? This could be a strong indicator of how prolific the self-rejection issue is today, projecting out of not being accepted in the home or the breakdown of the family unit.

Where self-rejection exists fruits such as guilt and self-condemnation will often be present. Guilt relates to believing that you have done something that you should not have done, or perhaps more likely in this situation, guilt believes that you have not done something that you should have. Hence the guilt is connected to the self-rejection via the mechanism of believing that you should do or be more and have failed.

Story

A number of years ago a man came to me presenting with diabetes. I asked him if he carried a fear of rejection, self-rejection and guilt. After he had thought about it for a while, he reported that he did. We did some brief *Truth Encounter* sessions over the next few weeks dealing with memories containing guilt that produced anxiety and self-rejection beliefs. At the conclusion of the ministry times I also prayed for his healing. After each session he reported that his blood sugar levels came down 2 points. I would not suggest that we make this a guideline for ministering to diabetics as it was an isolated case. However, we did target these emotions deliberately because there are ministries which consider diabetes to be rooted in the specific emotional dynamics of anxiety connected to rejection, fear of rejection, self-rejection, self-hatred, guilt, and depression [6].

We can readily see how this ties together. Depression often comes from hopelessness about ever being able to perform well enough or be enough to be accepted. As a result, you are constantly anxious and fearful about being rejected for not being or doing enough. You then reject yourself for being a failure and feel guilty about not pleasing others or achieving their standards.

So, to minister to these belief based negative emotions, the question is not so much do you have fear of rejection or self-rejection and guilt, as it is to why do you feel guilty and what do you believe that has led you to reject yourself?

Another lady came for ministry at one time with another autoimmune disease called Multiple Sclerosis. She was quite slim and had been a fitness instructor. As we went through the preliminary work up session explaining *Truth Encounters*, I commented to her that if she had been overweight, she may have had diabetes instead. She

---

[6] In His Own Image by Dr. Art Mathias. In my opinion, the specific fear that you are dealing with is fear of rejection, which is very often present with rejection and self-rejection.

related to me that her sister was overweight and she did, in fact, have diabetes. They both grew up in the same family environment and most probably held the same or similar rejection beliefs.

Outward signs of self-rejection

We have just discussed some potential inner workings of self-rejection; there are also some very obvious outward manifestations that may be encountered. Self-punishment for not being acceptable or not accepting yourself could present in behaviour such as *cutting*, or children banging their heads against the wall or hitting themselves. This self-punishment is a sure sign that they are angry and frustrated with themselves. Adults might try to self-destruct with alcohol or drug abuse. Others try to comfort themselves with food and can at times set up a self-destructive cycle. Now overweight, they consider themselves to be even less acceptable by the standards set up by modern media. Still others may go the other way with excessive gym work or excessive exercise or dieting to try to make themselves better and good enough. Some may have other performance and success-based goals such as career or wealth. These can also be to do with receiving love, acceptance, significance, value and worth from a performance-based world system which is for the most part rejective.

Cannot, will not receive encouragement

We have already mentioned self-pity. Many people cannot receive affirmation, the inner rejection belief regarding their unworthiness is like a force field that cannot accept any encouragement as being true. For some self-pity is a kind of distorted *good feeling* which is a kind of demonic counterfeit for love. Often people suffering from self-rejection will present as negative, pessimistic, and are unable to receive because of unbelief. The underlying belief is something such as; *if I reject me, surely you must too!*

Negative self-image and comparison

Commonly, self-rejection proceeds from memories and events where a person has been compared to a sibling, or another student, and as a consequence has felt that they are inferior. If this is the case then usually you will find that they still have a problem with comparison in order to rate their acceptability today.

The truth is that God does not mass produce humanity as we do cell phones where you can have a black one or a silver one and otherwise they are all exactly the same. Each one of us is an individual, one of a kind masterpiece that God created for Himself to spend eternity with.

2 Corinthians 10:12b, *"But they, measuring themselves by themselves, and comparing themselves among themselves, are not wise"* (NKJV).

Once we have received healing from beliefs stemming from comparison, it is wise to take the counsel of scripture and not compare ourselves with others. If we do, we will either decide that we are better and be swollen up in pride, or decide that we are lesser, and enter into inferiority and self-rejection. Just accept that you are an awesome individual creation that cannot be compared to any others. There are no other versions of you in existence, found in history or planned for the future. Thank and praise God as King David did for making you, you. That is not pride; it is acceptance of yourself and who God created you to be. You are the work of His hands; you did not after all create yourself!

Psalm 139:14-17, *"[14] I will praise You, for I am fearfully and wonderfully made; Marvelous are Your works, And that my soul knows very well. [15] My frame was not hidden from You, When I was made in secret, And skillfully wrought in the lowest parts of the earth. [16] Your eyes saw my substance, being yet unformed. And in Your book they all were written, The days fashioned for me, When as yet there were none of them. [17] How precious also are Your thoughts to me, O God! How great is the sum of them!"* (NKJV).

Distorted self-image

Self-rejection produces a distorted self-image. It can be like a belief based demonic hedge stopping people from receiving love, acceptance and belonging. It can cause people to reframe things that are said to them according to the inner heart beliefs that are held. Genuinely motivated suggestions for doing tasks another way or improving functionality from a friend, spouse or employer are heard, reframed by beliefs, and perceived as an attack on competency and worth.

My wife and I have ministered to many pretty girls who believe that they are quite ugly and unacceptable. This often begins as a child when they perhaps had a skin rash or similar, and possibly someone was unkind at school. Maybe they had a little bit of childhood chubbiness. The point is that the belief that they took to heart has distorted their image of themselves and consequently they now reject themselves. I mentioned this phenomenon whilst teaching on a school recently along with some other problems that apply here. A pretty young girl burst into tears and had to go out and receive ministry. I later found out that an incorrect self-belief about her looks was the cause of the outburst.

Sample rejection scenario
A person approaches you for help.

Step 1: Explain the process to the person, and what you are looking for, namely heart beliefs. This process could include having them read, view or listen to material explaining the ministry.

Step 2: The person comes for the actual ministry session.
Note: They already have the problem that they are struggling with so you don't need to come up with anything. It is not your job to fix their whole life, just try to help them with whatever is presenting at the time.

Listen to their story and the issue that they are bringing to you. Make notes of the things that they say that may be clues to what they believe. Writing things down is good as it means that you don't miss things that may need to be visited, and you don't need to interrupt their story.

Step 3: Example
    Fred: I felt very uneasy when I went to try out for the church choir!
    Me: Why do you think that you were uncomfortable in that setting?
    Fred: I think that I felt that I did not belong there, I was not a part of it.
This could indicate a possible belief such as; *I am not wanted*, or *I am not accepted*.

Step 4: We have them concentrate on the feeling produced by the thought that they do not belong, and are not a part of it; rejected by the group. We are looking for the earliest possibly historical place where they learnt beliefs that caused them to feel this way.

Fred: I have just remembered my first day of school. There was a group of kids playing and talking together and they ignored me!

Me: As you concentrate on the memory and feel that rejected feeling, why do you think that they ignored you?

Fred: Pauses and explores the memory. I think it is because I am not like them, I am new and so they don't want me. This must be true because they are all accepting each other, but I am on the outside!

Me: Let's ask the Lord what His truth, the real truth is. Lord what do you want Fred to understand about that time where he felt that he was not wanted because he is not like them, because he is new?

Fred: The Lord is reminding me, that these kids went to Kindergarten together and already knew each other. I couldn't get in to Kinder because they were full up.

Me: So, are you not wanted because you are different?

Fred: No, I am the same; I have just not built relationships yet. Later I did make some good friends there.

Me: How do you feel about the church choir now?

Fred: I feel excited about it now; I will be making some new friends it will just take a little time.

Me: Perhaps close in prayer thanking the Lord for His healing, or I may enquire as to whether or not there are other things which require ministry.

Clearly this example is not going to be as deeply painful as rejection often is. Some people may have very painful traumatic rejection situations from some kind of abuse or absence of love in the home. Other people may have a *profile of rejection* composed of multiple less painful beliefs.

CHAPTER 20
Pride

In this chapter we are going to examine the normal fruit associated with the pride tree.

Matthew 12:33b, *"... for a tree is recognized by its fruit"* (NIV).

What is pride?
We could say that pride is fallen confidence. God intended for us to have good self-worth and identity within the context of being satisfied with our own *individual* self. Pride is a condition where we now see ourselves as *above* other people and not equal. It is the imprint that Satan put on mankind tempting them with; *you will be as God*. This being your own god and making your own rules is clearly seen across humanity today. It began with Satan, and we see the five *I wills* of pride represented in scripture.

Isaiah 14:13-14, " *13 You said **in your heart**, "I will **ascend** to heaven; I will raise my throne **above** the stars of God; I will sit enthroned on the mount of assembly, on **the utmost heights** of the sacred mountain. 14 I will ascend **above** the tops of the clouds; I will **make myself** like the Most High"* (NIV, Emphasis mine).

This propensity for self-promotion is abundantly evident in the pride profile. We could say that pride is the enemy of success in anything we undertake. God is opposing our being conformed to the likeness of Satan and his nature, and his consequent expression in the Earth through our deception and subsequent co-operation.

James 4:6-7, " *6 But he gives us more grace. That is why Scripture says: "God opposes the proud but gives grace to the humble." 7 Submit yourselves, then, to God. Resist the devil, and he will flee from you"* (NIV).

Pride would have us have too higher opinion of ourselves, gathering credit or glory for ourselves. It encourages us to believe that we are over or *above* others and to consider ourselves as being superior. This gives us some insight into how Satan engineers it into our lives. It is a deception, and when we believe that we are *inferior* then the solution that he offers is to build an image that we convince ourselves is *superior*. The deception comes as it did with the tree in the Garden of Eden as; *this is what you need, this will make you happy.*

Once we have misinterpreted the situation and received this as being the solution to our inferiority, it leads us to sinful attitudes and practices towards our fellow man. It is the fallen self-life, old nature or 'flesh' exalting itself, as it was with Lucifer placing *self* on a self-made throne. Evidently most people are unaware that they are being influenced by, and hosting, a spiritual nature. It fits well with a performance based, climb the ladder of success society, which promotes achievement as a basis for acceptance and identity.

We would describe it as a *sin of the heart* which appears to be less tolerable to God than *sins and weaknesses in the flesh.* In the following passage, we see a man accepting his human frailty and sinfulness. Confession means, *say the same as,* and this man is accepting and confessing his shortcomings as measured against the ways of God, which is the basis of forgiveness. The Pharisee however saw himself as superior, or above the other man and consequently because of the attitude of his heart was not justified.

Luke 18:10-14, " [10] *Two men went up to the temple to pray, one a Pharisee and the other a tax collector.* [11] *"The Pharisee stood and prayed thus with himself, 'God, I thank You that I am not like other men; extortioners, unjust, adulterers, or even as this tax collector.* [12] *'I fast twice a week; I give tithes of all that I possess.'* [13] *"And the tax collector, standing afar off, would not so much as raise his eyes to heaven, but beat his breast, saying, 'God, be merciful to me a sinner!'* [14] *"I tell you, this man went down to his house justified rather than the other; for everyone who exalts himself will be humbled, and he who humbles himself will be exalted"* (NKJV).

People suffering from beliefs that hold inferiority and low self-image will either give up in self-rejection, and roll over, or gravitate to performance and achievement-based self-worth.

The Bible says that the pride of life is from the world, not from the Father. Remember the fruit of the tree in the garden of Eden was good for making you wise; knowledge puffs up, but love builds up; knowledge can make you look superior, but love will be building up others rather than self.

We have mentioned Peter failing when he denied Jesus, and as a result becoming humble, before God released power through him. It was necessary for Peter to understand his frailty and humanity for him to become humble, with a correct perspective of himself in order for him to be useable. He was then a *non-stick* Christian who would not let the glory and accolades be attributed to himself. He now knew who he was and made sure that everyone else was aware of his humanity as well, knowing fully that pride was the enemy of revival and harvest. As illustrated in the following passage, Peter refused to be lifted *above* anyone else, and made sure that the accolades and glory went to the right place.

Acts 3:11-12&16, " *¹¹ Now as the lame man who was healed held on to Peter and John, all the people ran together to them in the porch which is called Solomon's, greatly amazed.* ¹² *So when Peter saw it, he responded to the people:* "*Men of Israel, why do you marvel at this? Or why look so intently at us, as though by our own power or godliness we had made this man walk?* ... ¹⁶ "*And His name, through faith in His name, has made this man strong, whom you see and know. Yes, the faith which comes through Him has given him this perfect soundness in the presence of you all*" (NKJV).

Later we see the Apostle Paul making similar statements in Acts chapter 14. These early Christians knew their humanity and weakness, and that God would not let His glory go to another. They knew that they should not be seeking the praises and acknowledgement of man in lifting them *above* others. These men certainly refused to let the glory stick. It was a secret as to why God was able to place His power upon and through them.

Acts 14:9-12&14-15, "*⁹ This man heard Paul speaking. Paul, observing him intently and seeing that he had faith to be healed,* ¹⁰ *said with a loud voice,* "*Stand up straight on your feet!*" *And he leaped and walked.* ¹¹ *Now when the people saw what Paul had done, they raised their voices, saying in the Lycaonian language,* "*The gods have come down to us in the likeness of men!*" ¹² *And Barnabas they called Zeus, and Paul, Hermes, because he was the chief speaker.* ... ¹⁴ *But when the apostles Barnabas and Paul heard this, they tore their clothes and ran in among the multitude, crying out.* ¹⁵ *and saying,* "*Men, why are you doing these things? We also are men with* **the same nature as you**" (NKJV, Emphasis mine).

The fruit, or what will pride look like in behaviour and attitudes

Importance
You have to be somebody, you cannot simply be. You have to be important, regarded and valued. Many people and tasks will be beneath you, so as a result of your inferiority and rejection, you are now rejective. In a Christian environment this will probably be manifested as a person who cannot serve nor do small things. It is a breeding ground for super spirituality where people are too great in their own eyes to receive from other people and so propose that God talks to them directly. In turn it can be an opening for false prophecy where they feel that they always know best about that which God is saying. It will at times be in the form of correcting all of the *lesser* people who aren't doing things right (according to your standards).

Religiosity also comes into the picture. This happens as people learn all of the spiritual talk and jargon, know more scriptures, listen to more preachers than others etc. to make themselves be greater or above others. We call religion the *try hard* spirit, trying hard to be somebody. Religion declares, *this is what you do to be good enough, this is how you look and what you say!* Religion tries to be good enough by what you do, according to what you think will make you acceptable to man, and possibly be enough to please God.

Very often, as with the Pharisees, it is a man version of what God is supposedly looking for. He wants people who will worship in spirit and truth. This means that they will be very real, as Jesus was on Earth. We don't see Him with many of the religious or hyper spiritual activities that we see in churches today. If it doesn't look how Jesus was, I think we can safely discard it. He flew in the face of religious rules and practices, and we don't see Him having special manifestations to be more spiritual than others.

This can also be represented as masks, where the person presents as the *mighty anointed* or similar, but at home, off the stage or away from people they are entirely something else. The underlying problem is that they believe that who they *really are* is not good enough and inferior.

Presumption

Have you ever had those people come to visit, who sit down, put their feet up on your furniture, and proceed to change your television channel to what they want to watch? They will probably be overbearing, right about everything, full of their own opinions, arrogant and superior. The *language of the spirit* emanating from their actions and attitudes is something along the lines of; *I am and there is no other!* Have mercy on them. Although they can be annoying remember that usually underneath is a person who has been crushed or neglected, and full of a low self-image.

In 1 Samuel chapter 15 we see King Saul not fulfilling the instructions of God that he received from Samuel the prophet. He was anointed as King, but not as prophet. He wanted to please the soldiers and be popular. People with these issues will possibly presume to promote themselves to release or anoint people in a church environment, hence promoting themselves over existing authority. In the case of King Saul, Samuel noted that he was once *small in his own eyes.* In other words, his self-promotion and subsequent presumption and rebellion were proceeding from his low self-image.

1 Samuel 15:17, *Samuel said, "Although you were **once small in your own eyes**, did you not become the head of the tribes of Israel? The LORD anointed you king over Israel. 18 And he sent you on a mission, saying, 'Go and completely destroy those wicked people, the Amalekites; make war on them until you have wiped them out.' 19 Why did you not obey the LORD? Why did you pounce on the plunder and do evil in the eyes of the LORD?"* (NIV, Emphasis mine).

Rebellion against authority often runs closely with pride. This is because authority figures have not provided the identity needed for them to feel that they are sufficient. This is perceived as unjust or unfair and the response is to bypass authority as those in authority are not to be trusted. For Saul, who already suffered with low self-image, there would almost certainly have been heart beliefs leading him to this tendency. If he lived now in the dispensation of the Holy Spirit outpouring, he could have easily been set free.

1 Samuel 15:23, *"For **rebellion** is like the sin of divination, and **arrogance** like the evil of idolatry. Because you have rejected the word of the LORD, he has rejected you as king"* (NIV, Emphasis mine).

Judgment

These people will often be graceless, harsh, critical and unforgiving towards your shortcomings, imperfections or failures. The hardness and harshness are probably because, at heart level, they have not forgiven themselves for not being up to the mark.

Comparison

We have already mentioned this under the self-rejection heading, but it is a fruit of this tree. I would like to add that when comparison is coupled with low self-image it can lead to self-pity. *Poor me, everyone else is good enough, but I will never be as good as them. I will never be important, worthy or loved. I will never be good enough for love, compliments and attention.* This can be a down side, or depressive side that works in a manic depressive, or as it is now known a bipolar cycle. Swinging from feeling superior as a solution to your perceived inferiority, and then swinging the pendulum back the other way past centre into a depressive state where you feel that you can never be as good as others or be good enough.

Competition

Somehow, we think that if we can climb higher, run faster, gather more money or in some other way prove ourselves then we will feel better about ourselves. I was driving to school to pick my children up years ago, and a lady, who very much carried this whole profile, whizzed past in her car. I found myself accelerating, and then realized that I was being caught up in a competitive spirit and so I backed off. These people are often high achievers who will project onto you that you are not enough, don't do enough or have enough. They have arrived and you have not.

Once you are aware that it is a belief based emotional/spiritual dynamic that is around them, then you have the option. You can either be a tea bag and soak it all up and respond out of the feelings that it elicits in you; or be a golf ball, which doesn't soak up anything, and can be smacked around and abused quite a bit and remain impervious to its environment without losing its shape at all.

This principle is the same with anything that others are projecting onto you. If it is, however, causing a strong response in you it may be a good opportunity to *go up on the hoist*, so to speak, and get checked over for wrong beliefs or anything out of alignment in yourself.

We have a friend who is a single mother who was constantly wearing out and having to replace the front tires on her car. I suggested that she had someone look a little deeper, and it was found that there was a mechanical problem on her vehicle causing the scrubbed-out tires. Sometimes we do this in the church and just pray well-meaning prayers for each other expecting that we will go better now, when we need to look a little deeper.

The reason that Jesus was so impervious to anything that the devil threw at Him directly or through people, was that He had no wrong beliefs in His heart about Himself or His relationship with the Father. He also understood the ground that gave place to the devil in people that He dealt with that made them agents for the devil to use.

John 14:30, *"I will no longer talk much with you, for the ruler of this world is coming, and he has nothing in Me"* (NKJV).

Striving
Trying hard to have the upper hand, being contentious, struggling to be right or regarded, does not promote peace or unity. This possibly shows up in the marriage relationship more than anywhere else. Again, to not have your opinion valued strikes right at the roots of where this most likely all began. Striving may well struggle against the system and rules as well individuals. It is a part of the imprint on fallen man from the garden to want to throw off the rules and limits. This so that our humanity can have a free expression and realization of self. This is perhaps nowhere better illustrated in recent times than in the 1960s when the Bible was removed from the schools in the United States.

Without the guidelines regarding enjoying a prosperous life, morality and dealing well with your fellow man, it was not long before people became their own god. This meant 'self' deciding what was right and wrong, and as a result, we saw the emergence of sayings such as; *If it feels good, do it! If it's right for you, it's right. Look out for number one.* Etc.

Many statistics indicate little change for decades up until that time. After the change, for example, violent crime now multiplied more than 6 times by 1990. Divorce rates more than doubled by 1975, while unmarried couples increased by more than 3 times by 1983.

Single parent households doubled and premarital sex for teenage girls increased by 3 times by 1990. Pregnancies for unwed girls went up 7 times over the same period with a commensurate increase in abortions. All of this adds up to a lot of unnecessary misery. It really does work better if God is God and we live humbly as the created beings before Him.

Jealousy

Again, King Saul is our example. As we have previously stated, he was once small in his own eyes, or as we would frame it, he suffered from inferiority and low self-image. When David came along, he was exalted by the people. Jealousy occurs when someone else receives what you want. Because of his low self-image, King Saul needed to be praised by men. It ministered to his inner hurt and beliefs. So when David received more adulation than him he burned with jealousy.

1 Samuel 18:7-9, " [7] *As they danced, they sang: "Saul has slain his thousands, and David his tens of thousands."* [8] *Saul was very angry; this refrain galled him. "They have credited David with tens of thousands," he thought, "but me with only thousands. What more can he get but the kingdom?"* [9] *And from that time on Saul kept a jealous eye on David."* (NKJV)

This ungodly jealousy gave ground to an evil spirit which promoted a solution to the problem of David's popularity, namely his removal by murder. In today's world, and particularly the church environment this murder will usually come from the tongue by destroying a person's reputation.

It continues on in 1 Samuel 18:10 to say, [10] *The next day an evil spirit from God came forcefully upon Saul. He was prophesying in his house, while David was playing the harp, as he usually did. Saul had a spear in his hand* [11] *and he hurled it, saying to himself, "I'll pin David to the wall"* (NIV).

As time went by, we see King Saul relentlessly pursuing David, trying to eradicate him as being the threat to how he is perceived by the people. We can separate out his sinful attitudes and behaviour caused by his perceived beliefs and emotional needs, and his true self, which really loved David. I am reminded of the Apostle Paul in

Romans chapter 7 where he laments over the fact that his belief-based actions do not match that which he really wants.

Romans 7:15, *"For what I am doing, I do not understand. For what I will to do, that I do not practice; but what I hate, that I do"* (NKJV).

Certainly, this double mindedness was evident in King Saul at times; self-conflict evident, having just tried to kill David seemingly now lamenting his own state.

1 Samuel 24:15-17, *"¹⁵ May the LORD be our judge and decide between us. May he consider my cause and uphold it; may he vindicate me by delivering me from your hand." ¹⁶ When David finished saying this, Saul asked, "Is that your voice, David my son?"* **And he wept aloud.** *¹⁷ "You are more righteous than I," he said. "You have treated me well, but I have treated you badly* (NIV, Emphasis Mine).

Note:
Many of the presenting symptoms relating to pride issues discussed here were first noted in an excellent study called *Possess the Land* put together by Carroll Thompson from Dallas, Texas and Published by Carroll Thompson Ministries in 1977.

CHAPTER 21
Rebellion

2 Thessalonians 2:7, *"For the secret power of lawlessness is already at work; but the one who now holds it back will continue to do so till he is taken out of the way"* (NIV).

Rebellion or lawlessness runs very closely with pride. As we have already seen, Satan as Lucifer' no longer wanted rules. In his proud, self-elevated state he wanted to be above the laws of God and no longer wanted to submit to the authority of God and His commands. God of course would not tolerate this rebellion and Lucifer and those who cooperated with him were cast down to the Earth. He then tempted man to throw off the rules as he had and conform to, or be imprinted with, the likeness of his behaviour.

So, lawlessness or rebellion as we know it is when we won't come under authority and laws, or we set ourselves against authority. Our own will becomes our *god*, subject only to self, and we are no longer prepared to have rules and limits. I will re quote the passage from 1 Samuel 15:23 to make some observations before we move on to examine how the devil engineer's lawlessness into our lives.

1 Samuel 15:23, *"For rebellion is as the sin of witchcraft, And stubbornness is as iniquity and idolatry"* (NKJV).

Strong's concordance cites the Hebrew word; 'meriy' as meaning bitterness, i.e. (fig.) rebellion. The reason for this may be that when someone is embittered by injustice or unfairness it will produce rebellion as a predictable response. This will normally be directed towards those who are in authority, who are perceived as not being just and fair. In the case of the Garden of Eden, Satan was saying did God *really* say do not eat from that tree? He was craftily implying that God was keeping good things from them and did not really care about them. In a sense he was saying; *did God really give you limits, surely that's not fair!* God was painted as being unjust in keeping that tree from them and mankind doubted His love and character. It is not surprising that the way back to God for humanity is to accept His love, and the grace offered through His merciful character. God has given us the opportunity through Christ to reverse the effect of the fall and consequent separation from him. He has largely limited Himself on Earth to trusting in His nature and love and accessing all that He has for us by faith.

Sources of rebellion
We see rebellion and lawlessness enter into mankind at the fall as mankind doubted God's justness and fairness. We decided that we could be *like god* setting our own rules, providing for ourselves, and being accountable only to our own will and wants. Rebellion then is a predictable reaction to perceived or actual unfairness and injustice. We probably consider it to always be sin, but this is not always so; it is a reaction to a situation and what I term a *universal emotion* or response.

For example, the authority figures that Jesus dealt with were the religious leaders of His nation of birth. Jesus clearly rebelled against the heavy religious demands that these teachers were putting on the people. He showed what God actually wanted in relationship, not conformity to man-made rules. His desire was that we would respond to God and obey Him because we love Him. Jesus demonstrated the love, mercy and nature of God by meeting the needs of those who came to Him. This included those who had needs on the Sabbath, which infuriated the religious people of the time.

Matthew 23:4-5, "⁴*They crush you with impossible religious demands and never lift a finger to help ease the burden.* ⁵*"Everything they do is for show"* (NLT).

Jesus considered these religious burdens and demands on the people to be unfair, unjust and not representative of the Father. His response was rebellion against the existing system. He was not rebellious by nature but would not come under or submit to their unjust practices. We see that rebellion is a predictable response, or as I term it, *universal emotion* that any of us can experience when we are either exposed to stressors that produce that reaction, or if we are triggered by a perception of injustice if we hold unfairness issues. There are certainly oppressions and abuses in the world that we should be indignant about and push back against.

Rebellion 'as witchcraft'
As we explore this in the context of our falleness, why is rebellion as bad as, or like witchcraft? Those who practice actual witchcraft are taking control, that is not theirs, over the will and outcomes of other people. It is a perversion of the will, imposing your will on another. People in rebellion prefer their will and desires over those of another. They will struggle to submit to the position and will of instituted authority. Christian people with rebellion issues will want to bypass authority and usually consider that they have a *hotline* to heaven hearing directly and correctly from God.

There is a well-illustrated warning for us on two occasions in the book of Numbers. Firstly, with Aaron and his sister Miriam, who considered themselves greater than Moses because of his Ethiopian wife. We see yet again pride, and considering yourself above another, being linked to rebellion. As we have previously stated, Moses was usable because he was humble. After 40 years in the desert, he did not even want the significant leadership position that God had called him to. Being a leader does not necessarily mean that you are greater than others.

Numbers 12:2-3, "*² So they said, "Has the LORD indeed spoken only through Moses? Has He not spoken through us also?" And the LORD heard it. ³ Now the man Moses was very humble, more than all men who were on the face of the earth* (NKJV).

Rebellion inevitably will bring a curse and not a blessing, as is evidenced by the consequences of their heart attitudes.

Numbers 12:9-11, "*⁹ So the anger of the LORD was aroused against them, and He departed. ¹⁰ And when the cloud departed from above the tabernacle, suddenly Miriam became leprous, as white as snow. Then Aaron turned toward Miriam, and there she was, a leper. ¹¹ So Aaron said to Moses, "Oh, my lord! Please do not lay this sin on us, in which we have done foolishly and in which we have sinned* (NKJV).

I am amazed that Christians are not more careful in their attitudes towards their leaders, with examples such as these in the scriptures. Remarkably a few chapters later we see almost the same situation played out again. Someone has said that, *the one thing that we learn from history is that we don't learn from history!* We see the outcome of rebellion played out on Korah and his accomplices as they self-promote their own position.

Numbers 16:3, "*They gathered together against Moses and Aaron, and said to them, "You take too much upon yourselves, for all the congregation is holy, every one of them, and the LORD is among them"* (NKJV).

If we have rebellion issues it is advisable that we get them dealt with as quickly as possible for the sake of our future prosperity.

Numbers 16:32-33, " *32...and the earth opened its mouth and swallowed them up, with their households and all the men with Korah, with all their goods. 33 So they and all those with them went down alive into the pit; the earth closed over them, and they perished from among the assembly"* (NKJV).

I had a friend a number of years ago who became a Pastor. He visited me a little bit confused inquiring as to why he was now so unpopular, when previously everyone had loved him. I pointed out to him that when you take on a Senior Pastors role and represent authority, the people with rebellion issues automatically now unconsciously, see you as their *bad, absentee or uncaring dad, or disapproving school master*.

Sources of rebellion
Here are some potential beginnings of beliefs coming from authority figures. They emanate from real or perceived unfairness and injustice when it seems to a child that they are;

- not valued   - not protected   - not noticed   - not wanted
- not loved   - not cared for   - not affirmed   - not important

These we would consider to be omissions or deficits in terms of emotional nurture that would be justly and fairly expected. They are areas of identity that should have been put into the child that have not. When they are not present the child interprets the situation through their fallen tendencies, with no doubt some inspiration from unholy spirit, as being not fair. The next list covers things that have been done to a person, and should not have been, such as abuses which *were actually* committed and are unjust;

- Physical domination or violence
- Sexual abuse
- Emotional control or manipulation
- Attitudinal: nasty, angry or disapproving looks, shrugged off, indifference
- Verbal abuse: mockery, put down, condemned
- Inappropriate discipline, expectations, or workload

Both of these lists project onto the recipient attitudes, which result in beliefs such as; *you are not worth the time, you are a nothing, you are not of any value, I don't care about you* etc. Being made to feel this way really is not fair and is a part of broken heartedness that needs God's healing.

Possible struggles for those with rebellion issues

Lusts
People with rebellion issues often have trouble subjecting their flesh. They refuse godly limits and often lack self-control. Very commonly if they have grown up with injustice from authority figures they will take control of their lives as early as possible. Their inner thinking is probably something along the lines of; *If they won't look after me and care about what I need, then I will look after myself!*

This is probably the hardest time in history to be a teenager. Once you have decided to care and provide for yourself you will look to the World for what is available. You are now confronted with masses of addictive material including items such as drugs, cigarettes, alcohol, porn, illicit sex, unhealthy foods, media and much more. The deception behind bondage to addictions is still the same as it was with the temptation in the garden, with a spiritual entity suggesting; *This is what you need; this will make you happy and put you in a better place!* The tree of the knowledge of good and evil in that sense is alive and well. We know for Adam and Eve that it did not make them happy, and the same is very much true for us today.

Protecting our children
Ephesians 6:4, *"And you, fathers, do not provoke your children to wrath, but bring them up in the training and admonition of the Lord"* (NKJV).

We can protect our children from rebellion by treating them fairly, being caring and attentive to their needs, and not expecting them to be perfect in a hostile environment. It is not beneficial to try to isolate them from the world but rather teach them how to make good decisions and choices in the world.

When my children were in their early teens, they wanted to go to the pictures with friends from school who were going. I was informed by them that there were no sex scenes but a little bit of swearing. The age that they were, I had to weigh up the situation carefully. If I said no, then it would not be seen as fair because their friends were going. If I said yes, they may have heard some bad language, which doubtless they were already hearing in the school yard. The fact that they were being honest about the movie also demanded that they be respected and trusted to make their own decision at that age. I let them make their own decision and trusted their maturity in weighing the pros and cons.

Our children, now fully grown up, remain great friends that we often travel with. Understanding the roots of responses can help you to bring up your children in the counsel of the Lord. Is God unjust or unfair? Never, in fact His throne is established by being right in all His dealings and on justice. So, if we are to represent Him then we will be just also.

Psalm 89:14, *"Righteousness and justice are the foundation of Your throne; Mercy and truth go before Your face"* (NKJV).

Anger, bitterness, and resentment may also be additional responses and reactive emotions to injustice and unfairness. Self-pity could also be present. It is the *nobody cares about me* thinking that can proceed from not being dealt with properly. Lack of trust and insecurity about people's motives may also be evident, which can make it difficult for people with rebellion issues to come and submit to another for help. If you are dealing with somebody presenting with rebellion, my strong recommendation is that you reframe it around the root of the problem as injustice or unfairness issues. This is, not proposing that there is something wrong with them or their behaviour, but rather that there is something wrong with how they have been treated or dealt with by others, and consequently they will be far more likely to be willing to receive help.

Although all of this sounds daunting, and as if there is a lot to deal with, don't forget that all of these may be varying responses that come from one heart belief in one memory event. In some cases, it may be just a matter of minutes to resolve lifelong inner conflict and rebellious attitudes. Others have had a life of injustice and may hold a number of unfairness beliefs proceeding from different sources and may require more time.

Rebellion from rejection
Rejection is a source of rebellion as we see in the story of Cain and Abel. Cain felt that it was unfair that Abel's offering was accepted but his was rejected. In truth, Abel showed his heart towards God in bringing the best of what he had. People often feel that if we reject what they do or have then we reject them as a person. In reality, being a great musician or singer for example, is not who we are, it is a gift that we have. It was not Cain himself that the Lord did not accept; it was his attitude to the giving. We have to learn to have sufficient grace as God did to separate what we do from who we are. In any case, Cain rebelled against the warning of God and participated with sin in murdering his brother.

Genesis 4:3-7, "[3] *At harvest time Cain brought to the LORD a gift of his farm produce,* [4] *while Abel brought several choice lambs from the best of his flock. The LORD accepted Abel's offering,* [5] *but he did not accept Cain's. This made Cain very angry and dejected.* [6] *"Why are you so angry?" the LORD asked him. "Why do you look so dejected?* [7] *You will be accepted if you respond in the right way. But if you refuse to respond correctly, then watch out! Sin is waiting to attack and destroy you, and you must subdue it"* (NLT).

Although Cain had to suffer a consequence for his actions it was evident that the Lord still accepted who he was and cared about his safety.

Genesis 4:15, *"The LORD replied, "They will not kill you, for I will give seven times your punishment to anyone who does." Then the LORD put a mark on Cain to warn anyone who might try to kill him."* (NLT).

Rebellion as a 'Spirit'

Using the *Truth Encounters* principles, we are not looking for evil spirits but at times along the way we become aware that a problem, such as rebellion, is inordinate in its proportions, amplified or there is a stronghold indicating demonic involvement. We are still primarily interested in the beliefs that are held that produce the rebellion or other issues. Often when we expose the beliefs that are held is when the spirit is most likely to manifest and be easily cast out. I will deal with this in more detail in a later chapter. We are primarily focused on the person and along the way we may tell a spirit to go as a part of the process. If we have discovered and resolved the belief and exposed the spirit, the person normally now does no longer want to engage their will in hosting the spirit.

Most, if not all of us, have had some type of rebellious thinking somewhere in our lives because it was a part of our old nature stemming from the fall. In the event of somebody having a *spirit of rebellion* I have observed some fairly easily discernible behaviour. People who are captive simply cannot submit to another. In a church setting they may go from church to church airing their opinions, and whilst enjoying the spiritual climate cannot submit to any leadership. There can of course be other reasons for this as well. In relationships they cannot lay down their will in submission to another.

I recall one man who loved to serve in his local church in a variety of ways. But this service always had to be on his terms and his own decision and desire, or in other words, what *he* decided to do. If he was asked if he could help out with this or that the best that he could offer was; *I might*. Good man that he was, he simply could not submit. For him; *I might*, actually meant, *I will*, but he just could not bring himself to come under another will in compliance.

In that instance you will know that it is normally a spirit. People with this problem will often breeze into churches with lots of ideas and projects that they have that will bring people under their agenda and then disappear again. At times the source of a *spirit of rebellion* is the family line where it has passed through generations. Where this is the case, there is very often concurrent evidence of mental illness which we would consider to be a curse and not a blessing.

Autism and rebellion

I have only personally ministered to one autistic person who is now radically changed in terms of the behaviour that proceeded from the autism. At times and in certain situations there are some minor signs, if you know what you are looking at, of a residual tendency toward typical autistic behaviour. I am certainly not setting myself up as any kind of expert on autism and have not studied it in detail as a condition. I have only ministered to it on one occasion in a Christian context, applying Biblical principles. This involved ministering over time to many of the emotional areas that have been described in this book. This gradually eliminated the autistic behaviour. The areas of dramatic change include; rebellion, (as a spirit) self-hatred, violence, withdrawal, anger and insanity. This largely happened through rebuilding the walls of the personality with materials such as; acceptance, encouragement, fairness, godly control, security and reframing the person in questions boundaries.

I have had exposure to a number of other people suffering from autism in a general setting. In a number of those cases I have noted an observable *spirit of rebellion* in their fathers. By this I mean that their rebellion was demonic in nature from a spirit inside as opposed to the pressure to be rebellious from the outside of our beings that we all have or have had elements of. At the same time, I have seen other cases where this is not obvious in either parent but seems to be evident further up the family line. I am certainly not suggesting any kind of standardization based on the few cases that I know of, but simply offer what I have seen in case it helps anyone understand their own loved ones. I have also heard testimonies of autism symptoms improving and reducing through the prayer of faith.

Other Christian commentators have also observed the rebellion and self-rejection issues present with Autism. As we have previously pointed out, a result of rejection can be withdrawal as a countermeasure to extreme fear of rejection, along with self-rejection. At times the withdrawal from relationships is so extreme that the speech or ability to communicate is also not functioning. Some consider this to be an inherited deaf and dumb spirit stemming from Matriarchal control. They consider this ungodly order in the household to be the root cause of the problem. In addition to fathers with rebellion problems I have certainly observed some controlling women and role reversal in the generation lines of children suffering with these problems. Some report changes as these spiritual issues are dealt with.

Autism is one of many disorders that began to emerge after the family unit, from a Biblical perspective, began to disintegrate. Is it a coincidence that we can point to the rapid escalation of autism following the removal of the Bible in the U.S. in the early 1960's, as being the standard of reference? This impacted the world significantly with the proliferation of media from the U.S. and many following this nation as a role model. The problem is that rebellion against God's word and instructions still holds a consequence for subsequent generations, just as it did in the garden at the beginning. I am old enough to have personally witnessed the changes commencing in the 1960's where increasingly women don't work together in leadership, but instead rule the household. One study indicated that in 1975 the incidence of autism was 1 in 5,000. By 1985 it had become 1 in 2,500, 1995 1 in 500, 2001 1 in 250, and by 2012 1 in 88. A very alarming change as the family unit is reframed according to humanistic principles.

Note: The term 'autism' has been in use for around 100 years. It reportedly comes from the Greek word 'autos' which means 'self'. This then describes a state or condition where a person becomes an isolated self, withdrawn from social interaction.

Rebellion Summary
Failure to provide love and acceptance, nurture, encouragement and security leaves a void that the child feels that they need to provide for themselves. Nearly all rebellion problems begin in childhood and you can expect them to be networked with other negative emotional reactions stemming from heart beliefs.

Ministering to rebellion
You will need to go back and look for the origins of rebellion that exists against authority figures and others, usually the parents. In the ministry session we are looking for the feelings of injustice or unfairness. We are also being aware of statements emanating from

inner beliefs such as, for example, that's *just the way it is for me, nobody ever cares, it's not fair but it's just the way it is!* We have the person focus on the feeling or the statement which connect them to a feeling that is replicated in the past.

Having arrived at the earliest possible memory or impression, have them focus on the feeling and identify the belief, or if they are more cognitive and have the belief first as they look at the situation, have them concentrate on the belief and allow the matching feeling to emerge. Remember, your role is to ask questions to help them identify that which they believe.

Sample Rebellion Session

Me: "What seems to be bothering you Fred?"
Fred: "I've been struggling with angry feelings a bit lately when I come to church."
Me: "If you think about it, what exactly is it that is making you angry?"
Fred: Pause, reflection. "I think it is because the leaders never show any interest in the groups that I am starting around the church."
Me: "How does it make you feel as you think that nobody is doing that for you?"
Fred: "It's not fair; they don't care about what I am doing!"
Me: "Why don't you think they care about what you are doing?"
Fred: Reflection, some emotion. "I think it is because I am not very important...."
Me: "Fred, I want you to concentrate on that thought that you are not important. It must be a sad feeling so I want you to let yourself feel that feeling....and now I want you to let your mind connect you with other places where you have felt exactly that way."
Fred: Pause. "As soon as you said that I remembered when I was a little boy, all of the other kids getting a special meal brought home and I wasn't allowed to have any. I was probably about 4 years old."
Me: "So as you look at that situation, why do you think that you were missing out?"
Fred: "I feel a bit angry. They don't care about what I want!"
Me: "So does not caring about what you want mean that they don't care about you....?"

Fred:	"Yes, I am not important, I don't matter, and they don't care about me."
Me:	"Ok Fred I want you to concentrate on those feelings and see what the Lord has to say to you... His truth, which is the truth." (Then I pray inviting God to communicate truth through the Spirit of truth).
Fred:	"It seemed just like my own thoughts, but it seemed like God said that I am important to Him. And I just remembered that passage from 1 Peter 5:7 that says that He cares for me. As I continue to think about it, I have also remembered that I had been sick at the time ... and what I am sensing is that even though they didn't explain it at the time they didn't give me any because I might throw up!"
Me:	"So are you important? Cared about?"
Fred:	"God thinks so. And apparently my parents cared enough and thought enough about me to not want to make me sick."
Me:	"Fred I want you to look in your heart, not your head...is that belief that you are not important still there?"
Fred:	"No, which is strange because it has always been there...but I can't find it any more. I am important, and cared about."
Me:	"How do you feel about the leaders not paying attention to your groups now?"
Fred:	Ponders. "Well to be honest, I guess that I have never trusted them and let myself connect with them. I wanted them to take up my ideas; I was not interested in working with theirs. I suppose I just expected them to know how I felt which was a bit unreasonable of me I suppose."
Me:	"Do you feel alright about approaching them now?"
Fred:	"Yes, actually I feel a bit excited about what might be ahead for me!"

CHAPTER 22
Control

Godly control versus ungodly control

Clearly God wants His Kingdom run in an orderly way, not out of control but in an organized fashion, under instituted authority. This godly control of course is meted out in the right spirit and needs to be appropriate. We could say that we are to be responsible and have authority over certain areas, beginning with our own behaviour. For example, Adam was to be responsible for the garden and indeed the subduing of the Earth. He was given the list of instructions before Eve was created, so it fell to him to cover and be responsible for how she responded to the temptation. Instead of eating of the fruit he should have made some kind of statement such as; *God told us not to eat of that tree and so I am not touching it. Can I recommend that you don't eat it either and that you don't talk to snakes anymore?*

In our modern western society, we have seen a dramatic role reversal over the years since the Bible was removed as the standard for living in the early 1960s. Men became pleasure seekers who no longer wanted any responsibilities. As they increasingly abdicated their responsibility to being in long term relationship, and be committed to their wives, the spouses in turn became less and less secure about being looked after, provided for and protected. Whenever this is the case something rises in an individual with some kind of inner decision such as this; *If he is not looking after me/us, I better take over and look after myself and the family!* This understandable response has led increasingly to a role reversal in the home where the woman is the head of the house. It has been going on for so long now that it is almost a cultural norm.

We cannot blame the women at all; it is the failure of the men to fulfil their role, as with Adam, that has led to the problem. This is not to say that the man is to be domineering. Adams role was to hold up the standards and words of God, not to force Eve to do anything. She had free will as well, but if Adam properly set the climate of care, provision and protection for his wife, she most likely would have been more than content to work with him in his pursuit of God's will.

Some cultures now have a high percentage of households where the wife is leading. In 1 Kings chapter 21 we see King Ahab being too weak to appropriately execute his authority. The result was that his wife Jezebel presumed authority and control, and manipulated the outcome of the situation. To swing the pendulum all the way back past centre the other way, many nations have men dominated societies. Christians in these societies often use the Bible to strengthen their case of their wives being treated as second class citizens who must submit to them. This is actually a manifestation of a controlling spirit. The man's responsibility, in terms of how he sets a Biblical Holy Spirit led environment in the relationship, is the only part that he needs to worry about as an act of his free will. He cannot reasonably expect his wife to respond to him by doing her part, if he, as the covering, and the stronger member does not provide for her that which she needs.

Ephesians 5:25-29, "*25 Husbands, love your wives, just as Christ also loved the church and gave Himself for her, 26 that He might sanctify and cleanse her with the washing of water by the word, 27 that He might present her to Himself a glorious church, not having spot or wrinkle or any such thing, but that she should be holy and without blemish. 28 So husbands ought to love their own wives as their own bodies; he who loves his wife loves himself. 29 For no one ever hated his own flesh, but nourishes and cherishes it, just as the Lord does the church*" (NKJV).

It is not the man's role to force or manipulate the woman to submit to him. His part is only, by 'his own' free will and choice, is to fulfil God's intentions for him in the relationship. The woman in turn has her instructions in the Bible on how she should respond to his godly attitudes and provisions for her.

Although the Bible describes the woman as the weaker member [7], it also describes her as a helpmate comparable. If she is comparable, she is not inferior in the least. Clearly, she is weaker physically, and emotionally her hormonal state is up and down throughout her monthly cycles, whereas a mans is constant. She is the other half of God's perfect picture for us, together complementing each other with altogether different attributes and abilities. If we go into a church, for example, my wife can remember everything in the room,

---

[7] 1 Peter 3:7 Husbands, likewise, dwell with them with understanding, giving honor to the wife, as to the weaker vessel, and as being heirs together of the grace of life, that your prayers may not be hindered (NKJV).

whereas I have usually only noted where the door is so that we can get out again when it is time.

Women in general are more spiritually and emotionally open than men and will often pick something up intuitively in God more quickly than the gentlemen. However, along with this increased openness comes the potential for deception by other spiritual entities which is well evidenced with the story of Eve. God has created man as more cognitively based needing to apply logic and reasoning, weighing things up before he is prepared to receive them. Because of this I always value my wife's input and insight in all matters.

1 Corinthians 11:10-11, *"¹⁰ For this reason the woman ought to have a symbol of authority on her head, **because of the angels**. ¹¹ Nevertheless, neither is man independent of woman, nor woman independent of man, in the Lord"* (NKJV, Emphasis mine).

When God first called us to a deeper walk with Him my wife did not respect me and was quite rebellious. (I might point out that much of this was related to unresolved issues from her past!). Let me say though, at that time I was not particularly respectable and I needed to get into God's order myself! I had to learn how to appropriately deal with her and my family according to the Word of God. As I did that, over the years we naturally fell into our Biblical roles. But it began with me, as the covering, conforming to the Word of God before this could happen.

Still today I do not make my wife do anything. I respect her and her freewill and she can choose to follow me as I follow Christ or not, but I certainly would not expect her to submit to controlling attitudes towards her. I understand that just as Christ is the initiator of the ways of God to His bride, the Church, I am to be the initiator in setting the spiritual environment in the home. In fact, the Apostle Paul pointed out that the whole marriage picture was given to us so that we would understand the relationship of Christ and His bride.

Ephesians 5:31-32, *"³¹ For this reason a man shall leave his father and mother and be joined to his wife, and the two shall become one flesh." ³² This is a great mystery, but I speak concerning Christ and the church"* (NKJV).

God's plan is that we are one, working together, and this is His plan for a man and his wife and also a picture of Christ working together in harmony with His Church.

Areas of Godly control
Before we move on, let us briefly detail some areas that God wants us to be responsible for and have control over.

1. *Man over his family.*
This is not controlling your wife, as she is already at the age of choice, but is more in exercising fair and godly authority over children in a decreasing manner as they grow up and learn how to control themselves.

2. *Pastors and leaders in Churches.*
God wants His churches run decently and in order. This does not mean that a Pastor or leader can control his congregation; it means that he instigates God's order and sets the environment as loving, accepting, gracious and acknowledging free will and choice. Authority into people's lives is given by them and not taken from them. People either choose to submit to you as they learn to trust your love and motives or not. Many soulish people who have not read a Bible or have chosen to not obey it will remain carnal, and as in the garden will want the limits thrown off. They will be resistant to anyone suggesting to them what they could do.

This is their free will choice and they can deal with God over it. But it does not mean that they can run amok or that in any way we compromise the standards of God for them. The old saying is that people *vote with their feet*, meaning that if they are self-willed, they will take themselves in and out of church. We just need to respect them in that, but not let them get out of order in services. If they have come into a church they have come under the rules and standards of that church as with any other institution.

There are rare occasions where it is appropriate and godly to control adult people and override their free will and choice. Some instances that I can suggest are; drug addicts, violent people or criminals and people with mental illness. These people have no resistance to spiritual forces manipulating their lives and need help to control themselves.

Proverbs 25:28, *"Like a city whose walls are broken down is a man who lacks self-control"* (NIV).

Under normal circumstances God does not control anyone, and respects free will and choice, and so as His children, should we.

Ungodly control from insecurity
It was God's intention for mankind to grow up secure in identity, feeling protected, and provided for. When Adam and Eve took themselves out from under these attributes that were provided for them from God, they became insecure and fearful. To a large extent they now felt that they had to be *as God* for themselves, fulfilling these needs. It is now inherent in mankind to try to control his environment in order to feel secure. The problem is that this involves imposing your will on others which is never God's plan for how harmony and peace should operate. You will most likely find insecurity tangled up in every war that promises safety or a better future as an outcome.

The root of ungodly control in general terms is *insecurity*. This insecurity causes us to make things happen for our own provisions. It is demonic in the sense that it is a perversion of the *will* area of your being, imposing your *will* on others, beyond intended parameters. This is driven by Satan and is not from God.

1 John 5:19, *"We know that we are children of God and that the world around us is under **the power and control** of the evil one"* (NLT, Emphasis mine).

This insecurity leads to controlling others in ways that were not intended by God. For example, children who are grown up and are still subject to the will of the parents. They are not allowed to make their own decisions for themselves without the influence of the family. This is quite common in many European cultures where mum continues the mothering long after the children have grown up and become adults. Sometimes if a wife is not loved properly by her husband, she becomes insecure that there will not be anyone who will care about her, so she simply cannot let her children go even after they are mature people.

Insecure children growing up without firm guidelines and boundaries will even as early as 3 or 4 years old or younger, attempt to take control of their perceived needs. They are trying to make sure that they get what they think they need in terms of attention and provision using tantrums and other controlling behaviour. The truth is that the parent has been given authority to control the child in a godly manner, but in practice the child is now in authority because the adult is submitting to them. Submission giving authority to the one who is submitted to is a principle. Allowing a spirit to be given access to work through these children by their unwitting cooperation, becomes a serious issue.

Romans 6:16, "*Do you not know that to whom you present yourselves slaves to obey, you are that one's slaves whom you obey*" (NKJV).

2 Peter 2:19b, "*... for a man is a slave to whatever has mastered him*" (NIV).

Misuse of the capacity for control
Authority to have some measure of control is linked to responsibility. I could not, for example, walk into a church down the road and begin to tell people what to do. I am not responsible for them and consequently have no authority over them. The same goes for my family and so on. When you see people trying to get others to do things for them, they are exhibiting controlling behaviour.

I remember once visiting an event hosted by another church. The hosting Pastor was quite a controlling man who at one point in the service proclaimed; *All the Pastors will now come out and will pray for the people!* It was not what he was doing that was the problem, it was the spirit in which he was doing it. He was imposing his will to make something that he wanted to happen onto everyone removing their free will and choice.

This was insecurity on his part, that if he requested support, his desires may have been rejected. In the event that you submitted to such a statement you have now just placed yourself under his control and given him authority over you. Let me reiterate the words of the old Jazz song that is a good measure for discerning the spirit behind an action. *It ain't what you do; it's the way how you do it, that's what gets results!* If he had requested; *If there are any Pastors here that would like to come out and pray with people, would you like to do so now?* Then it would have been an entirely different situation, respectful and acknowledging personal sovereignty. I have known churches where people were too afraid to cut their sandwiches without asking the Pastor how it should be done. This is not a healthy, godly situation.

As a Pastor I never tell anyone to do anything. I do not own anyone. I respectfully request if they would be prepared to do this or that and am quite prepared to accept whatever response I receive. People submit to you because they want to, not because they have to. We respond to God as a response to the wonderful way that He treats us, and so it should be with us in relationships. Often people who are controllers seem to have used all of their capacity for control on others and consequently lack self-control and their immediate environment is in disarray.

Often controlling people will use the *God told me* or *thus saith the Lord* card to manipulate a situation and have their will carried out. After all who can challenge what God Himself has said! I tend to think that often when people are making these kinds of statements that you are dealing with the *'controlly' spirit* and not the *Holy Spirit*. They are hearing what they want to hear or feel they need to hear, to get what they want or remove their insecurity and thus open themselves up to deception. This will be obvious if the outcome of the use of the Lord's name relates to something that they think should happen.

As I understand it, blasphemy is when you take the Lord's name in vain. This does not necessarily mean swearing, it can mean saying that God said, when He didn't. People need to be more careful than they realize about how they use the Lord's name. Well-meaning mistakes about what we hear will attract grace, but manipulation and imposing your will or what you think should happen on others, attracts nothing but trouble.

In the church environment you may hear prophecies such as; "Oh my people you are not doing enough, saith the Lord!" This is most likely proceeding from the spirit of the person who is trying to make something happen that they think should happen. Usually upon examination they are people who have hard and often religious standards towards themselves.

Self-control

Listed as a fruit of the Spirit, or evidence that we are cooperating with and giving precedence to the leading of the Holy Spirit, is *self-control*. This is when we are able to discipline ourselves, not to be conformed to the World in some way through some kind of inappropriate *self*-indulgence. As usual, there is a demonic version of this where we make some kind of inner vow and control ourselves in a way that is not in a godly order.

Many years ago, I was at a seminar where we had to list our emotional intensity from 1-10. As I went along, I realized that I was scoring zeros. Initially I thought that I must be very spiritual because I never got, for example, angry. But I began to realize that I never wept, never laughed or never exhibited any emotion at all. I had made an inner vow to suppress or control my emotions, because, I believed as a child that if you laughed too loud or cried, it was not acceptable. *Little children should be seen and not heard* is something that many of us grew up under.

I do not blame my parents for this as it was the cultural norm at the time, however it did have its effect on me. I learnt that Jesus wept, got angry, had joy beyond all of His companions and indeed exhibited a full range of healthy, God given emotions. We can misuse self-control in a way that is the fruit of another spirit.

Note:
You never just don't have emotions. If you are holding them back underneath as I was, they will tend to come out in your body or behaviour as was the case with myself at that time, and as a result I had a disease. We can safely say, that not having emotions, can be just as big an indicator of wrong hearts beliefs and problems as excessive emotions.

Is God Controlling?

We are to be 'led' by the Spirit which denotes choice. Jesus began His ministry *led* by the Spirit into the desert and finished it in the garden of Gethsemane, deciding by His own free will and choice, to lay down the easy way in preference to the Father's will. It is perhaps notable that Adam and Eve chose to follow Satan in a garden where everything was going fine, and Jesus to reverse the effects of this chose to suffer to fulfil the Father's desires.

We could state that God is not controlling at all. He instructs us in the way and encourages us and empowers us to fulfil godly choices but does not make us do anything at all. Sometimes it would probably be easier if He did, but He is looking for us to respond to the Love that He initiates and choose Him. Jesus often included words such as; *if*, *then*, and *but*, which denotes choice. Put another way, He is saying that if you choose to walk this way then you can expect this to happen.

John 15:7-8, "⁷ **If** *you abide in Me, and My words abide in you, you will ask what you desire, and* **it shall** *be done for you.* ⁸ *By this My Father is glorified, that you bear much fruit; so you will be My disciples"* (NKJV, Emphasis mine).

Matthew 6:15, "**But if** *you do not forgive men their sins, your Father will not forgive your sins."* (NIV, Emphasis mine).

John 8:31, " ³¹ *To the Jews who had believed him, Jesus said, "***If** *you hold to my teaching, you are really my disciples.* ³² **Then** *you will know the truth, and the truth will set you free"* (NIV, Emphasis mine).

We know that Jesus was the perfect representation of the nature of the Father, so was He controlling? Not at all! The following passage helped me a lot in relationships, and also as a young Pastor, in realizing that it was not my job to make anybody do anything. It was simply to teach the way, if people were open to hearing, and then offer them whatever help they needed to get there. It would be completely understandable in these following verses, if Jesus had complained to the disciples that He had just invested years in training them and that therefore it is only reasonable that they remain with Him. But instead, He was completely releasing, not in the least bit controlling, and left the decision entirely up to them.

John 6:67-68, "⁶⁷ *Then Jesus said to the twelve, "Do you also want to go away?"* ⁶⁸ *But Simon Peter answered Him, "Lord, to whom shall we go? You have the words of eternal life"* (NKJV).

Control extremes and the big picture
In modern western culture, we see greatly diminished self-control with people being slaves to all kinds of addictions. There is almost an abuse of freedom, with virtually no discipline and few guidelines

for general living. It is all about you, what you want, and your rights. As someone has well said, the devil will always give you too little or too much. So as far as how you live, in today's society you can get drunk, have illicit sex, watch pornography, swear publicly, disrespect whoever you like, and in many cases do drugs and nobody pays much attention at all. While personally many people are out of control, at the same time the dark shadow of humanism is coming across our world.

This publication is not meant to touch on controversial subjects but we note that via media, technology and humanism, we are increasingly being controlled in what we may and may not do, and monitored in what we watch and where we go. Rules relating to religious expression are increasingly being imposed with yearly changes. Whilst it is true that *religion* is at the heart of many of the conflicts in our world today, true Christianity is not fundamentally a religion. It is not a set of practices or things that you do to be right with God, it is a relationship with God because you are right with Him through Jesus Christ.

Other more obvious *big picture* controlling ideologies include dictatorships, communism, and controlling religions. We see all of these actively working over cultures across our world today. It is not God's order. Let us get back to working with control in individuals, and particularly in the Church.

Branches that come from ungodly control

1. **Manipulation**
This could be in the form of kids threatening tantrums, wives withholding sex, or people saying that *God said*.

2. **Domination**
Violence or some kind of abuse is the typical outworking of someone misusing their authority or power.

3. **Standards**
"You must be how I want you to be and think you should be. You need to do what I want, how I want it or I cannot receive you! You must fit into my plans!"

4. Bitterness and unforgiveness
"I will not release you or forgive you for being how you are, or who you are, and not being and doing what I want!" This projects rejection because if what you want or do is not good enough then by implication you are unacceptable. That's not fair and so you can expect rebellion as a response to your control.

5. Self-willed; leading to intimidation
"If I don't get what I want, get my own way you will pay in some way or I will explode in anger....so look out!" (Intimidation)

6. Things have to be a certain way
This could come in the form of perfectionism or obsessive-compulsive behaviour which is an extreme form of insecurity and fear compelling you to control details of your life. Things have to be a certain way or there is a fear that something bad will happen. It can be learnt behaviour growing up in a household full of fears, or from a controlling environment where there would be some kind of pay out if things were not done according to the will of, for example, a parent with control issues.

Others have grown up not believing that they are cared about and will be looked after. They control those around them to make sure everything is done the right way to meet their needs. The demonic realm certainly can be working in areas of control. In order to identify heart beliefs relating to insecurity or fear, the best question that you can ask is; *what will happen if...?* If, for example, you don't check the door over and over, or you don't do things this way or that? It can be a tormenting bondage for many insecure people. If you don't do things how they think things should be done there can be some kind of violent, angry or extreme reaction. Sometimes these people will not trust others to do things for them because they believe that these things MUST be done a certain way.

7. Lack of self-control
We have already mentioned this; it is as if their capacity for self-control is directed outwards in getting others to do things for them, and as a consequence they have little or no self-control or authority over themselves.

8. Tendency to get others to do things for them
Controllers will always be getting others to do things for them. Remember they are insecure, so they are making sure that you care about them because underneath they believe that nobody does. For leaders, often many people are more than willing to help us; it is a good thing if we don't abuse that by getting them to do things that we could easily do ourselves.

9. Blame, fault finding and criticism
They should have done it this way or that way...my way!

Effects of ungodly control on relationships
We have already discussed the role reversal that is out of God's order for the home that comes as a result of insecurity. We see many couples, Christian couples, in conflict, wrestling backwards and forwards with each other trying to impose their will on each other. This creates instability and an insecure environment in the household which will generationally generate more insecurity down the family line.

Healthy relationships can only exist in the context of free will and choice, where you lay down your right to expect or demand anything from the other. Once you begin to live this way and treat each other this way you will soon find yourselves volunteering and preferring what the other partner wants. In my opinion the best place for sanctification of the will is in the marriage union. I always think that if you won't lay down your wants for your partner then you probably won't for God either. This is an important part of the dying to self process, where life is no longer all about you! When we release people into their own choices about methods, results, and how they want to do things, we are giving them respect and valuing them.
Galatians 5:13-15, "*¹³ You, my brothers, were called to be free. But do not use your freedom to indulge the sinful nature; rather, serve one another in love. ¹⁴ The entire law is summed up in a single command: "Love your neighbor as yourself." ¹⁵ If you keep on biting and devouring each other, watch out or you will be destroyed by each other*" (NIV, Emphasis mine).

While my wife and I were engaged we sold one of our cars to a delightful old lady who took us outside her home and gave us some excellent advice. She pointed up to her roof and made the following comments; *If I threw a rope over my roof and you were one each side of the house trying to pull it off you would have a big struggle and not make much progress. But if you both come around the same side of the house and work together it is as easy as anything!* So, rather than oppose each other contesting for our own will and way, if we lay down our side of the house and give our will to the other without expecting anything in return, then I can tell you from experience and 40 years of marriage that your life goes from being your worst nightmare to your greatest joy.

Luke 6:38, *"Give, and it will be given to you: good measure, pressed down, shaken together, and running over will be put into your bosom. For with the same measure that you use, it will be measured back to you"* (NKJV).

Practical outworking of ungodly control

1. It pushes away the ones that you are **trying to control**. If you are trying to conform somebody else to you, then you are not accepting them for who they are ... an individual.

2. It reads as an **unfair projection**. It proposes that they are not good enough as they are and should be something else. It suggests that what they want is worthless, implying that they are nothing.

3. **Love must come by choice**. If you make people do things to show that they care about you it is meaningless, because even if they do your will, in this regard you *know* that you made it happen. It was not something that they did for you just because they wanted to. In this sense a saying that is used in the musical world could be applied; *less is more*. Meaning, sometimes the right thing at the right time is more important than the volume of things done. It is more meaningful if people do less for you of their own accord, than doing a lot that you have compelled them to do.

4. **Controlling God**. Some movements even try to control God. There are extremes of faith where it is taught that if you believe hard enough and long enough that you can get God to give you what you want. Essentially this can be like witchcraft, where you turn God into some kind of vending machine who does your

will and becomes your Holy Spirit. Faith principles are for us to receive the promises of God which He initiated and already stated in His word as that which He has promised to give us. God will not be controlled; you may have to save up for that red sports car yourself.

1 John 5:14-15, "*¹⁴ This is the confidence we have in approaching God: that if we ask anything **according to his will**, he hears us.¹⁵ And if we know that he hears us--whatever we ask--we know that we have what we asked of him*" (NIV, Emphasis mine).

Other people who may have been given everything that they wanted growing up sometimes get angry with God when He does not do the same. You may see resentment and so on towards Him. This is usually rooted in resentment and anger that projects from parents who didn't seem to care about them, and now they believe that God doesn't either if He doesn't supply their *wants*.

5. **Legalistic religions**. There are religions and denominations that demand that you conform to their religious standards for acceptance. They can be very controlling in regards to who you marry, your finances, your spiritual disciplines and so on.

Probable sources of ungodly control

1. **Insecurity** - as we have detailed in this chapter, the most common reason producing ungodly control are areas in which we don't feel secure.

2. **Modelling** – at times growing up seeing a controlling mother or father can cause us to replicate the behaviour, believing that this is simply how you behave and act towards others. As we have previously stated, it is often attached to cultural expectations, and so we see that controlling attitudes can be learnt by osmosis soaking up the environment around us.

3. **Generational issues** - there can be a spiritual element where a weakness or tendency to gravitate towards operating in this manner is present.

What are we looking for in ministry?

Whilst aware of other possibilities, we are primarily looking for historical insecurity events matching the current need to control your surroundings. Having noted the fruit of control, you will probably have a much better response if you *ask* the person if they ever feel a little insecure, as opposed to *telling* them that they are controlling.

Associated inner beliefs that overflow from the heart

1. **Lack of attention** - *nobody cares about me*

2. **Lack of protection** - *I must look after myself*

3. **Abuse** - *I can't trust others to look after my needs, because when I do, I get hurt*

4. **Lack of provision** - *I must get things for myself, nobody really loves me or cares about what I need, so I must get people to provide for me. I must meet my own needs*

5. **Fears** - *I cannot let go of my insecurities and control, what will happen?*

Ministry protocol
1. Find where the insecurity began
The womb; (not wanted and therefore not feeling protected or safe?). A life event or theme in the home from early life experiences, osmosis growing up, or the family line.

2. **Deliverance** where applicable, concurrently with healing of the associated beliefs.

3. Sometimes teaching as you go with how to be releasing and **hold things loosely**. Some people are not aware of what they are doing, or that it is not God's order. Once you expose the discrepancy and give perspective it leaves them free to decide on their path.

Note:
You do not need to remember all of this to minister. It is to help you understand that controlling behaviour often flags insecurity beliefs. It is not necessary that you study every detail, just the basic principles.

Sample: Ministry to ungodly control that is presenting from insecurity.

Freda: "My husband says that I am very controlling."

Me: "Give me an example of why he would call you that."

Freda: "Sometimes he gets home later than he should from work. He complains that I am always at him to be on time. He says he feels controlled and can't even stop off at the supermarket on the way home."

Me: "What do you feel will happen if he isn't home on time?"

Freda: Ponders. "Mmmmmm I guess I feel that there will be nobody there for what I need and it's not fair."

Me: "I want you to concentrate on those thoughts that it is not fair that nobody is there for what you need, and see if you can remember another time as early as possible in your life where you felt just like that."

Freda: "As soon as you asked me that, the memory of my first day of school came into my mind. All of the other kids were picked up but my mum didn't arrive for ages."

Me: "As you look at that situation what is the strongest way to describe what you believed as a result of that event?"

Freda: "I guess I believe that I am not important and so nobody is bothering to be there for me. I feel unprotected."

Me: "As you concentrate on that feeling let us see what truth the Lord has for you?" Prayer; "Lord what would you like Freda to know. She believes that she is not important enough to be there for, she feels unprotected."

Freda: Pause. "It seems like my own thoughts but it seems as if He is saying that I am important to Him, and that He has set His affection on me, and the scripture that He will never leave me nor forsake me has come to my mind."

Me: "Do you still believe that you are not important enough to be there for?"

Freda: "No, I am very important. I also just remembered that my mum had a flat tire and that is why she was late. But I knew that and it didn't seem to fix the problem before."

Me: "That is probably because you took in the belief when you were very upset and emotionally vulnerable. It is what you perceived to be true at the moment of weakness that counts. That conclusion was deeply stored in your heart and as a result it is the inner thought that remained."

"How do you feel about your husband getting home late now?"

Freda: "Fine. I can't believe that it mattered so much to me. It seems a bit ridiculous. He should be able to do some errands if he wants to."

3 LEGS of the 'Jezebelic Spirit'

Rebellion and ungodly control are like witchcraft because they are all about you imposing your will on another and making what you want happen.

1 Samuel 15:23, *"For rebellion is as the sin of witchcraft, and stubbornness is as iniquity and idolatry"* (NKJV).

We have already explored this passage in terms of the rebellion aspect. The word normally translated as *stubbornness* here is the Hebrew word; *patsar* which according to Strong's concordance means; to peck at, i.e. (fig.) stun or dull:--press, urge, stubbornness. Along with rebellion, you have this sense of *pecking at, pressing,* or *urging,* in order to have what you want and impose your will on another, which we would describe as ungodly control. All of this contributes to the *I* syndrome or the fallen *self* on the throne problem that is described in the Bible as the *Flesh or sin nature*. We can perhaps summarize it in this way with some easy to remember I words. These may help you to recall the normal roots of the tree problems that we have just discussed;

PRIDE as   "I will make myself above"
                 (Comes from inferiority, or insignificance)
REBELLION as   "I will not submit to another"
                 (Comes from injustice, unfairness)
CONTROL as   "I will have my way"
                 (Comes from insecurity)

There have been a number of books written giving a lot of detail in regards to the type of fruit that is associated with what is described as a *Jezebel spirit*. Whilst there is no Jezebel spirit mentioned in the Bible there is the example of behaviour that we find in the story of Jezebel that does often have a demonic element. When these spirits are in place, they may respond to any name given when the authority of Christ is exercised.

In my experience the three elements that summarize Jezebelic responses are pride, rebellion and control. From these, all of the other fruit proceeds. Most of us either have or have had one or more of these expressions in some measure and they were not directly held by an evil spirit.

We can of course, point the finger and describe and avoid people with this behaviour and run them out of the Church. However, if we look past the fruit as God does, and see the hurt in the heart, we will have grace for them and seek to minister to the beliefs producing inferiority, injustice and insecurity. Many times, they are not open to help because they have difficulty admitting that they may have a problem. They may struggle to trust and submit to someone for ministry. If this is the case then, of course, dealing with their attitudes must be wisely negotiated to protect the Church family.

Many of these people have been hurt and abused more than most, and they are looking for genuine love and understanding. Often, we have to grow in love and grace to reach the person, moving past their offensive attitudes to reach the real person underneath. As the saying goes; *they don't care how much you know until they know how much you care.* We then have to grow in grace and love before these hurting ones that God wants free will open up to us.

1 Peter 4:8, *"Above all, love each other deeply, because love covers over a multitude of sins"* (NIV).

Proverbs 19:11, *"A man's wisdom gives him patience; it is to his glory to overlook an offense"* (NIV).

Jezebel
People with unhealed Jezebelic behaviour will present doing the types of things illustrated in the Bible. In 1 Kings chapter 18 Jezebel kills off the Lord's prophets. Today Jezebelic Christians will try to assassinate Pastors, leaders and genuine ministries or authorities. This will usually be with their tongues, through attacks on the spirituality or abilities of the leaders. They often try to gather people to themselves by starting groups in or out of the church bypassing permission from those in authority. In this sense they can instigate divisions in the Church. You will often hear that God told them. They will usually appear to be very spiritual as was Jezebel.

In 1 Kings chapter 19 she intimidates Elijah, the man of God. Jezebelic people will often threaten and intimidate people who will not do what they want. Jezebelic people commonly want to bypass the normal processes of being acknowledged in a church and sometimes seek to get in close to senior leadership. From there they can manipulate and influence things in the direction that they desire.

In 1 Kings Chapter 21 we see Jezebel very close to senior leadership in the form of King Ahab her husband. When he was too weak to exercise his kingly authority over Naboth in the purchase of his vineyard, Jezebel stepped in and *made it happen*. These are some of the qualities of her actions that we need to take note of in light of what we can expect from unhealed people with Jezebelic mindsets. She is not submitted to Ahab's leadership. She assumes authority that is not hers. She manipulates and controls people to get what she wants. She instigates lying, false accusation, slander and murder. What began as assassination with the tongue in this case ends up playing out in actual murder as Naboth is removed from the scene. Ultimately Jezebel is cursed for her activities and meets a very sad end.

We certainly do not want to see anyone not finish well, so we need to see these hurting ones as God does, looking inside to the inferiority, injustice and insecurity that they have been exposed to. Graciously, we need to be extending the hand of help rather than the pointing finger of accusation and judgment.

- Section 3: Discernment -

CHAPTER 23
Principles of Anger

Many years ago, we lived in a city in inland Australia. It was a very dry area redeemed only by a large river supplying irrigation. At one time we moved into a very old and neglected house. There was nothing alive in the garden and all that remained was one small seemingly dead tree about 5 feet tall. I was going to pull it out but a visitor looked at it and said that it was still alive and that if I watered it that it would recover.

I faithfully began to stand out in the yard in the cool of the evening hosing my 'dead' tree. As I stood watering one night the thought came into my mind; *why don't you play golf anymore?* It was a strange question because I had not played for more than 15 years at the time and was no longer really interested in the game. I considered the question for a while and responded; *I would get too angry.* The next question came into my mind; *And why did you get angry?* After thinking it through for a few moments I replied; *I got angry because I was frustrated.* The next inquiry was; *And why did you get frustrated?* I pondered this for a few moments and came to the conclusion that it was because I could not do what I should be able to do.

The understanding then came into my mind that I became frustrated because something was not how I thought it should be, namely, in this case meeting the standards that I had for my performance on the golf course. When the frustration came to fullness it boiled over in anger. Anger is not a problem in itself; you don't just get angry, or be an angry person, it is coming from something that you believe. From this watering session I established the statement in my mind that *anger comes from unmet expectations or standards*, and more than 20 years on, I have found it always to hold true.

This could relate relationally to a situation such as newlyweds making adjustments with each other. They both come into the marriage with a set of standards and expectations about how the house should run, learnt from their growing up environment. For example, the husband gets frustrated, and then eventually angry because his mother always used to do the dishes straight after their meal. His new bride on the other hand grew up in a household where it was social time after dinner and the dishes were done later in the evening or in the morning. They would both be frustrated and angry with each other trying to enforce their standards and expectations onto each other. The solution is of course to decide to pull down whatever standards and requirements that you are putting onto each other. This holds true for all anger where you are trying to apply your rules to each other. It even extends to people having to meet the unreasonable religious standards of the leaders or denominations in a church environment. Whenever somebody comes to me with an anger problem, I know immediately that I am looking for whatever it is that they believe or perceive, that *isn't how they think that it should be.*

When you apply this to *Truth Encounters* you are looking at anger beliefs coming from events where things were considered to not be how they should be. Perhaps this could be a father who never attended school events with their child. The child feels that this is not how it should be, based on what other fathers are doing. These unmet expectations or standards are probably out in front of a deeper belief such as; *I am not worth being there for, therefore I am worthless. Or I am not as worthy or valued as the other children whose dads make the effort to attend.* Usually when you resolve the hurt belief behind the fruit of anger, the anger is resolved. There can of course be multiple situations and beliefs.

God and expectations
We can be thankful that God dealt with any expectations and standards that could have been applied to us through the cross. Jesus met all of the requirements of the law on our behalf so that God could extend grace to us and we could come as we are, fully accepted and with access to the Father.

In relationships as we learn to be conformed to the likeness of Christ in this, and remove any standards or expectations that we may have learnt from family or society, we find our relationships will flourish. If there are areas where we have difficulty extending this grace, then we are looking for inner beliefs that are being triggered when we are dealing with others.

Anger as a 'universal emotion'

The principle of anger being a predictable response to things *not being how we think that they should be* is not always sin, and not always inappropriate. At times it is the right thing to do to show disapproval of activities that *are not how they should be*. This is well illustrated when Jesus became angry at the money changers making His Father's house into something that it was not intended for. It should have been a house of prayer, but it was made into a den of thieves.

Matthew 21:12-13, *"[12] Then Jesus went into the temple of God and drove out all those who bought and sold in the temple, and overturned the tables of the money changers and the seats of those who sold doves. [13] And He said to them, "It is written, 'My house shall be called a house of prayer,' but you have made it a 'den of thieves'"* (NKJV).

Self-anger

When there is anger towards others, as with other emotions, it is most often inward as well. If someone comes for ministry and their spouse is for example, reportedly making them angry, because they make them feel as though they are not good enough in some way; as well as being angry at the spouse, they are also most likely angry at themselves for not really believing that they are good enough. If they thought they were enough they would not be hurt by the spouse's treatment. So, you are looking for the memory and the pain that related to them 'supposedly,' not being what they are meant to be. Anger is the response and not the problem, so once the hurt relating to the expectations and standards is resolved the anger will disappear.

Anger and health

Ephesians 4:26-27, *"[26] In your anger do not sin: Do not let the sun go down while you are still angry, [27] and do not give the devil a foothold"* (NIV).

Whether anger is internalized or outward towards others, it is a good idea to take the loving advice of scripture and resolve why we are angry as soon as possible. There are various biological actions that cause us harm if we remain angry. Without taking the time here to go through the mechanisms involved, strong or chronic anger can reportedly lead to problems such as strokes or other physical complaints.

Summary
Whenever somebody comes to me reporting anger issues, I am immediately questioning them in regards to what may be in their lives or in their environment, and then in their history that is *not how they think that it should be.*

CHAPTER 24
Unforgiveness, resentment and bitterness

'Present tense' forgiveness

The bible gives us clear instruction to forgive others. This means that if someone does something that offends you today' then under the guidelines of scripture, we are to forgive them as many times as is necessary. This lifestyle should begin as soon as we know that this is the counsel of scripture. It is the nature of God towards us and we are to go and live likewise. If our next-door neighbour throws his empty beer bottles over the fence every night then we need to choose to forgive him daily for the offense. (There is nothing wrong with dropping by and in love requesting that he stops doing it or some action may need to be taken!).

Forgiveness comes before love. We cannot fully love anyone while we hold onto the things that they have committed towards us, or for that matter, the things that we think that they should have done and haven't. God had to deal with suffering a price for our offences first, before He could extend forgiveness and relationship. In much the same way when people are mistreating us, we have to take up our own crosses, absorb the hurt, and deny ourselves retaliation in order to perpetuate love and grace in the spirit of the gospel.

When my wife and I were first married, for many years, we had a love/hate relationship. That is, we did love the person who was inside behind the behaviour, but we did not love the attitudes and hurt that was coming to us from the other person. As we dealt with the issues and learnt to be gracious and forgiving, no longer demanding conformity to each other's standards, our relationship began to blossom.

Matthew 18:21-22, " [21]*Then Peter came to Him and said, "Lord, how often shall my brother sin against me, and I forgive him? Up to seven times?"* [22] *Jesus said to him, "I do not say to you, up to seven times, but up to seventy times seven"* (NKJV).

I have been taught that seventy times seven in the Aramaic language in this preceding verse means in an ongoing manner. This means a lifestyle of forgiveness. We once had a couple visit us who had terrible relationship conflicts. Before I began to look into their inner issues, I noted that they could not forgive each other for anything. For example, he could not forgive her for being a woman and not being able to operate machinery as he could. She would not forgive him for not understanding her emotional make up and so on. They simply refused to not hold each other to account for their shortcomings, failings and imperfections.

In our first few years of marriage, I would become frustrated that my wife wasn't as organized as I was, and she could never find her car keys or handbag. Later I began to realize that very creative people are sometimes a bit random in the structure department. After learning forgiveness, I now think it's cute and funny, as long as she doesn't touch my keys!

A 'record of wrongs'

1 Corinthians 13:4-5, "*⁴ Love is patient, love is kind. It does not envy, it does not boast, it is not proud. ⁵ It is not rude, it is not self-seeking, it is not easily angered, **it keeps no record of wrongs**"* (NIV, Emphasis mine).

A record of wrongs is when you have a list of grievances against someone. Years ago, I would have considered that I had no unforgiveness towards anyone in the world. That is, I certainly had no deep pain driven hurt or resentment. However, one day I noticed that whenever a particular person came up in conversation that I could not help myself from mentioning various occasions when this person had, in my opinion, acted inappropriately towards us. As I spoke, out would tumble this list of offensive actions that I held. I realized that I had kept a record of wrongs. I made a deep decision to be like our Father in heaven and remember their sins no more. Some people say that God forgets our sins, but I believe that by a deliberate act of His will He chooses to not remember them anymore. I decided to not remember them anymore and began to pray for this person's prosperity, and that God would do for them everything that I would like Him to do in His dealings with me.

Almost immediately my *record of wrongs* list disappeared and was no longer accessed when that person came up in conversation, rather I would find myself saying only positive things. (This was now in effect, *blessing* them, which biblically means *speaking well of them*, rather than cursing them). Could I resurrect the list by trying to remember those grievances? Probably, but now I would have to try to remember, and this is something that I had wilfully decided not to do. For many people, this kind of dealing with resentment and unforgiveness is not possible without healing being done first.

'Past tense' forgiveness
We have talked about the Bible's instruction on forgiveness. So now we know how we should respond to hurts, grievances and offences. Many people come to us having been taught that they must forgive, and as a result, they have spent much of their lives endeavouring to do so but feeling guilty and condemned because they just can't seem to get there.

The problem is that the unforgiveness resides in hurt received from historical sources. These situations will make up the majority of times that people will come to you with unforgiveness, resentment and bitterness issues. Under these circumstances we do not initially request that the people forgive those who have offended against them. The reason that they struggle to forgive is because they do not really know what it is that they are forgiving the perpetrator of their unforgivness for.

Let me explain it in this manner. Imagine if someone has suffered, for example, sexual abuse. Clearly, they know that the abuse is the source of their resentment. They most likely are not, however, aware of the beliefs that are causing the pain in them. Let us take a common belief that often emanates from this kind of abuse; *I am ruined, I am no longer like other people*. This belief then, is at least a part of the source of the pain, along with other inner thoughts from the event. Once it is discovered, identified and healed by the Spirit of truth, we then ask them how they regard the offender. When the healing is complete and the hurt is resolved, over and over we see that forgiveness comes easily. The abused person may now make some kind of comment such as; *Well I kind of feel sorry for them that they had that problem. Something must have happened to them to make them like that!*

This holds true of people who have been emotionally, physically, and verbally or in other ways suffered abuse. It also stands fast in situations where for instance love, acceptance and encouragement have not been given as well. You may hear comments such as; *I know that mum/dad did not get much love themselves, and now that I see it, I feel sorry for them that they had nothing to give!* Usually if a person is all about themselves, they are nursing wounds of some kind. As we get healed of our own issues, we now begin to become aware of the needs of others, making us increasingly available and useable to God.

Unforgiveness of self

As with other emotions, there is an inward version of this; unforgiveness towards self. This is where we have a *record of wrongs* regarding our own failings, imperfections and shortcomings. In some instances, we can simply forgive ourselves and move on once we realize that we have held ourselves to account. Most issues that people come for ministry for in this regard may be deeply rooted in an event where a heart belief has come in such as; *I'm not as good as others, I am useless, I am not loveable* for some reason and so on. These need to be healed before you can accept your own self as a normal human being who doesn't always get things right. Again, with healing we hear self-forgiveness statements come such as; *I was only a child; it was ridiculous for me to think that I should know how to do that! Actually, I am ok; it was my parents who had the problem in expecting me to be perfect.*

Progression of a lack of forgiveness towards others or self

For some people, if they refuse to forgive, and they stew on the matters, they will develop eventually into resentment. When resentment becomes deeply seated it can grow into bitterness towards others or self. This is the very toxic form which can end up growing into hatred and can be implicated in various diseases. The old saying; *It is eating them up like a cancer* certainly in my experience is quite accurate. I have witnessed personally as bitterness, self-bitterness and resentment have been strongly present in a number of cancer cases.

A number of years ago, I recommended to a lady that it might be very beneficial for her health in the long run to deal with her unforgiveness which had led to resentment and bitterness. She didn't seem to believe me and was not prepared to let go of her attitudes. Two or three years later she developed cancer and died. I believe that this could have been prevented. Sadly, there are others as well who have not heeded the warning and suffered this or other maladies.

We have also seen cancer healed and know of many others healed by other ministries when the person has come for prayer and help. For some, when the bitterness progresses to hatred it often involves rebellion or retaliation against the perpetrator of the offence. This then can at times involve trying to destroy the other person in some way with the tongue which is not advisable. In the event that the person you are bitter against is yourself, there will be some kind of self-destructive, self-harming, self-punishing behaviour as we witness in modern epidemics such as cutting.

God's perfect order is that you are loving and forgiving towards others, and also towards yourself, but often we need His healing before we can live this way. The Lord knows this very well, which is why He promised to heal the broken-hearted and set the captives free if we will come to Him.

Matthew 22:39b, *"You shall love your neighbor as yourself"* (NKJV).

CHAPTER 25
Dealing with Fear

We now consider two types of fear:

1. Circumstantial fear

What I term *circumstantial fear* is anxiety that is relating to a current event, such as a storm, a particular financial situation, or some other present tense happening. These do not relate to anything that you already believe from fearful times in the past.

For example, we were recently booked to run a number of healing schools in Kenya at the same time as they were running elections. These are often volatile and violent times in Kenya and many people including some Kenyan ministers warned us not to come. My wife and I both prayed about it and together had peace about the trip and so decided to go and fulfil our commitments anyway. When we arrived many of the Pastors commented that we must be very brave. The truth is they had been through anxious times with elections before, but we had no precedent or beliefs about potential harm to influence our decision. So, we were not actually brave, we simply had an absence of fear which is not the same thing. Courageous people push through their fears despite difficult circumstances.

I recall reading once that Napoleon's bravest general at one time could not mount his horse because his knees were shaking so violently. Reportedly he looked down at his legs and said something along the lines of; *If you knew where I was taking you next, you would shake much more than that!* He was not prepared to submit to fear and let it dictate his activities. I am sure that once he was in battle the fear would have been displaced.

A practical theology of dealing with 'circumstantial fear'

The Bible gives us a theology of how to respond to fear in our present circumstances where there is no historical precedent. It shows us how to practically deal with fears that are new situations, by displacing them in choosing trust and having faith in Him. This of course assumes that we are free from fear beliefs stemming from the past. I am told that there are 366 *fear nots* in the Bible. That is one for each day of the year and even leap year is covered. In the event that you are captive to a fear that came to you before you knew how to respond, or had God in your life, then you most probably need to be set free by a *Truth Encounter* with the Holy Spirit.

Before we examine how to be set free at heart level from historical fear beliefs let us first examine what our mindsets or *default position* should be in regards to submitting to fear. There are some excellent pictures of this that Jesus gave us in the gospels. In Matthew 14, we see the story of an event that produced fear in the disciples that had no historical precedence. The setting is that Jesus had just fed the five thousand people multiplying five loaves and two fish. I believe that one aspect of what He was doing was to move the Apostles from the basic principles of the World in terms of what was possible, to understanding that all things are possible with God. God is never confined or limited to the program that this World runs on.

I take heart that the Apostles were a little slow picking this up. After the feeding, rather than travel across the lake with them as He usually would, He made them go ahead.

Matthew 14:22, *"Immediately Jesus **made** the disciples get into the boat and go on ahead of him to the other side, while he dismissed the crowd"* (NIV, Emphasis mine).

I believe that He did this purposefully in order to challenge their believing and God picture with yet another supernatural act. As you read the following verses keep in mind that they had never seen anyone walk on water before and so had no previous beliefs from any such experience.

Matthew 14: 25-31, *"25 During the fourth watch of the night Jesus went out to them, walking on the lake. 26 When the disciples saw him walking on the lake, they were terrified. "It's a ghost," they said, and **cried out in fear**. 27 But Jesus immediately said to them: "Take courage! It is I. Don't be afraid." 28 "Lord, if it's you," Peter replied, "tell me to come to you on the water." 29 "Come," he said. Then Peter got down out of the boat, walked on the water and came toward Jesus. 30 But when he saw the wind, he was afraid and, beginning to sink, cried out, "Lord, save me!" 31 Immediately Jesus reached out his hand and caught him. "You of little faith," he said, "why did you doubt?"* (NIV, Emphasis mine).

Their response was automatically fear, where Jesus was trying to move their default position to being faith. Notably Peter did have enough trust and faith in Jesus to step out on His word. The principle here is that while he looked to Jesus he was doing fine, but when he heeded his circumstances, he was not fine. We could say that faith makes you float and puts you above or over your circumstances, but fear makes you sink and puts you under the power of your circumstances. Faith can make us walk over our situations because it is centred in a supernatural or above natural being. Fear will make you subject to natural outcomes, submitted to your surroundings and senses.

Jesus talks to the storm
In Mark Chapter 4 we see Jesus assessing where the disciples were up in terms of their moving from circumstantial fear to a faith response in God. We call fear the *what if spirit*. As an opposite to faith, real fear believes that another spiritual being can have the final say in outcomes, producing something negative. I have been at sea in storms and you can imagine some of the thoughts behind the fear in the boat. *What if* Peter's repair on the hull doesn't hold? *What if* we cannot bail the water out quickly enough? *What if* Luke's knots don't hold on the mast, he is after all a physician? *What if* Jesus doesn't wake up and tell us what to do. There may have been a whole myriad of beliefs and thoughts that together gripped them with fear.

Mark 4:39-40, "*³⁹ Then He arose and rebuked the wind, and said to the sea, "Peace, be still!" And the wind ceased and there was a great calm. ⁴⁰ But He said to them, "Why are you so fearful? How is it that you have no faith?"* (NKJV).

Jesus attributed their fear to their lack of faith. We will either submit to or come under one or the other. In regards to new situations, it is always a choice which we will make. Many times, how we decide to respond is based on our previous experiences of God coming through for us.

Jesus always seemed committed to releasing His disciples into the supernatural potential of the faith dimension. He took them through many situations that were possibly places of choosing to believe. One such time, was after feeding the 5,000. He now fed the

4,000 in the hope that the dawning of understanding would come to them. We can all thank God that He is so patient with us in our journey out of fear into faith. He is in fact the author and finisher of our faith (Hebrews 12:2). Whatever page we are on in the book of the pilgrimage into faith that we are on, we can be sure that he will complete the good work that he began in us (Philippians 1:6). In any case the disciples were not yet thinking about the supernatural potential of faith. We can take heart, later of course when they understood, they turned the world upside down.

Matthew 16:8-9, " ⁸ *But Jesus, being aware of it, said to them,* **"O you of little faith**, *why do you reason among yourselves because you have brought no bread?* ⁹ **"Do you not yet understand**, *or remember the five loaves of the five thousand and how many baskets you took up?* (NKJV, Emphasis mine).

Jesus pointed to remembering previous things that God had done, as the means by which to reprogram your expectations to a place of faith. We could perhaps summarize our part in releasing God into our situations, and that which He wants to do through us, something such as this;

Unbelief	expects	nothing to happen.
Fear	expects	something bad to happen.
Faith	expects	something positive to happen.

Defining fear under another name
You may know fear in one of its many forms, for example, anxiety, stress, distress, worry, tension, restlessness, dread, apprehension or insecurity. Additionally, we might add in hopelessness, helplessness, doubt or unbelief. They are forms of fear because they do not include the presence, power or willingness of God to resolve whatever we are confronted with.

To summarize fear, we could define it as; *An expectation of a negative outcome.*

I was doing some study quite a few years ago on what different people had to say about fear. Some books cited the existence of over 5,000 known fears. I wondered how I might manage to remember all of these fears. A thought came into my mind; *fear is whatever you are afraid of!* Hardly a blinding revelation, but nonetheless it resolved the issue once and for all for me. When we are ministering to others or even examining our own selves, it is not necessary to work through a list, simply identify what it is that the person is afraid of.

Good fear
We have used the term *a universal emotion* as being a predictable feeling or response that can be distorted by the devil as a consequence of the fall. God gave us fear as a protective instinct. As a result, we don't normally play on highways or near cliffs. We don't as a rule, kiss snakes on the lips, this is simply not smart.

I am not sure of the origins, but I recall the story of a Pastor who was visiting town and decided to drop in on a member of his congregation. When he arrived, even though the door was not locked nobody responded to his knocking. He amused himself by leaving a note on the door which he considered was very clever.

Revelation 3:20, *"Behold, I stand at the door and knock"* (NKJV).

On Sunday, after the service, one of the deacons approached the minister with an envelope that had been addressed to him and which was found in the offerings.

Genesis 3:10, *"I heard you in the garden, and I was afraid because I was naked; so I hid"* (NIV).

We can say that there is *good, wise* God-given fear that protects us. This includes the fear of God which helps to protect us from negative outcomes. The distorted version of fear deceives us, that we need to protect ourselves, when it is in fact not necessary or beneficial. It is the fear of things that we are not meant to fear, or times when we can exercise faith to displace fear, that I am talking about.

Fear began in the garden, where man no longer believed that God had their best interests at heart, and was keeping things from him. In essence they doubted that He was good and really loved them. This was unbelief, or probably more aptly, wrong belief which is the basis of all of our anxieties. As a result, as we understand and receive God's love and acceptance both in our minds and hearts, we find ourselves being freed from our many fears. I have sometimes asked for a show of hands, in congregations where we are ministering, of people who have no fear at all. As yet I have not seen a hand raised anywhere.

1 John 4:18-19, "*[18] There is no fear in love; but perfect love casts out fear, because fear involves torment. But he who fears has not been made perfect in love. [19] We love Him because He first loved us*" (NKJV).

Equally we could say that the antithesis or natural enemy of fear, faith, also proceeds from believing that there is no longer any need to expect negative outcomes for us. This knowledge of His love for us, both mind and heart, receives that God has shown His love first by redeeming us and paying the penalty for our transgressions.

Fear as faith in reverse
I recall a fine sounding worldview that goes something such as: *Hope for the best, expect the worst, and take what comes.* Thinking such as this proposes that we really have no input into our destinies and outcomes. It denies or discounts interaction and results proceeding from the abilities of God or submitting to satanic spiritual powers.

Let us contrast Job with Daniel's friends, Shadrach, Meshach and Abednego. In the case of Job, everything was going well. He was highly regarded, wealthy, healthy, and had, by all appearances, a good family. Then everything around him began to fall apart. To what did he attribute and note as a precursor to these happenings?

Job 3:25, "*What I feared has come upon me; what I dreaded has happened to me*" (NIV).

In contrast, we see Shadrach, Meshach and Abednego, and everything was not going well. However, they still refused to bow down to anyone or anything other than God. They refused to fear and chose to put themselves under God's ability in faith regardless of the outcome. This took them out from under the potential outcome that Satan would have had for them and put them under the supernatural power and provision of God.

Daniel 3:17-18, " *[17] If we are thrown into the blazing furnace, the God we serve is able to save us from it, and he will rescue us from your hand, O king. [18] But even if he does not, we want you to know, O king, that we will not serve your gods or worship the image of gold you have set up"* (NIV).

The outcome of their faith decision, and choosing to refuse fear in their circumstance, was finding the Lord in their trial with them, and the final result being them having favour and witness with their oppressors. Notably, they were not spared from the trial but were triumphant in the midst of it as a result of their choice.

Daniel 3:25, *"He said, "Look! I see four men walking around in the fire, unbound and unharmed, and the fourth looks like a son of the gods"* (NIV).

I was in Nigeria a number of years ago and there was a lady who was directing witchcraft type stares at me in order to create an opening through fear in me. I remember thinking, not arrogantly but confidently; *lady, do you think I am going to submit to fear from you when God is for me!* Later in a church service, she was delivered by the local minister of the spirit associated with her practices.

I will spare you the whole story of how I ended up in a first-class seat on the way to England at one time, but I did. Seated beside me was a doctor who was calmly reading a book. As I looked out from my high window on this 747 my attention was drawn to how the engine was wobbling around on the wing. For a moment I felt anxious, until it occurred to me what was happening. I inwardly made the statement; *I like flying, go and find someone else to bother!* Within seconds the doctor that I was sitting with suddenly became very agitated and left his seat and went out and I assume vomited. My guess is that there was someone in the aircraft quite close to us with fear issues that were of a demonic nature, and this spiritual dynamic was reaching out trying to impact us. As we go through life we are challenged with situations where we need to make faith choices and refuse to submit to the pressures of the enemy.

Note:
These are rare isolated incidences to illustrate how to respond to our presenting circumstances out of our understanding of Biblical perspective. 99.9% of my fears have been historically rooted which I will explain in a moment.

Programming

It takes only the briefest examination to see that the devil is busily programming the world with fear via media. Horror movies, violence, end of the world films, plane crashes, disasters, and so on litter our screens. Shows where people are cut up to be examined, medical series, and so on abound. Those who have time to view television or other media are inundated with fearful images and themes. Personally, I fly too often to be interested in spoiling my journeys by watching air crash investigations or the like. We are filled with the possibilities of *negative outcomes* daily, ranging from global warming to a world financial crisis. This may have more impact than you realize.

I recall reading conclusions from researcher Brandon S. Centrewall who was looking at the effects of television on programming. He discovered that homicide rates in the U.S., where gun laws are comparatively loose, from the time that they had television in 1945 through to 1974, increased 93%. As a reference, they also looked at Canada who had very strict gun laws and had television over the same period of time, and saw almost the same rise of 92%. South Africa did not have television until the early 1970s, and so over the same period homicides went down 7%. After 1975 with the introduction of television, their rates went up 130%. We can reasonably conclude that it was the programming in behaviour of the human soul through media that produced the changes and not the access to guns.

Some time ago, before I became full time in ministry, I worked part time to help support us. I met with a client at one time and upon enquiry as to how his previous day had been, he responded with; *Terrible thanks, I was admitted to hospital with panic attacks!* I felt prompted to ask him if he viewed horror movies. When he responded *no*, I thought I had missed it. Then he followed on with the comment; *I used to, I used to watch a lot.* Indeed, we need to be very careful about what we fill up on, and are exposed to, as the seed will bring its harvest.

Setting the 'default position' of faith

It seems reasonably obvious that God did not give us or intend for us to be subject to a spirit of fear. We must realize that Satan is the instigator of bringing us into the bondage of fear. This invisible enemy will be seeking to bring to pass the object of our fear as we accept and submit to his plan for negative outcomes for us. Moving from fear to faith, as far as how we think in our minds is often a progressive journey as we hear from the counsel of God instructions such as; *Do NOT worry about your life, what you will eat, tomorrow, and so on. Do NOT be anxious. Cast ALL your anxiety on Him.* (Matthew 6:25-34; Philippians 4:6; 1 Peter 5:7, NIV). If God says *do not* then I do not see another way to live other than His perfect order.

Joshua 1:9, *"Have I not commanded you? Be strong and of good courage; do not be afraid, nor be dismayed, for the LORD your God is with you wherever you go"* (NKJV).

Joshua was going to be confronted with many potential opportunities to worry and fear negative outcomes. In all five times through the book of Joshua he was instructed to be strong and make the choice to be courageous. Repetition makes a deep impact on our memory. When it is reinforced with decisions to obey and make this our *default response*, it becomes a part of our thinking and being.

In Australia we have a lot of bushfires. A study on resident's responses to these fires showed that those who meditated and rehearsed their fire escape plans, acted out accordingly when the stressful challenges came. Those who had no plan of how to respond tended to be overwhelmed and panicked, at times resulting in their deaths. It has been well said that fear and faith are equal in that they both expect an outcome. It becomes vital as to whether we are under Satan's deception and responding to perceived fear; as he gives us his perspective on potentially negative events, or faith, allowing God to produce His outcomes.

Remember fear exists because we have a negative expectation in regards to God's attitude towards us, or our worthiness to receive from Him which relates to our next area, *historical fear*. Every time that we expect or entertain a negative outcome, we are submitting to a spiritual power that is challenging God's word and nature, just as it happened in the Garden of Eden.

Perhaps the first ever fear was, fear of missing out, based on the tree of the knowledge of good and evil. Today the fear of missing out is called the new phenomenon abbreviated as FOMO. It is related to people addicted to media who cannot go for very long without checking their media for fear of missing out on the latest post etc.

Renewing our 'minds' in regards to fear

If we do not live progressively in the counsel of scripture in regards to dealing with fear, there is a strong chance of you ending up with what we term a *fear profile*, where your practiced fear thinking becomes a permanent part of you; your default position. We need to discipline ourselves, filling our minds with the instructions of scripture in terms of how to deal with circumstantial fear.

The bottom line is that God is *the power* and he is right behind His word to perform it. The devil, on the other hand, is a created being who is limited to creating scenarios and perceptions to deceive you into submitting to fear. In scripture, there is usually an antidote to fear along with the acknowledgement of the pressure of fear to impact us. There are examples of declarations that we can make to reinforce our decisions to make faith our default position and automatic response. I will list a few examples for your consideration;

Proverbs 29:25, *"The fear of man brings a snare, But whoever trusts in the LORD shall be safe"* (NKJV).

Isaiah 26:3, *"You will keep him in perfect peace, Whose mind is stayed on You, Because he trusts in You"* (NKJV).

Psalm 56:3-4, *" ³Whenever I am afraid, I will trust in You. ⁴ In God (I will praise His word), In God I have put my trust; I will not fear. What can flesh do to me?"* (NKJV).

Psalm 118:6, *"The LORD is on my side; I will not fear. What can man do to me?"* (NKJV).

Effects of fear

Spiritually	Robs us of our faith, therefore removing our power and potential.
Mentally	Confusion, mind racing, trying to solve the problem.
Emotionally	Takes our peace, torments, feels bad.
Physically	Many negative effects on the body and health.
Fruitfulness	Makes us unfruitful, binds us and stops us walking into our *promised land* of abundant life and limits that which God can use us for.

The problem with us accepting fear as a reasonable response, is that in order to do so we have to downsize God and His love and power to match our beliefs. We have to believe that He is not in control, cannot protect or provide for us, or does not really love or care about us. In that instance, we have to re-define fear in our lives as doubt and unbelief.

We often think of fear as being adrenaline releasing heart pumping anxiety of some kind, but many times it is low grade in the form of daily stress, worry or anxiousness. This every present kind of fear is usually emanating from heart beliefs that we hold from sources located in our history.

2. Historical fear

We have just spent a considerable amount of time on examining the instructions of scripture in regards to how we should deal with present tense or potential future fear circumstances that we may encounter. However, the vast majority of fear projects from beliefs we hold which we have already learnt in negative events, or fearful environments in the past. Even if we are presented with a potentially anxious situation in the present which does not have precedence, if we still hold unresolved fear beliefs from the past, we will automatically have expectations of a negative outcome by interpreting the possibilities of the event based on our previously existing beliefs. As a result, virtually all people who come for ministry presenting with fear and anxiety issues need to be set free from the beliefs that they have learnt from past experiences.

We have two types of fear, being circumstantial or historical in nature. We also have two kinds of fear beliefs. As we have detailed in the *Truth Encounters* section, we can hold beliefs that come from situations that relate to the events where we learn them, and also beliefs that relate to our identity. These beliefs are also marked and distinct in the area of fear.

Fear from Situational beliefs

Phobic type fear, or phobias, where people have specific fears tend to fit into this category. (*Phobos* is the Greek word from which fear is translated in the New Testament). For example, a person may present with a fear of tight spaces or elevators. As you have them focus on their fear you are looking for a memory that holds matching feelings or circumstances as with those that they are currently experiencing. Their fear of tight spaces is not going to be to do with their identity, who they are, or whether they are good enough. We might ask them a question such as; *What is it that you are afraid of happening in the enclosed space?*

They could perhaps respond with something such as; *I will be trapped and I won't be able to get away.* I would then enquire as to what will happen if they can't get away. You may get for example a response such as; *I won't be able to breathe, and if I can't breathe, I will die.*

These beliefs can, many times, be established before going to the memory, or later in the memory examining the matching feelings. I would ask them to really embrace the feeling and ask them if there is a historical place where they felt exactly like this. That is, they are trapped, can't get away, can't breathe, and as a consequence in the memory, they believe that they will die. This is the actual belief producing the fear, in this case, *that they are going to die.*

This could have come from a situation such as the story we related in an earlier chapter where a boy gets hold of the football in a game, and then has several heavy guys on top of him pressing the football into his chest. It is a matching set of circumstances to potentially being in an elevator or on an aircraft for instance. You could be trapped, not in control of the situation, and in the end as a consequence you could die. Mostly anxiety attacks or panic attacks come from these underlying beliefs. We see people set free from these attacks as the subsurface beliefs are identified and dealt with.

In the case of our footballer, once we have identified the belief producing the emotion and the source of the thoughts with the matching circumstances, we ask the Lord for His truth. We tend to deeply encode the belief in the intense moment. The Lord may say something such as; *I didn't let you die, it was just a moment and you were free, I will always watch over you,* or some other kind of freeing truth. God is very creative in how He sets the captives free.

At times there may be a spirit attached to the fear. If that is the case you will become aware of the probability by the intensity of the fear. Don't make casting out demons a part of *your method* in dealing with these fears. If there is a spirit there, it may simply leave when the truth sets them free. Do be aware of the possibility. I never go into ministry thinking about demons, looking for them, or expecting that deliverance from them will be a part of the ministry. To me it would be like going shopping and expecting every time that you were out that you would have to deal with somebody who was going to be rude to you. I just go out to get what I am wanting, and at times a person becomes involved that I have to deal with who, for instance, is trying to take my parking space and prevent me from getting where I want to go.

In the case of ministry, the problem is still the problem, and that is the belief producing the negative emotion. We continue to go after the belief and if there is an evil spirit involved powering up the fear response, we simply tell it to go in the name of Jesus. Think of it as shooing away a fly while you are trying to cook a barbeque. A spirit is only as big as you make it in your thinking. Either you believe that the Bible is true and you have complete authority over them in Jesus name or not. If you believe that Jesus' is the name above all names you will have no problems. I will explain more on this is section four.

We can summarize dealing with these kinds of fears by saying that we are simply looking for a situation where the belief/s were taken in. If you recall, we talked about the Amygdala area of the brain which is reportedly considered to be the fear centre. When a negative incidence occurs, it responds with something such as, *you better make a good memory of that so that we can watch for it and prevent it from happening again!'*

Some people say that fear is;
False **E**vidence **A**ppearing **R**eal

This is true to a large degree in that fear is usually a projection towards something that *might happen* based on previous experience, rather than something that definitely will happen. The World may well end, but we actually don't have much to do with when that could happen. Certainly, fear will not prevent it from happening or change the time of that possible occurrence by one second.

Fear from Identity beliefs
As you understand by now, what we term *identity beliefs* relates to who you are, how you are, and what you consider to be true

about yourself. I will not go into a lot of detail here because we have already detailed these in the preceding chapters; the sources of negative self-beliefs which we may now fear being reinforced. These project from incidences producing rejection, inferiority, injustice, insecurity, abuse and so on. I will suggest a few common beliefs that people may hold as a result of being exposed to these negative influences; *I'm weak, stupid, inferior, can't do it, not as good as others, not wanted, don't belong, am not worth caring about, am a nothing, not important* etc.

Once life has programmed these negative inner thoughts into you, you now fear that they will be proven to be true. You may fear that people will discover these *supposed* weaknesses in your person. Additionally, you may fear that people will not want you, or think poorly of you because of these *perceived* shortcomings. For example, if you believe that you are a failure and cannot meet people's expectations, you will fear disappointing people and not being able to do those things that they require. The freedom from the fear regarding these beliefs about yourself comes once you no longer hold them as being true about you.

Situation or phobic beliefs will trigger if you are suddenly confronted with a stressor that you cannot avoid. Many people control their environments so that this will not happen. If you are afraid to drive in the city you will possibly catch the train and as a result have no anxiety when you go to town. However, identity-based fears are hard to avoid because they are often ever present in your dealings with other human beings. In my opinion and experience, these are usually the fear, stress or anxiety beliefs that are mostly implicated in disease.

Two categories of fear
At the time that I was pondering on the long lists of fears that were offered to us, I came to the conclusion that broadly all fears seemingly fall under one of two categories.

Fear of harm
This would obviously relate to being hurt or abused physically or in some other harmful way and would include anxieties projecting from accidents and traumas. It could also take in situations such as fear of no protection or no provision or even lack of finances. These

would all mean that some kind of harm to your state of being would be the result. Fear of being out of control may stem from places where you were out of control and some kind of hurt was the result.

Fear of rejection
The other broad category I would consider many fears to come from is fear of rejection. Under this we will find such subtitles as *Fear of man, fear of failure, and fear of embarrassment* etc.

> Why would you fear man?
> > He may not accept you for who you are.
> What will happen if you fail?
> > People will reject your efforts and consequently you!
> Why would you be embarrassed to begin with?
> > This is because some kind of weakness or supposed inferiority has been exposed with the expectation that people will reject you because of it.

In our minds:
We know that we should not even care about the 'praises of men'.

We know that being accepted and loved by God is not conditioned to our performance, abilities or success in man's eyes.

We know that God will be pleased by our faith, in not submitting to fear but rather trusting Him in everything, and trusting Him and stepping out in service.

However, knowing this in our minds and wanting to hold these attitudes and produce corresponding actions does not remove the heart beliefs that oppose our freedom. We really do need God to set us free to be all that we can be for His glory. I don't find people who want fear or who don't want to be free to serve the Lord. Most hate it, and long to be free. It is not however, a matter of merely changing your thinking or reading books and becoming experts on fear. I have not seen anyone set free that way. It is the truth at heart level that makes you free.

Romans 7:15, *"For what I am doing, I do not understand. For what I will to do, that I do not practice; but what I hate, that I do"* (NKJV).

Physical manifestations of fear

Earlier in these writings, I described some physical outworking of fear problems in the body such as allergic reactions, skin problems, asthma and so on. I will not go into further detail here, only to say that these problems are evidence of the spiritual issue of fear working out in the body via the beliefs and emotions, and then finally producing a physical manifestation in the physiological balance of the afflicted person.

I was working in *Truth Encounters* with a young lady one night and as we moved into her anxiety-based beliefs she broke out all over with little lumps. Initially I thought it must have been because earlier in the day she had been at the river with friends, and there are a lot of mosquitoes there and she must have been repeatedly bitten. As we talked about the lumps it became apparent that it was hives resulting from touching into the places of anxiety that she had in her memories. The Bible describes us as doors and gates. Both God and Satan are looking for an expression from the spiritual realm into the natural realm through what we believe. Our thoughts, decisions, actions and reactions make an opening to the spirit world. This young lady's case was a demonstration of a spiritual/emotional malady having expression in the physical realm.

Psalm 24:7, *"Lift up your heads, O you gates! And be lifted up, you everlasting doors! And the King of glory shall come in"* (NKJV).

Wholeness in our souls, and consequently our bodies, is an expression of the spirit of God having worked in us.

3 John 1:2, *"Beloved, I pray that you may prosper in all things and be in health, just as your soul prospers"* (NKJV).

Sample ministry: Situational or phobic fear

Me: "What can we help you with today?"
Fred: "Well I have a fear of flying."
Me: "So what are you afraid might happen when you get on an aircraft?"
Fred: Ponders "I feel as though I will be out of control"
Me: "I want you to focus on that thought and the feeling that goes with it and see if you remember a time in your life where you felt just like that."

Chapter 25: Dealing with Fear

Fred: "I remember being pushed down a steep hill in a little cart we had made. The big kids put me in and sent the cart racing down the hill towards the trees."

Me: "What did you believe might happen while you were afraid?"

Fred: "I guess I felt that I was going to get hurt and nobody could stop it happening. I was terrified!"

Me: "Let's hold that belief up to the Lord that 'nobody can stop what's going to happen, and I will get hurt.'" (Prayer asking the Lord to bring His truth)

Fred: "I just remembered that actually one of the big kids ran after me and eventually did stop the cart before it hit the trees."

Me: "So what does that mean to you?"

Fred: "Well it means that God will always find a way to protect me. He is always in control."

Me: "So think about flying now, are you still afraid of being out of control?"

Fred: Pauses "No. I am still a bit fearful though it is nowhere near as much!"

Me: "Alright focus on the residual fear and see if you can work out what you are afraid of."

Fred: "I have been on a plane before and it felt like there was nothing solid underneath me....it was a scary feeling."

Me: "Okay, I want you to concentrate on the anxious belief that there is nothing solid underneath you." "Lord, would you help Fred to connect with a place where he felt just like that before?"

Fred: "As soon as you said that I remembered being on a cliff edge when we were kids and it caved in underneath me. I slid down the face of it and into the river."

Me: "So you felt as if there was nothing solid under you? And what was the consequence or fear expectation about that situation?"

Fred: "I thought that I was going to die!"

Me: "Alright, I just want for you to embrace that anxiety and belief in that memory that because there is nothing solid under you, you will die."

Fred: Pauses "Do you know, that is just not true. What came to mind was the scripture that talks about the circle of the Earth. It's just hung out there in space with nothing under it just because God put it there and supports it, nothing under it, but still suspended."

Me: "So if you think about there being nothing solid under you on a plane how do you feel about it now?"

Fred: "You know it's really okay....!"

Me: "How do you feel about flying now Fred?"
Fred: "Do you know, it's weird but I think that I am a bit excited!"

Perhaps we might say a prayer thanking the Lord or certainly make a comment about how amazing our God is in setting us free and acknowledging Him as being the one who has done the freeing. Either way, God is glorified as He fulfils His promise and the session closes.

Sample ministry: Identity belief-based fear

Me: "What seems to be the problem?"
Fred: "I have been asked to do communion in church next Sunday, but I am petrified and haven't been able to sleep!"
Me: "I want you to imagine yourself up there in front of all those people. As you feel that anxiety I would like you to examine it and try to work out exactly what it is that you are afraid might happen."
Fred: Pause "I am afraid that I might not be able to do it properly."
Me: "I would like you to feel that anxiety about not doing it properly, and as you do let your mind connect you with a place that held those feelings. It will be somewhere where you actually couldn't do what was expected."
Fred: Ponders "I remember in school when I was about 7 years old. The teacher wanted me to write some cursive text on the blackboard, and I wrote it back the front. The teacher made a big fuss over it making fun of me in front of the whole class and I recall being incredibly embarrassed."
Me: "As a result of not being able to do it, and the intense embarrassing moment in front of the class, what conclusion about yourself did you come to?"
Fred: Pause, thoughtful "I'm dumb. I must be dumb because I could not do it right."
Me: "As you feel that embarrassment and the belief that you are 'dumb' because you could not do it, let us ask the Lord what the real truth is."
Prayer: "Lord Fred thinks that he is dumb because he could not do the cursive writing on the board. What do you want him to know about that situation?"

Fred:	"Well, I didn't hear any thoughts. But I just sort of understood that none of us had actually been taught cursive yet. And the teacher liked to mock us and make fun of us. She sort of deliberately put me in that position to make sport of me."
Me:	"So are you dumb because you could not do it?"
Fred:	"No, the truth is that none of us could yet. I am feeling that I was alright, there is nothing wrong with me, but I think that the teacher had some issues. I forgive her."
Me:	"Picture yourself doing communion on Sunday, how do you feel about messing it up now?"
Fred:	"I actually feel fine about it, I will work out how to do it as best I can and really everything doesn't have to be perfect. After all, we are all family."

Note:
A situation such as public speaking typically may evoke a response from more than one historically learnt fear producing belief. As each one is ministered to the intensity of the anxiety normally goes down. If you just process the beliefs one by one eventually you will achieve peace. It is of course normal to be a little nervous if it is a new situation.

- Section 3: Discernment -

CHAPTER 26
Guilt and shame

Romans 8:1, *"There is therefore now no condemnation to those who are in Christ Jesus, who do not walk according to the flesh, but according to the Spirit.* (NKJV).

Guilt is a fruit that will tie into areas such as self-rejection, inferiority and performance anxiety. By that I mean anxiety over our ability to perform to people's expectations. Usually we reject ourselves because we have learnt that we fall short in some way. As a result, we often feel as though we should have done more, been better, been able to please or do what was expected of us and so on. A consequence of these perceived failures is often low self-image, and guilt or shame.

As we have previously stated, we could summarize that guilt and shame are connected to something that we didn't do that we feel that we should have, or, something that we have done that we shouldn't have. If we have dealt with things that we should not have done from our previous years, we should have received Gods forgiveness' and also our own.

Clearly if we are still doing something that we know that we shouldn't be doing, and could stop in our own strength then guilt is probably an appropriate emotion. In that instance it is not condemnation because we can always repent, but it may well in fact be conviction. Guilt is often tied to other emotional issues and even implicated in depression. It can be one possible trail back to the initial memory for truth and healing.

- Section 3: Discernment -

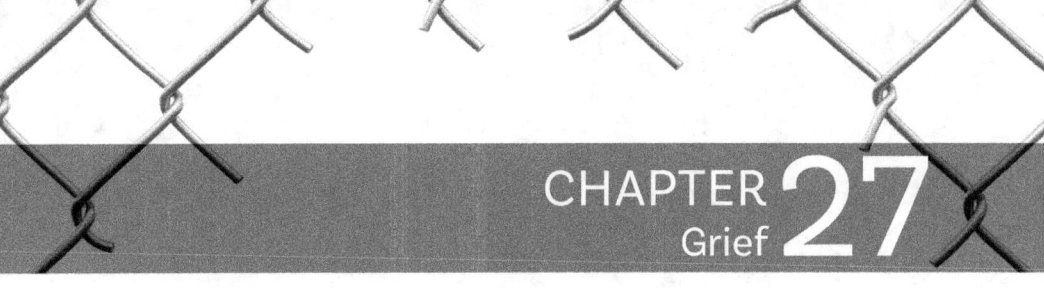

CHAPTER 27
Grief

Grief is normally associated with loss of some kind. This could include loss of your identity and self-worth if, for example, you have been sexually abused. It could also relate to loss of a relationship or loved one. As with any other belief-based emotion the goal is to identify the thoughts producing the sad feelings.

Psalm 31:9-10, " *9 Have mercy on me, O LORD, for I am in trouble; My eye wastes away with grief,* **Yes, my soul and my body!** *10 For my life is spent with grief, And my years with sighing; My strength fails because of my iniquity, And my bones waste away."* (NKJV, Emphasis mine).

We take note from the preceding verses, that grief has an impact on both soul and body. At times, we minister to people who look constantly sad. It is wonderful to see the joy come into them when the Lord sets them free.

SECTION 4

DEALING WITH THE DEMONIC ELEMENT

- Section 4: Dealing with the Demonic Element -

CHAPTER 28
Spiritual dynamics and setting the captives free

There have been very few weeks over the last 30 years where we have not been dealing with demons in some setting or another. We have come to some understandings as to how they generally operate over that time. As we begin to discuss the connection between evil spirits and ministering to people, I want to make a couple of points very clear up front.

Firstly, we do not go into a ministry session looking for demons, generational problems or entry points from any other source. If we come from a *methods*, or *this is what you do, follow this process* type training, we will often gravitate to being directive and pre-empting what the problem might be. I have seen ministries that work through a particular list of *demons*, or we *break this* or *that* as their standard ministry model, and, many times, they see very few or limited results.

We begin with *what is your problem*? Along the way we may become aware of demonic power being involved. Even when these spirits are discerned, our primary interest is the *ground, terrain, activity,* or *belief* that gives them place and not the spirit itself. The devil and His demons are completely and utterly totally defeated and there is no other way to regard him.

Luke 10:19-20, "*[19]I have given you authority to trample on snakes and scorpions and to overcome all the power of the enemy; nothing will harm you. [20] However, do not rejoice that the spirits submit to you, but rejoice that your names are written in heaven*" (NIV, Emphasis mine).

If you accept the preceding and following verses, then our complete authority over Satan is obvious. The only thing that remains to be done to ensure your freedom is to identify the *topos* or ground that the devil has been given to stand on and resolve it.

Colossians 2:15, "*And having disarmed the powers and authorities, he made a public spectacle of them, triumphing over them by the cross*" (NKJV).

We can accurately say then, that for a believer, the devil is not the problem, rather it is the area of our thinking or inner believing that gives him ground and deceives us into moving our will to participate with him. So, we really are not *demon focused*, instead we are targeting the presenting problem that a person carries, being aware that at times it might be empowered and amplified by an evil spirit. Our mission, in co labouring to set the captives free, is to resolve wrong believing and areas of deception working under the ministry of the Spirit of Truth.

Luke 11:20, *"But if I cast out demons with the finger of God, surely the kingdom of God has come upon you"* (NKJV).

Examining beliefs at a heart level is the quickest way that I have seen to expose the ground held by many evil spirits. The beliefs themselves may be the ground for the demons, or the resultant sin choices and behaviour may give them place.

The spiritual or unseen realm

As we begin to look at this area, we should not have a problem with seeing the world as being manipulated from an unseen realm. I can only imagine the thousands of mobile phone calls, SMS messages, radio waves, emails, television station transmissions, Facebook pictures and so on that are all around me in the invisible realm at any given time. Add to that the unseen power of gravity, prismatic color, temperature, magnetic fields, static electricity, etc. etc. etc., there is indeed a great deal that we cannot see that affects our world. I cannot see how a television remote changes the channels or another *bipper* puts up my garage door, but they do! All of these examples, and we have not even mentioned unseen spiritual beings interplaying and manipulating the world system through mankind.

What are demons or evil spirits?

Although many people have various theories about what demons are and where they come from, the Bible does not specifically state any of this. It does however reveal their nature and activities, and also how we are to deal with them. By observation however, we can say that they are bodiless spirits. The terms *demon*, *evil spirit*, or *unclean spirit*, according to the famous Bible teacher Derek Prince, are interchangeable. To be demonized is considered to have or be under the influence of an evil, unclean spirit or a demon. Some early translations used phrases such as, *possessed with devils*, or *possessed with the devil*.

Note:
Devils' is considered to be a mistranslation for demons as the person of the devil is *diablos* speaking of Satan himself and used only in the singular. Demon is translated from *diamon* or *diamonion*.

Some took this to be that the devil possessed the entire person, whereas in reality, *demons* often possess or have control of areas of the human personality or body. In truth, a believer is redeemed and possessed only by Christ. The control of these areas is certainly by degrees ranging from one part of the person having strongholds, through to many areas. Mostly demons are not always manifested or seen all of the time.

A long time ago I worked with a man who, in a given situation, would exhibit demonic facial and behavioural changes. He was in fact a good man, who had an unresolved problem area that appeared only on rare occasions when particular circumstances presented. At the other end of the scale, I have worked with an extreme case where all that was constantly visible was demons and where the person virtually was completely run by the evil spirits. This is extremely unusual and I have never seen another case even close to this level of demonization. Usually the demons hold areas of a person in the soul or body.

I liken the personality to your neighbourhood. Most of the houses are fine, but there are one or two residences that are noisy and have wild parties. Sadly, we cannot normally arrange evictions for these neighbours as we can with demons. So, we can say that these spirits without bodies can hold areas that have become available to them for inhabitation. The demons do not have a choice in this as it is whatever is yielded to them through some kind of agreement, weakness or cooperation from the host.

'In' a spirit
The late Derek Prince pointed out that a passage such as Mark chapter 5, verse 2 could also be rendered as a man *in* an unclean spirit rather than *with*.

Mark 5:2, *"And when He had come out of the boat, immediately there met Him out of the tombs a man with an unclean spirit"* (NKJV).

A lady came to a home group that we were running in the mid-1990s complaining of having had an unusual outburst of anger. Armed with the information from Derek Prince's observation about being *in a spirit*, I proceeded to ask her if she had been near anybody who was an angry person. I had known her for a number of years and she had always presented as very calm and amiable. She responded that she had been with a man who was a very angry person indeed, and that she had had the outburst in his company. People who carry demonic spiritual dynamics will often have an almost magnetic spiritual atmosphere that you need to avoid being pulled into. It is trying to illicit a reaction in you to have some measure of control over your behaviour. For example, rejection rejects, pride will make you feel inferior, rebellion will treat you unjustly and disrespectfully to try to create the same responses in you that gave the spirits place in the host. That certainly does not mean that you will automatically receive that spirit, but it does mean that it now has had an expression through you as well as the host.

The spirit realm is a 2-way street. One day I was sitting in a group with some other Pastors and I was getting clear visions and strong words of knowledge for members of the group. Whilst I do have words of knowledge and so on, normally visions for me would be more like impressions. After a while I realized that I was seated beside a well-known and regarded prophet. I concluded that my proximity to him had me *sitting in his gift* and that was the reason for the abnormal pictures etc.

In summary we can say that we need to be aware of the spiritual dynamics of people that we are dealing with and that discernment is our best defence against receiving or responding to someone else's junk. We can see it many times as being something beyond the normal levels of a person's problems, to the amplified or unnatural tangible invisible influence of an unseen entity. If you are aware, you can often see the presence of a spirit on a person as a facial expression of for example, grief, low self-image or lust. You can also see them in body language such as pride and arrogance, perhaps rebellious or aggressive attitudes.

Although demons do not have a body, they seek a *house* or host to inhabit. They exhibit all the normal faculties of a soul. They showed *knowledge and comprehension* of knowing Jesus and also Paul. They displayed thought and decision or will when they decided to return to their house. In James chapter two it says even the demons tremble which indicates that they have emotion. Legion in Mark chapter 5 knew who he was as a soul, and in this case had sufficient power over the vocal chords of the man to speak, communicate and express himself.

At times you will be aware that speech coming from a person is demonically influenced even though there is not complete control as in the case of the demoniac in Mark 5. In these cases, it will be more of a mixture with the person's own personality and there will not likely be a complete voice change. This could be something in the order of; *I hate you!* or *I'm such a loser!* where the intensity of the emotion or statement may be an indicator of a resident spirit. Even at the minimum end of the scale, as we have already pointed out, Jesus identified the source and inspiration behind Peter's comments in Mathew 16:23 as having originated with Satan, although operating from outside of his person.

Activities of Demons
The late Derek Prince compiled the following list of the activities of demons from both scripture and personal involvement with deliverance ministry. In my experience it is completely accurate.

1. Demons Entice or tempt. (James 1:14)
2. They deceive. (I Timothy 4:1-2)
3. Spirits enslave. (Romans 8:15) [This would include besetting sins]
4. They torment. (2 Timothy 1:7; 1 John 4:18)
5. Demons drive or compel. (Luke 8:29)
6. Evil spirits defile. (Titus 1:15)

Demons work to deceive, oppose, destroy and rob us of peace and produce disharmony and division at every opportunity.

CHAPTER 29
Unholy spirits, are they inside or out?

Spiritual influence from Outside

Spiritual pressures that come from outside of us largely come through the programming of the world. This could be in the form of cultural dynamics, for example, the western world is highly sexualized in our times. As a consequence, we are bombarded with ungodly sexual themes and images which proceed from demonic influences. These are *coverings* or spiritual powers that have found cooperative people or groups to work with and follow them. This submission gives them power. It is highly unlikely that the devil or his cohorts are watching you or following you personally. His attacks on you will usually come through people who are unwittingly following him. They are thinking that how they are behaving or dealing with you is simply something that *they* independently want to do; after all the devil doesn't exist.

So, we have extremes, with some people thinking that the devil is able to attack you as a spiritual being without the use of a host person or some kind of medium such as media. Then at the other end of the scale, the devil just doesn't exist at all. In the case of Jesus' dealings with Satan through Peter, Jesus pointed out that the access came through Peter's *man* thinking which was programmed into him by the world system.

Matthew 16:23, *"But He turned and said to Peter, "Get behind Me, Satan! You are an offense to Me, for you are not mindful of the things of God, but the things of men"* (NKJV).

By implication, the things of men are the things of Satan, the influencer and controller of the fallen world. Notice that Jesus did not say *come out*. Peter did not have a demon inside him, rather he was submitting to the spiritual environment and training coming through his society. We see in the story of Job that he attributed some of the thinking and comments coming from his friends to their lack of discernment in regards to what spirit they were being inspired by. This may have been a shock to them as quite probably they thought that all of their ideas were coming from their own wisdom.

Many of the thoughts that we have, very possibly proceed from some kind of spiritual influence that we are open and attentive to because of our training. This is certainly true when we renew our minds to the ways of God and through His word conform to His Spirit.

Job 26:4, "*Where have you gotten all these wise sayings? Whose spirit speaks through you?*" (NLT).

Again, we see that the way of thinking that gave place to the devil, and a consequent door through their minds and then mouths, was a non-biblical mindset from worldly wisdom. We also note, to attack Job with negative thoughts, which incidentally may well have affected him, required hosts for the spirits to get at him. The fact that he was able to discern the source was protective for him in not receiving what they were trying to put on him.

We have, in a previous chapter, cited Jesus pointing out to His disciples that they were unaware of the type of spirit that they were being influenced by.

Luke 9:55, "*But He turned and rebuked them, and said, "You do not know what manner of spirit you are of*" (NKJV).

Yet again we see that He did not cast a spirit out of them because it was not resident inside them. It was worldly thinking inspired by the proud Satan controlled environment that they were still operating in.

Can Satan attack you at will?
Many Christians seem to have the idea that Satan can attack you out of a *clear blue sky* so to speak, anytime that he wants. This thinking suggests that he can attack you at will without some kind of agent to work through or exposure to some kind of medium or prior programming to tempt you. Their concept proposes that the devil might suddenly decide to attack you with fear, or to hold you back in your walk, just because he chooses to. In my experience I have never seen anyone attacked by fear who was not presented with a potentially anxiety inspiring situation, or more commonly holding a previously existing fear belief from a historical source.

To believe this would be to believe that someone who has never suffered with bitterness or lust for instance could suddenly be attacked with resentment for no reason or struggle with immoral thoughts. To take this further, this kind of thinking proposes that you could, without contact with another human being, or any kind of advertising, exposure or encouragement suddenly be overcome by a power drawing you into alcoholism, drugs, violence, and the occult or horror movies. This is absurd really, but there are a lot of people who spend time on *spiritual warfare* against a non-existent threat.

Believing that the devil can do this is giving him much more power than he actually has. He is roaming around, but he tempts through media or temptations to cooperate with him through some kind of peer pressure or reaction to offences from other people. Jesus preached repent, in other words change your thinking about what you allow yourself to join with and be exposed to, saying that the Kingdom of heaven is at hand to cooperate with.

Isaiah 14:16, *"Everyone there will stare at you and ask, 'Can this be the one who shook the earth and the kingdoms of the world?'"* (NLT).

Satan is not omnipresent as is God. He is limited in his ability to personally monitor individuals. In the case of God who *is* omnipresent, I knew of him because a person taught me about Him as a small child. In my teenage years and early twenties, I had largely walked away from Him and scarcely gave Him a thought. Even He did not put *God thoughts* into my mind. He eventually used a person to refire my faith. So, normally in the first instance, even God does not approach a person who has no knowledge of Him without the use of a person.

Romans 10:14, *"How then shall they call on Him in whom they have not believed? And how shall they believe in Him of whom they have not heard? And how shall they hear without a preacher?"* (NKJV).

In conclusion, we could say that as we resolve our fallen nature tendencies by dying to that which the world offers, and deal with deceptive beliefs held at a heart level, the devil has no place from which to bother us. I know many mature and free Christians who are only aware of the devil in the setting of getting others free of his influences. The only power that he actually has, is in what he has already trained you to believe, such as to live in fear, or, that you are not acceptable and so on. These beliefs give him access to how you respond to life and deal with others, which now gives him opportunity to provoke or tempt others through your ungodly activities and attitudes towards them. The other way he can affect you is in what you choose as a result of your beliefs. This may outwork as it did in the garden in thinking that something sinful and forbidden is what you need to make your life better. Indeed, the Apostle Paul knew that the people's eyes were closed to the deception and activities of Satan, and that this was the source of his power over them.

Acts 26:18, *"... to open their eyes, in order to turn them from darkness to light, and from the power of Satan to God, that they may receive forgiveness of sins and an inheritance among those who are sanctified by faith in Me'"* (NKJV).

In all of this, participation and submission to him are an unwitting form of worship in that you prefer his guidelines for living over God's. In this sense, the devil inhabits the praises of his people!

Ephesians 2:1-3, *"[1] As for you, you were dead in your transgressions and sins, [2] in which you used to live when you followed the ways of this world and of the ruler of the kingdom of the air, the spirit who is now at work in those who are disobedient. [3] All of us also lived among them at one time, gratifying the cravings of our* **sinful nature** *and* **following its desires and thoughts**. *Like the rest, we were by nature objects of wrath"* (NIV, Emphasis mine).

Most of what we believe was programmed into us growing up. And this, through *people* who were giving us thinking and believing that did not line up with God's ways. Therefore, it becomes reasonably obvious where most of our problems begin from, and where the solutions for freedom lie.

Collective human spirit
Sometimes what we think is an evil spirit is actually the collective power of a cooperative human spirit which is open to working in the devil's ways. For example, drunken parties, drugs or orgies, or the agreement of the corporate human spirit of our society on matters such as; *fornication is not sinful* or *pornography is normal and acceptable*. This is human spirit streaming in behind the devils wishes because it suits the self-indulgent fallen nature. It is a power

dynamic which creates a spiritual environment in much the same way as football matches or rock concerts have a spiritual/emotional atmosphere as the human spirit opens up and gets involved. That is not suggesting that football or a music concert is demonic, only that it has an atmosphere that has a corporate spirit emanating from a dynamic of collective human spirit in unison that can be felt and caught up in.

Random attacks from Satan
So, am I saying that God or unholy spirits cannot put thoughts in your mind from outside your person? No. What I am proposing is that it appears that neither God nor His opposer randomly put thoughts in your mind without eliciting or evoking your attention by some means. If you watch a horror movie and then have bad dreams in your sleep it is because you gave Satan your attention and handed him your mind. He is going to try to get to you through the world system, people and through your existing beliefs.

In much the same way we choose to communicate with God in prayer and seek Him for His counsel. So then when we open ourselves to His input, we ask, seek, knock, then we receive something, otherwise we probably won't hear much. Once we have committed our lives to Him, He has every right to give us His thoughts if we are looking to Him and giving Him our attention. For example, if I am seeking Him for a sermon, I will get more inspirational ideas than if I am engaged in a building project at home and my faculties are focused there. I often have a notebook or at least a pen available in a church service because as we are all giving Him our attention, and He is near inhabiting our praises, I often easily get thoughts and inspiration. But these are times of deliberate focus on Him. The door is wide open as we are choosing to communicate with Him.

Of course, if His Spirit resides *inside* of us and we are one in spirit with Him then he has full access to our faculties all of the time. In much the same way, if we have a spirit inside of us holding onto an area of our thinking then that demon will be a constant influencer towards those kinds of thoughts.

The devil has no power whatsoever, or ability to attack us or put thoughts in our minds without us beholding him, thinking about him or being attentive. Many Christians are deceived into thinking that he has power to attack us and that if we say this or that, he will test us. Or if you press in to God or are active in the gospel he will go after you. This is deception leading to fear.

My wife and I have ministered the gospel and taught on healing and deliverance in many developing countries. We have never feared anything happening and have never had any oppression or attacks on us, ever. That is not arrogance; it is simply what the Bible says. If God is for us, who can be against us? If you think that the devil can attack you then you are putting your faith in him as being greater than God, and that he is not defeated at all, which is faith in reverse, that we know as fear.

If that is the case, you may be right, because you are giving him power that he does not have through your deception. We never even give the possibility that the devil can touch us a thought. In fact, I don't think about him at all, beyond recognizing his activities through others that need help so that his works can be destroyed. God is the power and we are in Him. His ability to protect us is unchallengeable. When the Lord says that it is time to go home it is time. God Himself oversees all of our circumstances; He allows them for our shaping and refining.

Luke 10:19, *"Behold, I give you the authority to trample on serpents and scorpions, and **over all** the power of the enemy, and **nothing** shall by any means hurt you"* (NKJV, Emphasis mine).

Jesus suffered not because the devil was able to overpower Him, but because He was yielded to the Father's will in suffering for our sake. The same could be said of Paul and the others. They chose to put themselves in harm's way for the cause of the gospel. It was their will and not that of the devil that caused their tribulations. They wilfully exposed themselves to human beings through whom the devil could operate, in the hope of saving them.

Matthew 26:53-54, " [53] *Or do you think that I cannot now pray to My Father, and He will provide Me with more than twelve legions of angels?* [54] *"How then could the Scriptures be fulfilled, that it must happen thus?"* (NKJV).

Satan means the adversary, enemy or opposer which can be applied personally to the devil, but also encompasses all of the spiritual opposition to God working with him. So, attacks that come from the devil will usually come through people who are submitted to him in some area. This could be in the form of someone rejecting or being violent towards you and range through to a fellow teenager showing a schoolmate pornography on a smartphone. Either way his attack has not come from nowhere but rather evil spirit has found a manifestation in the natural realm through a *door* or *gate*. Jesus said that the *gates of hell* will not prevail. In other words, those who let the devil use them for his work, whether unwittingly or not, won't have the victory over believers who constitute the church.

Matthew 16:18, *"And I also say to you that you are Peter, and on this rock I will build My church, and the gates of Hades shall not prevail against it"* (NKJV).

Someone once said that both God and Satan are looking for a manifestation in the Earth. Like Peter, at times we can be double agents, where one moment we are exhibiting the Spirit of God in love, gentleness, kindness and so on. Later we find ourselves working for the other side and giving him an expression through criticism, fault-finding, or rejecting someone. We truly do need to make our focus worshipping God. Our behaviour and attitudes being doors and gates for His Spirit only, giving Him a manifestation in the Earth.

Psalm 24:7, *"Lift up your heads, O you gates! And be lifted up, you everlasting doors! And the King of glory shall come in"* (NKJV).

We need to come to the truth about whose spirit we are allowing to work through us, and often that requires receiving truth in the *inner parts* or *heart* before we are able to know what manner of spirit that we are of.

John 4:24, *"God is Spirit, and those who worship Him must worship in spirit and* **truth***"* (NKJV).

Spiritual influence from Inside
When a spirit finds a way inside a person it has much greater influence over them, and becomes entwined in the personality or body. This is true of the Holy Spirit indwelling a believer as well.

Obviously, there is no comparison between the power of the Holy Spirit and a demon, but in many ways, the Holy Spirit also limits His power in us, and through us, to wilful cooperation. Whether speaking of the Holy Spirit or an unholy spirit we could say that when they are inside, they have greater access and influence on our thoughts and faculties. The Holy Spirit normally comes inside when the person is ready and open to His presence. He does not force His way in. On the other hand, a demon will take any opening possible to find a way into a host person.

Jesus gave us the example of the wineskins. I believe that when a person is born again, he now has a new sensitivity to God and the Kingdom of heaven. This would be likened to a new wineskin. He now has a new soft regenerated human spirit which can expand and grow in the things of God. The Bible uses the picture of the New Wine as the Holy Spirit being poured out. We need a new spirit or a new wineskin to hold the new wine, which is the Holy Spirit who will continue to mature, ferment and expand in us when He comes inside.

Matthew 9:17, *"Nor do they put new wine into old wineskins, or else the wineskins break, the wine is spilled, and the wineskins are ruined. But they put new wine into new wineskins, and both are preserved"* (NKJV).

The Bible teaches us that we are one spirit, joined to the Lord. The Greek word translated here is *kollao* which literally means glued or stuck together. This powerful joining makes it impossible to be closer with Him in spirit.

1 Corinthians 6:17, *"But he who is joined to the Lord is one spirit with Him"* (NKJV).

It is worth pointing out that the Strong's concordance cites an element of the word *Charis* from which *grace* is translated, as *the divine influence upon the heart*. This sheds a different light on the grace of God. A large part of this grace is His influencing us away from ungodly behaviour and serving Satan. Because of the presence of the Holy Spirit, we can have *the mind of Christ* if we choose to listen.

Let me propose that whether you are a Christian or not, if you have a demon inside you, then you can have the mind of that evil spirit as well. It is not that the evil spirit is more powerful than the Holy

Spirit; it is that you choose to follow it for some reason. When the Apostle Paul encourages the believers to work out their *salvation* he did not exclusively mean their passage into heaven. He knew that this was provided for through redemption. Salvation is translated from the Greek word *soteria*. Strong's Concordance presents it this way: 4991. *Soteria, noun; rescue or safety (phys. or mor.):--deliver, health, salvation, save, saving.*

Paul was implying that you need to work on your deliverance from the devil. This, we are proposing, is by receiving light and truth which will result in your healing in every area of your being.
Philippians 2:12, *"Therefore, my beloved, as you have always obeyed, not as in my presence only, but now much more in my absence, work out your own **salvation** with fear and trembling"* (NKJV, Emphasis mine).

Again, we see the Greek word *sozo* translated as *saved*, carrying in it the sense of more than simply being saved for eternity: *4982. sozo, to save, i.e. **deliver** or protect (lit. or fig.):--heal, preserve, save (self), do well, **be (make) whole*** (Emphasis mine). It also points to deliverance from the opposer, as well as healing, and importantly being made whole, which is the result of sanctification through truth.

Ephesians 2:8-9, *" 8 For by grace you have been **saved** through faith, and that not of yourselves; it is the gift of God, 9 not of works, lest anyone should boast"* (NKJV, Emphasis mine).

We can conclude that a major part of our freedom and protection from evil spirits, whether they are inside or out, is by responding to the divine influence of the Spirit of Christ and receiving healing, deliverance and wholeness from His ministry.

1 Thessalonians 5:23, *"Now may the God of peace Himself sanctify you completely; and may your whole spirit, soul, and body be preserved blameless at the coming of our Lord Jesus Christ"* (NKJV).

If demons are influencing us from outside of the body the Bible instructs us to resist them.

James 4:7, *"Therefore submit to God. Resist the devil and he will flee from you"* (NKJV).

If they are operating inside the body, we are to cast them out in the name of Jesus Christ.

Matthew 8:16, *"When evening had come, they brought to Him many who were demon-possessed. And He cast out the spirits with a word, and healed all who were sick"* (NKJV).

Sometimes I hear people say that a Christian can't have a demon. I think the question is more like can a demon have a Christian, or at least an area of one? As an obvious example, most statistics that I have heard, cite that well over 50% of Christian men regularly look at pornography. I rest my case.

A demon under every bush
Some people who are excessively demon focused may be looking for a *demon under every bush!* Whilst that may be true to some extent, it is not a healthy way to approach this area of ministry. There is probably a spider under every bush as well but we don't really pay much attention unless it relates to something that we are doing.

The other end of the scale is to ignore the possibilities of demons altogether and come up with some unbiblical theology that excludes them. A common one is that a Christian cannot have a demon. This is often based on the premise that God cannot exist with evil and so He cannot infill a believer and have the devil remain. However, He does indwell believers and most often sin and sickness remains and dwells with Him. He is not condoning or participating with it, but nor is He removing Himself from it. At the beginning of the book of Job we see God seemingly casually chatting with Satan. Apparently, He has no problem being in the presence of an evil spiritual entity.

Let me propose that not only can a believer have a demon, but in fact deliverance from them is our *bread* or a provision for us that is not available to others.

Mark 7:27, *"But Jesus said to her, "Let the children be filled first, for it is not good to take the children's bread and throw it to the little dogs"* (NKJV).

In this passage the woman was looking for deliverance for her daughter from a demon. Jesus was pointing out that it was something that was for the children of God. She showed herself to be just such a person, coming ahead of time under the new covenant of faith as a means to receive God's provision. It is worth observing that the daughters' problem was a demon, but that the result of it leaving was healing. Sometimes the work of an evil spirit produces sickness of some kind.

Matthew 15:28, *"Then Jesus answered and said to her, "O woman, great is your faith! Let it be to you as you desire." And her daughter was healed from that very hour"* (NKJV, Emphasis mine).

Being set free from demons then, is a part of God's children's provision. Consequently, Jesus instructed the disciples as a part of their job description to deal with them. So, to not be prepared to use His name and authority in this way could be seen as disobedience to His command.

Matthew 10:1, *"He called his twelve disciples to him and gave them authority to drive out evil spirits and to heal every disease and sickness"* (NIV).

I was once dealing with a man who had come into our church from a denomination that taught that a Christian could not have a demon. He began sharing this point of view with a young believer who was influenced by him at the time and was also a part of the church. The problem was that the young man who he was imposing his doctrine on had had a powerful deliverance the evening before and had witnessed his wife being set free as well from an Occult spirit. This would be *expert* on demons quickly changed his position from a *Christian can't have a demon*, to, *that's not how I do it!*

To say that a Christian cannot have a demon is a bit like saying that they cannot have sin or sickness. The overwhelming evidence is that they both can and do, although the intention of God, as modelled by Jesus, is that they should not have either. Respectfully might I suggest that we could perhaps spend a little less time on matters such as how the Sunday service looks and a little more time on delivering the promises of God to His people? That is not to say that the service isn't important, but if that is all we have to offer those who attend how biblical are we?

CHAPTER 30
The Strong man's goods

A number of years ago I was pulling down an old house on our property in order to build a new one on the site. In the meantime, we had a large shed and I set up my office and a lounge room in there. There was also a lot of furniture stacked in there. While I was working outside some of the children came out screaming that there was a snake in the building. Now I could have taken the attitude that I would just deal with it if it showed up. However, I felt that it was my duty and responsibility to find where it had come in and seal that off and then expose it and deal with it so that it could not cause harm.

As I have said, if we become aware that a *demon* is in the house, we have a duty to those that we are responsible for to find out where it came from and evict it as soon as possible. Sometimes when I go camping, there will be a mosquito in the tent. I will not rest until I have tracked that thing down and eliminated it before I try to sleep. I know that in the night with its buzzing, it will rob my peace and ruin my functionality and mood for the following day. Consequently, it is prudent for me to deal with it as soon as possible. First, as with the snake I have to expose where it is hiding and block up the place where it has come in!

Exposing the enemy through teaching

It has been proposed that fully one third of Jesus' recorded ministry to people in the gospels was dealing with demons in some way. We know that before He ministered, He often taught the people. A number of years ago we were ministering in a large church in the Pacific and immediately prior to lunch I had taught on rejection. There was a young lady who brought the meal to us at the Pastors house, and as she put the food in front of us, I noticed that she had tears in her eyes. I commented to her; *The rejection teaching touched you didn't it?* She responded that it did. I asked her if she wanted me to pray for her and she indicated that she did. Across the table I took authority over the spirit of rejection and commanded it to go in the name of Jesus. She had a manifestation and I asked her if it had gone. She informed me that it had and so we proceeded to eat our lunch. The point is that this was easily done because she saw her problem. If the setting had been right, *Truth Encounters* would have been a good option for further healing. If she had not understood the source of her issue and the spiritual element of her problem, most probably nothing would have happened.

In the mid-1990s an intellectual lady came for some ministry advice. As she described her problem it became evident to me that she was also carrying a spirit of rejection. I explained this to her and how it worked but she was struggling with the concept, and so thanked me and left. Several months later she returned and confirmed that she now believed that what I had explained was true. Now that she had seen the spiritual element of her problem it was only a matter of moments and she was free. She later reported that she was now able to get on with people whom she formerly struggled with and generally felt better.

I want to make the point that if I had tried to cast out the spirit without her having a realization that it was present, I would have been wasting my time. God will not necessarily set her free because I want her to be free. He will set her free when, by her own will, she wants Him to free her, which will normally require her understanding her need. If this were not the case then God would automatically set everyone free of everything without the consent of their free will and choice. Even the demoniac in Mark chapter 5 came to Jesus and fell down before Him. Jesus often said things such as; *do you want to be made well?* (John 5:6).

Another factor that I would like to mention regarding this lady's ministry was that at that time we did not minister *Truth Encounters* and although she reported improvement and that the power had gone out of her rejection she was still not completely whole in that area. A few years later she returned for further ministry in which the *truth made her completely free.*

What are the strong man's goods?
A strong man's *goods* or *possessions* are those things which he holds that strengthen his position. The Greek word translated as *goods* or *possessions* is *huparchonta*, which also means *that which one has* or *his property*.

Luke 11:20-21, "²⁰ *But if I drive out demons by the finger of God, then the kingdom of God has come to you.* ²¹ *"When a strong man, fully armed, guards his own house, his possessions are safe"* (NIV, Emphasis mine).

Let me suggest that he is fully armed with areas of deception that protect those areas that he considers his property, possessions or goods. These possessions that give him *a place* are the beliefs that we hold that cause us to serve him and participate with him. For example:

- A spirit of bitterness will hold hurts and beliefs resulting from being hurt or abused.
- A spirit of rebellion will hold beliefs relating to injustice.
- A spirit of pride will hold beliefs relating to inferiority.
- A spirit of self-pity will hold beliefs to do with nobody caring about the host and so on.
- The one who is stronger is the Spirit of truth, because truth overpowers the power of deception just as light dispels darkness.
- So is the spirit the problem or, is the property or possessions that he holds that give him a place, the issue?

Ephesians 4:27, "*... nor give* **place** *to the devil"* (NKJV, Emphasis mine).

Ephesians 4:27, "*... and do not give the devil* **a foothold**" (NIV, Emphasis mine).

Giving the devil a foothold or a place to stand, through what we believe and the resultant way that we act, is the true nature of the problem. Again, we look to the original Greek language and see that *foothold* and *place* come from the word *topos* which means a location, a home, or even an opportunity. So often through what we believe we consciously or unconsciously yield a portion of our personality, soul or body for the demon to stand on.

Being *fully armed* relates to his ability to protect his position. For example, if his possessions which give him place are beliefs relating to inferiority then his ability to defend those beliefs are the pride response that comes from those beliefs. Now he is safe because the host will not go to anyone for help because their pride will not allow them to be *under* another person. Remember this is because the solution to inferiority that the devil suggests is to make you *over* or *above* everyone else in pride. This means that you believe that you know more or better and have more wisdom than anyone else. If we continue to use the same examples the *fully armed* component of injustice beliefs is the rebellion reaction. Now the person is captive because they cannot submit to another.

In the case of a control spirit, the person's insecurity is the issue. To trust another would mean that they are no longer in control, and this is the defence of the strongman and so on. This is why ministering to the root heart belief, rather than trying to cast out the demon by attacking his defences is a far more effective and permanent way of dealing with the spirit. He is now weak and easy to cast out because he has lost his *possessions* which gave him a *place* and so this is also a gentler approach for the person.

Many times, the spirit is attached to sinful behaviour, attitudes, reactions and responses that are retaliatory by nature. The name of the demon is the name of ungodly sinful activities such as unforgiveness, resentment, bitterness, ungodly control, rebellion, pride, hatred, self-rejection, fear of rejection and so on. I need to point out that all of these can and do exist without the presence of a demon inside the host. Either way the beliefs need to be dealt with to remove the areas that the devil can work through from outside, or that are strongholds of evil spirits on the inside.

Two of the main ways that the demons have a place then, is firstly by holding people captive to pain and hurt coming from heart beliefs. Secondly, they are from responses that you believe will resolve the issues proceeding from these beliefs. This could, along with the emotional reactions that we have described, include things such as lustful or immoral activities, violence, addictive behaviour, theft, lying, criticism, and so on.

How right was Louis Pasteur when he made an observation relating to the destructive power of the unseen enemy that we now know as germs! *The germ is nothing, the terrain is everything!* In a spiritual sense we could replicate this principle by saying that the demon is nothing, the environment or beliefs that give him place are everything. The only hold he has on us to use us, manipulate us, and keep us in bondage is some area of deception or wrong believing in the mind, heart, or both. The *germ is nothing* and consequently our focus is not on him, he simply *flags* the real problem. Once we know the type of root belief and likely circumstance that it was learnt in, we can deal with the terrain.

The 'dung' god
Jesus described Satan as *Beelzebub* which means the *dung god*, or *the lord of the flies*. This gives us a great perspective on how God regards demons. They are nothing, they are just like flies. The only power that they have is whatever you are deceived into giving them, which is why when you know the truth it will set you free. I think that most of us who started out with a *cast out the demons* focus, and neglected healing the broken hearts, would agree with me that many times we would shoo away the flies on Monday only to find that we had to do it again a week later. Some people would stay free, or have a measure of deliverance but many, even though they may have had powerful deliverances and manifestations, would return bound again.

Whereas when we take the *Truth Encounters* model, we see them completely free in the area ministered to, and are often not even aware if there was a demon there or not because we took his goods in which he trusted in. It is much gentler for the person than attacking a fully armed spirit if we remove that which he trusts in. In short, clean up the dung and there is no further reason for the flies to be there. They need food and the dung heap as their place. The fly is nothing; the dung is *everything*!

Swept and empty
When Jesus used the picture of that which the spirit considers to be *his house, or place that he inhabits* He states that if this abode, which is based on the possessions of the demon is left empty, then it is likely that the evil spirit will return. Why is this?

Let me propose that the property of the demon that gave him place was the deceptive beliefs that the host or person held. So, if the house is left empty and not filled with God's truth through the ministry of the Spirit of truth, then there is nothing stopping him from returning. If knowing the Truth will set you free, and if this is done by the Spirit of Christ, then you will remain free indeed.

Matthew 12:43-44, "⁴³ *When an unclean spirit goes out of a man, he goes through dry places, seeking rest, and finds none.* ⁴⁴ *"Then he says, 'I will return to my house from which I came.' And when he comes, he finds it empty, swept, and put in order"* (NKJV).

Repentance and deliverance
Once a spirit has established a strong hold on your hurts or sinful reactions, he is going to replay them as inner thinking or addictive and often repetitive behaviour. He is also going to amplify your responses and the intensity of emotion that you hold. People with demonic powered beliefs may often not be able to control their feelings and have an inordinate response in how they react to stressors.

When we talk about repentance, people normally consider it to mean to turn from your sin. This turning is actually a by-product of repentance. The word translated as *repent* from the original Greek language is *Metanoeo* and it means to *think differently* or *reconsider*, or *to change one's mind*. When we think differently about what we are doing, reconsider our ways and then change our minds, the by-product will be turning from sin. In the first instance we need to know that our thinking and resultant deeds are wrong in the first place, and we do this through learning the ways of God from His word. In the epistle 1 John and chapter 3 we see that Jesus came to destroy the works of the devil.

1 John 3:8, *"He who sins is of the devil, for the devil has sinned from the beginning. For this purpose the Son of God was manifested, that He might destroy the works of the devil"* (NKJV).

Having established that Jesus came to destroy the works of the devil that were operating in and through mankind, we now observe that He came preaching; *repent for the Kingdom of heaven is at hand.* Why?

He did this because in order to destroy the devil's works in us, he needs us to stop cooperating with our enemy by our own will and volition. He needs for us to think differently, reconsider our ways and change our minds to living the ways of the Kingdom of God. We do this by renewing our minds and then deciding that we want to be hearers and doers of the word. But as we have described in an earlier chapter the Apostle Paul had set himself in this stance as he outlined in Romans chapter 7, but was unable to do that which he had decided to do with his conscious mind. He needed a change of thinking at heart level as well before he could be fully repentant, and this is a gift of God through healing ministries such as *Truth Encounters* and deliverance.

2 Timothy 2:24-26, *"²⁴ And the servant of the Lord must not strive; but be gentle unto all men, apt to teach, patient, ²⁵ In meekness instructing those that **oppose themselves**; if God peradventure will give them **repentance to the acknowledging of the truth**; ²⁶ And that they may recover themselves out of the snare of the devil, who are **taken captive by him** at his will"* (KJV, Emphasis mine).

As in the case of Paul, these people oppose themselves because how they want to act with their minds is not in agreement with how they do actually act, which is based on the deceptive beliefs that they hold in their hearts. The final result is that they remain in bondage to the devil acting out his will and manifesting his nature. They are doing this even though they are believers, in part because they believe that their actions are *just what they want to do*, and are not aware of the devil's involvement. In 2 Timothy chapter 2 and verse 25 it refers to the change of thinking or repentance coming as a result of acknowledging *the truth*.

Our mission is to gently instruct them and teach them the truth about the roots of their issues and how they can receive freedom from captivity. Mostly evil spirits have a place in us through something that we believe either consciously or unconsciously. This could include not believing that a part of the problem is a demon.

Spiritual 'armour'
Whilst we are mainly focused on the issue, or the 'dung', it is good to be aware of the possibilities of spiritual interference, which is why I am writing this whole section.

Story
At one time a lady travelled a long way to receive *Truth Encounters* ministry. Before we began the ministry session, and following

a prompt, I prayed for her and she received the baptism in the Holy Spirit as evidenced by her speaking in other tongues. As we proceeded to go through her memories, we identified the beliefs in her heart, as we normally would, and God communicated things to her that were consistent with what would normally happen.

This is the only time that I have ever seen this, but at the end of the session she reported that all of her problems were the same and that her new Holy Spirit tongue seemed ridiculous to her. Again, I felt prompted to ask if I could pray for her against a spirit before she left and she responded that this would be alright with her. I took authority over a spirit of doubt and unbelief and commanded it to leave and come off her mind and emotions. Nothing obvious happened.

A couple of days later she was booked to come in for another session before she made the long journey home. I was not particularly looking forward to this time together because all that we usually saw God free people through did not seem to have had much effect on her. When she arrived, she alighted from her vehicle beaming and reported that she was all healed and loved her new prayer language. The spirit of doubt and unbelief had been blocking her from receiving any of the things that had happened in her prayer session. Once the spirit was gone, she had a download and was completely set free. Following is an excerpt from the testimony that she emailed to me a week later;

"Steve and Em, wow you would not believe the changes in me!! But then of course you do believe!! Praise the Lord...here we go...just overflowing with the Holy Spirit like the incredible hulk, just wants to burst out, the heaviness, anxiety, confusion, sadness, back pain, sleeplessness...all gone, zapped, now light, joyous, calm, strengthened."

And so, it went on, including no longer needing her medication for a physical problem. The point is that, if we were not aware of the possibility of a spirit or spirits being involved, it is unlikely that she would have received her healing.

Chapter 30: The Strong man's goods

Story

On another occasion I was ministering to a young lady who had suffered considerable sexual abuse. God was faithfully setting her free from the beliefs that she held from the painful memories. As the Lord resolved one particular memory, she reported joy and peace in regards to her new freedom. She asked me a question not relating to emotion from the event. In this instance she had been sodomized and her question was in regards to whether or not I thought this could have been implicated in a problem with moving her bowels. I shot up a quick thank you prayer as I had missed it, and could have left her with this problem for life.

I related to her that there may well be a spirit of infirmity that attached to her as a result of the ungodly act towards her. At this point some of you may be thinking why should she get a spirit when she did not do anything wrong? This is a reasonable question so let me briefly digress.

If you went to your neighbours' house and they hit you over the head with a piece of wood, who sinned? They did. Who has the lump on the forehead? You do. Sin creates an opening just as when parents deeply or repetitively reject their children, and the child receives a corresponding spirit. It would be rare for a person to ask for or want a demon; something has happened to them, usually that they did not ask for.

In the case of this young lady, she was a victim of an ungodly sexual bond and along with the emotional trauma this created an entry point for the spirit. I will explain this more fully under the heading *integrity*. I simply addressed the spirit of infirmity that had come in through the lustful activity and told it to go. She looked a little bit uncomfortable for a moment and then told me that it had gone. A few days later I received a phone call from her and she reported that her system was now working perfectly. Again, if we were not aware of the possibilities of a spirit operating, she could have gone on through life with the problem.

A lady once came to me after a meeting where I had spoken and ministered in their church. She asked for some wisdom for a lady that she was looking after who was bitter and angry against God because her husband had died. I suggested that she tell the lady that; *God does not always get what He wants*. He does not want wars, children abused or people saying nasty things to each other. He has in some sense limited Himself in evidently giving all of His creation free will and choice. He is not pleased, and eventually will judge using the Word of God to measure. Even for believers He in some measure has limited His activities to faith which is based on how we see His character.

CHAPTER 31
Names of demons and touching the spirit realm

Some people feel that they need to know the names of all the demons and get them right before they will leave. You can simply say something such as; *you spirit that is attached to this or that, leave in the name of Jesus.* There are books around with pages of lists of the names of demons. At one time I remember reading a book with one of these lists and thinking how will I remember the names of all these evil spirits? A scripture that I had read came to remembrance in my mind about the *lying spirits* in 1 Kings 22:22. In this passage the prophets were looking to say what the Kings wanted to hear in order to receive their acceptance and favour. The usual reason that people tell lies is a fear of rejection and it is the most common reason that I have found that causes people to lie.

I have dealt with a number of people where this has become a demonic problem and they simply cannot tell the truth even when they want to. The basis of freedom in these people in the first instance came with resolving the rejection beliefs, but I digress.

In the case of the prophets wanting to please the Kings and say what they wanted to hear, this opened them to having a spirit attached to them.

1 Kings 22:21-23, " ²¹ *Then a spirit came forward and stood before the LORD, and said, 'I will persuade him.'* ²² *"The LORD said to him, 'In what way?' So he said, 'I will go out and be a lying spirit in the mouth of all his prophets.' And the LORD said, 'You shall persuade him, and also prevail. Go out and do so.'* ²³ *"Therefore look! The LORD has put a lying spirit in the mouth of all these prophets of yours, and the LORD has declared disaster against you"* (NKJV).

What I learnt from studying and meditating on the passage is that the spirit was not a *lying spirit*, it was just a generic nondescript spirit. It was only able to attach itself to that which was yielded to sin, in this case lying. It could not go and be a spirit of lust or bitterness because that was not the area of the personality or body that was being made available to sin. So, the name of a spirit is simply the area of the person that they hold. If it's bitterness, its bitterness, lust, lust, lying, lying and so on. It exists there because it has access to the person in some way, often through their unwitting yielded ness in following sinful behaviour, attitudes and responses.

Many in the church seem to have this idea that the devil already has spirits with special names, functions and job descriptions in stock that he can send at will to attack people. You can almost imagine how some might think this would look in the spirit world; *We are running low on spirits of bitterness in New York, could you send 5,000 more please? And we need another 10,000 spirits of lust to drive the porn industry in London!* In all probability a spirit that may have previously functioned as bitterness because of the participation of its last host, could well have a role of insanity or mental illness in the next person that they are able to inhabit.

When they run through generation lines, they seem to be able to promote the same beliefs and ground to operate on that was in previous generations. As a result, you may see issues such as ungodly control, lust, unforgiveness or rejection run through families, with corresponding physical maladies, until someone receives freedom from Christ Jesus.

Touching the spirit realm
When I was a young man, we used to go camping in canvas tents. This material was excellent at keeping out the rain and weather. The only problem that it had was that to some extent the material seemed to soak up the water to the point of saturation as a part of its ability to have the rain runoff. So, if you touched the material anywhere when it was raining that was now a place where it leaked. The spirit realm is very much like this. We are always surrounded by spiritual elements and wherever we touch it, that is where we have given it access to leak into our environment.

Let me suggest some areas where we may create openings, and if there is demonization that goes with it then the following list of examples could all be the names of demons. We could address them as; *you spirit that has been involved in holding Fred into 'rebellious' behaviour.* (This assumes that we have dealt with the injustice beliefs already or concurrently.)

These are some sample areas of the human person that spirits may influence or affect:

- Emotional breaches;   fear, bitterness, rejection, inferiority. Etc.
- Mental problems;   doubt, unbelief, fantasy, withdrawal, insanity. Etc.
- Moral issues;   pornography, fornication, adultery, lying, theft. Etc.
- Relational disharmony;   mockery, criticism, judgment, religion. Etc.
- Spiritual alliances;   the occult, false religion, witchcraft. Etc.
- Physical bondage;   addictions, lusts, altered states, violence, infirmity. Etc.

These are all potential areas of exposure to the spirit realm if we touch it or there is an opening through which it can enter. You will note that virtually all of these are tied to thoughts coming from beliefs, which precipitate and present in decisions. This should re centre us on the need for truth at every level of our being so that we can make good protective choices.

- Section 4: Dealing with the Demonic Element -

CHAPTER 32
Breaches

Integrity

Most probably when you hear the word *integrity* you think of a business man or similar who conducts their dealings in an upright and trustworthy manner. The word integrity actually means; *the state of being entire, or whole.* As an example, if you could imagine your skin as a God given barrier to protect you from the elements as well as various bacteria and diseases. While my skin holds its unbroken integrity and remains whole you could pour, for example, hepatic B virus over my arm and I would not be harmed. But if you created a small cut or opening in the wholeness of my skin then I would become infected and get sick.

We have already mentioned that the word for being *saved* is *sozo* and that a part of the meaning of that word includes to *deliver or protect* and coming to *wholeness.* The more whole we are in regards to truth about God, ourselves, how to deal with others, and the spiritual world that we have, the more delivered we are. This is our best protection against possible infection from the spiritual realm and this is why children are the most vulnerable, because they have the least amount of truth and understanding. They need our spiritual protection and instruction to bring them up in the counsel of the Lord.

When we have a break or breach in our spiritual or emotional integrity, it is a potential entry point for a spirit. This could be a time of fear or trauma. It could be a time of abuse where our understanding of the situation is overwhelmed and we are out of control. It could also be at a time where we are on drugs or drunk, and our normal resistance and mental integrity is weakened and now we do something sinful that we would not normally do.

In a ministry setting we are aware of possible breaches in our wholeness of some kind that may have given place to a spirit. We are looking to repair the breach in the walls of the human personality so that the people again have normal resistance to spiritual inroads.

Isaiah 58:10-12, "¹⁰ *If you extend your soul to the hungry And satisfy the afflicted soul, Then your light shall dawn in the darkness, And your darkness shall be as the noonday.* ¹¹ *The LORD will guide you continually, And satisfy your soul in drought, And strengthen your bones; You shall be like a watered garden, And like a spring of water, whose waters do not fail.* ¹² *Those from among* **you Shall build the old waste places**; *You shall raise up the foundations of many generations; And you shall be called the* **Repairer of the Breach**, *The Restorer of Streets to Dwell In"* (NKJV, Emphasis mine).

Walls were intended to keep the bad things out and protect the good things inside. Physically, a healthy body will include a good immune system that can deal with all of the attacks that may come. In much the same way a healthy soul carries its own protection. Some spiritual and emotional building materials that are used to strengthen the walls of the human personality and keep the temple in good condition are such items as; love, acceptance, grace, truth, value, significance, encouragement, worth, freedom, respect, honour, forgiveness, kindness, protection and so on.

We children of God have been given the privilege of working with the Holy Spirit to help repair people's lives, and for Him to receive the glory for that which He does in them. This is well illustrated in the following beautiful typology from Isaiah.

Isaiah 61:3-4, " ³ *To console those who mourn in Zion, To give them beauty for ashes, The oil of joy for mourning, The garment of praise for the spirit of heaviness; That* **they** *may be called trees of righteousness, The planting of the LORD,* **that He may be glorified**. ⁴ *And* **they** *shall rebuild the old ruins,* **They** *shall raise up the former desolations, And* **they** *shall repair the ruined cities, The desolations of many generations"* (NKJV, Emphasis mine).

Integrity to integration
Many people are unaware of, or unable to discern the spiritual dynamics that may be at work inside of them. Often times they leave getting help until it is too late and they have a trail of hurt children and broken relationships or a physical problem.

A long time ago I developed a low-grade tooth ache in a slowly rotting tooth. As with most people I didn't particularly like the dentist's chair and so I put up with it for several years. Eventually it did get worse and I did go to get it taken out. I recall the very irate dentist sweating profusely as he wrestled for a very long time with his pliers on this rotten tooth. He became increasingly frustrated as pieces broke off as he struggled to remove the offending article. As he wiggled the last piece loose, interspersed with grunts I recall him saying between pushing it back and forth; *Don't EVER, EVER leave it this long. again!*

Very often we minister to people who have a trail of relational or other damage behind them. You can't help but think that if they had done something much sooner their lives and those around them would have been much more abundant. Sadly, the modern church is often either not equipped to offer help to them or prioritizes other activities. Jesus spent His time healing people and setting them free, and everything else proceeded from that.

Working in the darkness
In Australia we have termites or white ants as we know them. We used to live in an area where they were highly active. They are not unlike the demonic realm in the sense that they work in the dark and hate being exposed to the light because they will die. We once owned an old house that had an infestation. Very often the first sign that they were there was a hole in your skirting or architrave where, when you pushed on it, your finger would go right through. By that stage the damage was done and your framing was usually extensively damaged. The only way to avoid this was through regular examinations from an expert who was equipped to detect them and knew the signs to look for.

I do not say lightly that today there is evidence everywhere that the body of Christ is quite badly infested. We need to train up an army of helpers to get her into an irresistible condition to attract a hurting world. God can of course resolve all issues if He is given the opportunity to do so.

Once a spirit has breached the integrity of a person through some means and come inside, it will entwine itself with your personality. From experience I would say that a demon is limited to work in you in the area or place that has given it ground. By this I mean that a spirit that causes you let's say, to be violent, has no ability to lead you into false religion or lustful behaviour. Its function and area of influence is limited to that which has given it access and place. If the member of your person that is given to the devil is, for example, your sexuality through choosing to view pornography, then it follows that lust will be the stronghold outcome rather than say bitterness.

Romans 6:12-13, "*¹² Therefore do not let sin reign in your mortal body, that you should obey it in its lusts. ¹³ And do not present your members as instruments of unrighteousness to sin, but present yourselves to God as being alive from the dead, and your members as instruments of righteousness to God*" (NKJV).

Although many times a spirit will come to us as a result of the sins of others which have created breaches in us, in the preceding verse we see that at times the demon has come as a result of opening a door through our wilful cooperation. This happens even though we may be unaware of the spiritual implications at the time. If we continue using the common problem of pornography as an example, a person may or may not receive a spirit of lust from a one-time viewing. However, if people have continued and repeated exposure, submitting to the spirit power behind the offense, you can be reasonably sure that they are giving a strong place in their sexuality where a spiritual stronghold will be established and make a *home*.

People who have become bound by this have reported the replay of images and an amplification of their sexual urges and chemical responses as a result of the thoughts. So, is this a spirit of lust that has brought its nature in, or is it just a generic spirit which now holds a specific area of your being, namely your sexuality? Again, the scriptures point to the likelihood that it is not the nature of a spirit that has a hold on you; it is rather an area of your own person that has been yielded to the spirit and distorted.

James 1:14-15, "*¹⁴ But each one is tempted when he is drawn away **by his own desires and enticed**. ¹⁵ Then, when desire has conceived, it gives birth to sin; and sin, when it is full-grown, brings forth death*" (NKJV, Emphasis mine).

I am not suggesting for a moment that every time you sin that you are going to receive an evil spirit. I am proposing that all sin is not from God, so anytime that we sin we are serving Satan and, at times, this could open us up to demonization. For the most part the *ground* for demons entering is prepared and made available in the earlier years of life from conception to adolescence.

Entwined
Let's continue examining sexuality as an easily understood area of our person that can be open to demonic activity through some form of immorality. Once engaged in lustful behaviour the spirit inside has entwined itself with your sexuality and you have, to some measure, become one with it in your thoughts in regards to sexual matters. As a result, the sexual ideas, desires or tendencies are influenced by the demon inside of you.

We could say that it has come in through some kind of breach in the integrity of your person and has now moved to being integrated with your sexuality. If you are unaware of this influence then you now think that it is only your thoughts and ideas that move you towards ungodly sexual activities. So, you do not hesitate to go ahead with this behaviour because you simply think that it is what you alone want. You think it is just your thoughts that you are having.

The same could be said for retaliatory or revengeful thoughts that you may be having if you hold unforgiveness. You simply think that it is what you want, and what will please you, and so you don't hesitate to act out further in sin. This could apply to any area of distorted behaviour or attitudes that we are in bondage to, and that are replayed or amplified as an expression. We need to discern it by identifying that which is out of order with Gods plans for our attitudes and actions. This is done by measuring these thoughts and deeds by the Word of God and the counsel of the Spirit of God.

John 6:63, "*It is the Spirit who gives life; the flesh profits nothing. The words that I speak to you are spirit, and they are life*" (NKJV).

It is often difficult to receive deliverance and separation from an integrated spirit until the person understands which part of their thoughts are not actually them. After all, why would you want a part of yourself cast out?

Let us propose a case of say somebody addicted to smoking or excessive food intake as possibly a form of comfort for inner pain from identity beliefs. Now they feel prompted to have a cigarette or go to the refrigerator. If they think that it is simply their own thinking then they won't hesitate to go ahead and act out. But if they realize that it could be a demon within them compelling them to continue in behaviour that will result in them being robbed of health or bring on premature death, they may be ready for separation. The devil is a liar, a thief and a murderer; he will always be working against you reaching your potential for abundant life.

In regards to the examples that I have used, I would say that, in my opinion, only a percentage of smokers have a spirit attached to their addiction. Most of the smokers that I know of, wish that they could give up. This is strong indicator that their will and thinking is not completely compromised or influenced excessively. I have at times heard people say of cigarettes; *I just love them!* Most people would say that they enjoy some of their smokes but a lot of them are just out of habit. On more than one occasion when I have heard the, *I just love them statement,* I have commented to the host that actually maybe they do not love them, and that it is probably a spirit that they are entwined with that loves them, and that this in part is what is speaking out of them.

I have on a couple of occasions offered to cast them out. Each of the times when I have said this, the spirit has risen in their throats. In every instance the men have said *not now* being shocked at the revelation that their habit was perhaps spirit driven. Evidently, they needed time to decide whether or not they actually wanted to stop and work out what was what, and decide whether the spirit was a friend or an enemy! Later I know that one of them did give up, others I have not seen again.

In the case of food addictions as a means of comfort, clearly not every time will it be an evil spirit. If it is extreme and out of control then it is a possibility that this is a part of the problem, most likely along with rejection and other emotional issues. Once we have integrated with a spirit, we can use terms such as participating with, following, or cooperating with the ungodly internal entity. We have to begin by changing our thinking about it in repentance and then fall out of agreement with our working with it as a basis for being set free.

Physical or mental problems
Once a demon has integrated and amplified, for example emotional issues, you can expect some kind of outworking in the physical body and or mental health areas. For instance, there are various reasons that people hear voices, but very often it is echoes from things learnt in painful memories that are demonically replayed.

Remember, dealing with the connected inner beliefs is the basis of the freedom and not merely shooing away the flies.

A lady was set free from a spirit of rejection. The rejection had been the foundation for bitterness and resentment in her life which in turn affected her physiology. By the age of thirty years old if she was sitting down for more than a couple of minutes when she stood up, she would hobble around until she could get her arthritic ankles moving. Her father was the same and his mother before him. Perhaps a month after her deliverance someone noticed that she no longer *hobbled* when she stood up and it was realized that she was healed. The point is that nobody prayed for her to be healed from the arthritis. It was a cause and effect healing and a by-product of being set free from rejection. Almost 30 years later she is still healed and has never *hobbled* again, whilst others in her family who never received ministry have chronic arthritic and associated resentment issues.

As we have dealt with emotionally rooted issues, whether demonic or not, we have seen many physical ailments such as asthma, hormonal problems, inflammatory issues, allergies and so on simply disappear. All without any direct prayer. We can include various *mental illnesses* with all kinds of interesting names that detail the fruit associated with the malady. The point here is that we need to be aware of the possibility of a spiritual component relating to a person's problems and be aware that evil spirits don't respond to counselling, you can't get them saved or disciple them, and you can't inner heal them! The ground needs to be dealt with and they need to be evicted. I recall ministering to a 70-year-old lady who was set free from an unclean spirit. She was sad as she made the comment after receiving her freedom that it had ruined her and her husband having fullness in their married life.

Infirmity
Luke 13:11, *"And behold, there was a woman who had a spirit of infirmity eighteen years, and was bent over and could in no way raise herself up"* (NKJV).

Apparently, prior to eighteen years earlier, the woman did not have a spirit of infirmity and she was healthy and well. Something happened! Strong's concordance informs us that the Greek word *asthenia* from which we have the word *infirmity* contains the following meanings: *Feebleness (of body or mind); malady; frailty: disease, infirmity, sickness, weakness.*

We can conclude that whenever we are praying for a disease, sickness or malady that has taken hold as the result of a weakness in the body, there is a strong possibility that a *spirit of infirmity* is holding the body into that condition. It has most likely taken hold when the physical integrity or wholeness of the person was weakened and breached through trauma, or longer-term hormonal imbalances caused by emotional 'dis' ease from faulty heart beliefs, or some other kind of breakdown of the body's normal defences such as immune problems.

People are healed after a simple prayer commanding the spirit to go. Many times, the emotional components of the disease need to be ministered to, and also beliefs emanating from trauma dealt with to take away the ground that the spirit holds. If we don't do this then, although the spirit is gone and healing may result, we have left the door open, so to speak, and they may end up with the same or another sickness. If people prayed against the spirit of infirmity more, and the recipients of the prayer understood what this meant, we would see many more people being healed. Not surprisingly this can extend to physical injuries where a weakness has occurred through events such as accidents. We could say; *you spirit that has come in through weakness* leave and expect the same results.

I recall that Smith Wigglesworth used to command spirits to come out of the damaged knees of miners and this would result in healing. May I suggest that this is probably because their knees were weakened over time through their work, and the weakness was created by their form of employment? I have prayed with individuals commanding a *spirit of infirmity* to leave without seeing anything obvious happen, and later heard that the person involved discovered that they no longer had their illness.

In summary, we could say that arthritis is a kind of infirmity or weakness created by beliefs producing emotional and consequent hormonal imbalances. The same could be said of cancer, migraines and many other illnesses. We could say that cancer is one kind of infirmity or weakness, migraines another, arthritis another and so on.

Insanity
The majority of this publication is directed towards how to become increasingly sound of mind and whole of body. To be insane simply means to be unsound in mind.

Hosea 9:7, *"The days of punishment have come; The days of recompense have come. Israel knows! The prophet is a fool, The spiritual man is **insane**, Because of the greatness of your iniquity and great enmity"* (NKJV, Emphasis mine).

We see various mental illnesses which have a spirit of insanity involved. People such as drug addicts' risk being open to this problem through opening the door by voluntarily going into altered states that make their mind not sane, not sound or whole and seeking unreality as a means of pleasure, or escaping from life or pain.

Let me tentatively propose that the modern church, in seeking the *power of God* for the wrong reasons, may unwittingly at times open themselves up to insanity. Where leaders have low self-image issues, they may seek to be the *most spiritual* church and have *more blessing and power from God* than other churches. This competitive spirit may open them to readily embracing any manifestations as being from God, and consequently create an opening for other spirits. These extra biblical manifestations are not outlined in the Word of God as something that will be a function of the Holy Spirit, as are for example gifts.

I fear that this may be another expression of a religious spirit. You may recall that we call the *religious spirit* the *try hard spirit*. When the pendulum swings too far one way this will be legalism where you try hard to be better than everyone else by getting everything right and keeping the letter of the law. At the other end of the scale when the pendulum swings back past centre the people involved will be trying hard to be the more spiritual and in their own eyes superior to others. Trying hard to be good enough for God or others is usually a sign of an inner belief that you are not enough and this inferiority opens us to pride. I thoroughly believe in the power of God and enjoy seeing people, touched, healed and delivered.

A number of years ago some churches that I know of embraced some such manifestations where people would be gripped by strange movements and actions. Some friends that I knew reported that they did this every week, but that they also saw some of the people who were manifesting at these meetings drunk and smoking at the hotel the following evening. Apparently being touched by the *power of God* was not affecting any change in these individuals. My personal experiences of seeing the power of God is mostly in the Holy Spirit bringing healing or deliverance as it was demonstrated with Jesus. I understand that making these comments will make me unpopular with some people but let me explain a little more fully why I offer these observations.

Around 27 years ago we took in a 9-year-old insane boy who was virtually totally demonized. Particularly in the first few years as we worked through the different dimensions of his problems, we witnessed all kinds of crazy laughing and strange manifestations. To say the least we became very familiar with full blown insanity. One night I attended one of these meetings and witnessed virtually the same behaviour through these well-meaning Christian people. At one point as many of them were on the floor under the influence of this spirit suddenly the crowd parted and I had a few second snapshot of a well-known man doing exactly the same crazy laughing as our foster son had been doing. It is indelibly imprinted on my mind to this day. I am not referring to the laughter movement that went through many churches on which I have no comment.

My intention is not to hurt anyone or diminish them as good people, children of God or excellent ministers of the gospel. I am simply trying to alert areas of the body of Christ that may not be aware of this, and that not every spirit is the Holy Spirit. I cannot see any way that making people behave in this way would bring glory to God. If I was an unbeliever and walked into such a meeting, I would probably conclude that if I became a Christian that there would be a reasonable chance that I might end up with epilepsy or similar.

Possible entry points
We have already covered some of these major topics in detail.
- Trauma or loss of mental or emotional integrity
- Sin responses, or reactions coming from emotional pain or abuse such as bitterness, hatred, or rebellion etc.

- Sin *solutions* stemming from efforts to resolve emotional pain; Lusts, excessive use of substances such as food, alcohol, drugs, or escape into media and unreality, immoral relationships, addictions etc.
- Involvement in the Occult, witchcraft, or false religions as being the worship of other gods.

Generationally inherited spirits
In a sense all sin is generational, because it began with Adam and Eve and has travelled through the generations up to this point in history. Often the drawing to the family weaknesses opens us to also committing the same sins and giving place to the devil through our own submission and compliance.

We were working with a Chinese lady one day and she was having emotional healing and deliverance from various spirits. In the course of the Holy Spirit setting her free her body began to contort into various unnatural shapes. Once she was free from these generational demons my wife asked her if this was some kind of dragon spirit because of the particular way her body had conformed as they exited, and she confirmed that it was so.

I was watching a current affairs program on television a number of years ago and they stated that chemical and genetic habits passed through the sperm and ovaries from mum and dad to the child. The report went on to say that they have not worked out how yet, only that it must be so because of the evidence in behaviour. It would certainly be a difficult thing to understand if you remove the spiritual element. In other cases, there have been twins separated at birth that have grown up distantly and exclusively of each other who have both independently exhibited the traits of their parents.

'Soul ties'
Another area that we have not touched on and has become popular in church jargon is an opening for demonic entry that has been dubbed a *soul tie*. Although difficult to find under that terminology in most modern translations, the principle refers to some kind of connection of the soul whereby some ungodly element passes from one person to another.

So, if we replaced the term *soul tie* with the word *relationship* then you discover that the whole Bible from cover to cover is talking about the interaction of the souls of humanity, and the consequent impact that it has upon us.

A godly *soul tie* or *relationship* then would be something such as parents ministering love and acceptance to their children, or believers building each other up and encouraging one another. But clearly there are many negative things that can be imparted to us from the souls of others in relationships.

1 Corinthians 15:33, *"Do not be misled: Bad company corrupts good character"* (NIV).

So perhaps at the least end of the *soul tie* scale we could suggest something such as a boy in year 4 at school looking to a lad in year 6 who he thinks is *very cool*. The older boy swears and uses bad language so as a result of the younger boys' agreement and coming in line with wanting to be like the very cool year 6 lad, he also begins to swear. So, something ungodly, sin, has just passed through their relationship. In this case, when the younger boy gets a little older, he decides that actually it is not cool to swear and decides to stop. This change of thinking or repentance as we know it, then breaks the tie.

At times, if the connection is stronger then, the relational joining can be an opportunity for a spirit to pass. This could be through an illicit sexual relationship, where a spirit relating to the one flesh joining sits over the connection, holding them together. People report suffering from depression or having suicidal thoughts or lust problems that they have never known before, but that their partners in the ungodly act suffer from.

1 Corinthians 6:16, *"And don't you know that if a man joins himself to a prostitute, he becomes one body with her? For the Scriptures say, "The two are united into one"* (NLT).

We were once ministering to a man who confessed an illicit adulterous relationship from, as I recall, around 12 years earlier. As he was sharing what had happened his mobile phone suddenly went off and it was this lady whom he had never had contact with in all of that time. Evidently his thinking and talking about her had enlivened an existing connection in the spirit. Jesus often healed or delivered people without needing to be present because distance is not relevant in the spiritual realm.

Another man once came to me reporting that he still had dreams about a girlfriend that he had been with before he was married many decades earlier. He was a good Christian man with a lovely wife whom he loved, and together they had a large family. It troubled him and he wanted to be free. As we discussed what had happened, he revealed that this girlfriend was immediately before his conversion. When he came to the Lord, he asked her if she would ever be interested in God, and the response was no. With his new-found faith he thought it through and decided that she was not for him and broke the relationship. So, the mind and will part of his soul had disconnected but his emotions had not because he had loved the girl. The Lord set him free with the realization of what had happened and the dealing with the emotional component.

If someone is struggling with some kind of *relational* or *soul tie* to another then their part in their freedom is to voluntarily disconnect from any memories of the other person. For example, I have ministered to a number of men who have had previous sexual partners who, now married, feel as though when they are having marital relations with their wives that there are 3 of them in the bed. These men are usually still allowing themselves to think about this past partner from time to time which keeps the tie alive. Our advice with any kind of soul tie is for them to remember them no more. This means pleasures, adventures together or whatever memories might bind them, and get rid of any articles that might promote these thoughts from the past.

The critical element of breaking the tie is not the spirituality of the minister or the power of God, it is the will of the person to disconnect. If they are genuinely prepared to do that then if you feel that there is a spiritual power involved then you can address the spirit that binds them together, or anything that is known of that has come to them through the other person. Again, *breaking soul ties* or *generational links* is not the first place that I would go as a method, but rather is something that you deal with as it comes up in the course of resolving areas where they require the Lord's healing and freedom.

Objects as 'links'

A number of years ago in the course of ministry it was revealed by a lady of around 45 years old that we were working with, that she talked to her teddy bear. As she explained about her relationship to the toy it became apparent that her connection with it was more than a natural emotional fondness. The discussion about the bear had come up as we were finding it difficult to break her free from a spirit connection of witchcraft to her adoptive mother, who gave her the teddy and practiced the craft. The next time she came in she brought the toy with her and really struggled with the thought of relinquishing it. Eventually she gave it to me and when she did the spirit came out of her. Now instead of being possessive of the bear she became indignant and went into our lounge room and threw it in the fire. I am not in the habit of removing people's childhood toys from them but in this case, it was a tie to the witchcraft coming through the mother.

Transference

Some people fear that a demon can simply pass to you for no reason, and this is very much not the case. As we have already described there has to be an opening in the wholeness of the person. This could be through someone wilfully opening the door, through to something such as an ungodly tie or cooperation and alliance in sin with another person. It could also come as transference through the generation line or through an opening such as submitting to significant fear. This fear could come through the violent or abusive behaviour of another acted out on you, or fear generated through some kind of occult ritual or witchcraft type activity.

The idea that you could be near another human and without some kind of breach in the integrity of your person, that a spirit could just pass to you is not the case. I have previously mentioned taking in a demoniac boy who was initially completely run by evil spirits. Our children and other foster children, sat with him, slept in the car or at times the same room as him. They sat at the same table with him to eat, and particularly in the early days there were usually fully manifested spirits operating. Nobody ever received anything from him although he had a great many quite powerful spirits still within him.

Proverbs 26:2, *"Like a flitting sparrow, like a flying swallow, So a curse without cause shall not alight"* (NKJV).

Manifestations

Some people get hung up on the type of things that they expect to see when a person is delivered of an evil spirit. They may feel that there should be loud shrieks or the person slithering across the floor. There is a wide variety of manifestations that may happen ranging from those types of lively encounters to seeing nothing at all, with the person simply reporting that something left, they feel free, lighter, peaceful or joyous. This is in part to do with the type of spirit that you are dealing with, and sometimes how much you have undermined its position before you have told it to go. If it is emotionally based, it will be much easier on the host if you do the healing work first. Sometimes upon commanding them to leave you may see an unexpected eruption of emotion which can be quite deep if the pain has been traumatic. A spirit may rise in their throat and come out with coughing or some other kind of appearance such as involuntary deepened breathing.

The more dramatic manifestations are often connected with involvement in activities such as witchcraft or the Occult.

We leave all of those things to the Holy Spirit as the finger of God. Our job is just to be obedient as God's mouthpiece and command them to go. Don't be surprised by what happens or doesn't happen, the main thing is that the person is free.

One night I was praying for a man in the kitchen at church and when I addressed the spirit that was troubling him, I did not see anything happen. I said to him, not to worry about not seeing anything, it must go and that I sensed that it had. He replied; *Oh no it went alright, it came in from my shoulders and went out through the top of my head!* This was an unusual manifestation, but don't be surprised by anything when you are dealing with the spiritual realm.

Getting started

Not long after I began studying books about demons we took in a little girl as a foster child. To begin with, if I approached her, we would see her face twist up and contort. This was unusual because I normally had a great rapport with little children. We concluded that most likely she had previously suffered some kind of abuse from a man. Eventually I won her over and she would not let me put her down. Some months went by and eventually her mother was moving to another district and so she needed to be placed in care in that area.

From what we had read, and now understood, it was apparent that her ongoing issues were demonic in nature. This put me in the very uncomfortable place of either stepping out with my little bit of faith, or leaving her with issues that may hamper her for the rest of her life. When we put her to bed one night, I took authority over the spirits that we perceived were there and commanded them to go in Jesus name. She responded with a massive prolonged yawn and then turned over and went to sleep.

At that time, we lived next door to my wife's sister, who at times she would go to visit. Normally when she did this our little foster girl would have facial contortions and manifest. The day after prayer my wife proceeded to go next door and the little girl had no response whatsoever and sat happily playing with her toys. It was a miracle. My wife had been praying that her next foster parents would be Christians as well, which turned out to be the case. They later reported that she was a perfect little girl not exhibiting any of the behaviour that we had seen before the prayer event. So, although we have talked a lot about understanding the work and activities of demons here, at the end of the day you fix your attention and concentration on the Holy Spirit, and in the name of Jesus and tell them to leave.

The name of Jesus
It's good to remind ourselves that spirits don't respond to our name, and that God really doesn't need us to set people free. A number of years ago we had a particularly powerful time delivering a lady from demonic power which included a physical healing. I remember afterwards walking around the back of the church hall and feeling a bit like I was God's man for the hour. I did not like the feeling of pride and prayed to the Lord to get rid of it because I could not make it go away.

Later that evening we were conducting a training session and discussion time on deliverance. We put on an old Derek Prince VHS on the subject which was probably 10 years old at the time. We had seen it many times over the years but on this occasion when we got to the end part of the tape, where he commanded various spirits to come out, the lady sitting beside me manifested a demon, and it came out and she was free. It was quite humorous because the pride that I had felt in the afternoon was gone as well. It was as though the Holy Spirit was saying; *I don't really need you I can use anything!*

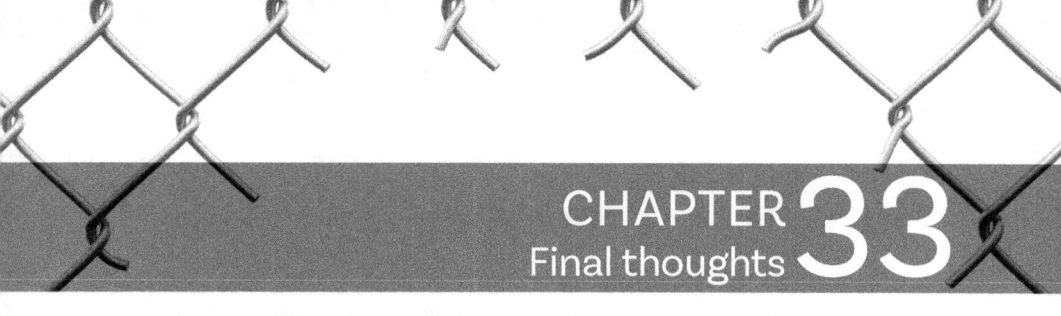

CHAPTER 33
Final thoughts

Our part in the session

We have already stated that the key to helping people come into the provisions of God is all about positioning them to receive. In the case of deliverance, if nothing is happening with the person, or if there is but they are not getting free then most probably it isn't to do with your spirituality, and certainly not with the authority of Christ. Let me suggest some areas that you might need to work through which could be blocking their ministry outcome:

1. Revelation

If they have not understood the nature of their problem and been able to accept the spiritual component, they may struggle to get free. Jesus taught them first.

Hosea 4:6, "*My people are destroyed for lack of knowledge*" (NKJV).

2. Confession

To confess means to say the same as. When we say the same as God does about our problem, rather than to deny it or try to justify it, then we are in a good place to receive freedom. If, for example, we have a demonic element to bitterness, but in our minds feel that we have every right to hold our unforgiveness and bitterness then we may struggle to receive our freedom. We are not falling out of agreement with the spirit and into agreement with the word of God.

3. Repentance

If we are not prepared to change our thinking or reconsider our ways then we may block our freedom. In the case of inner thinking, we may need the beliefs dealt with, before we can cooperate for the deliverance. For example, if we have had a fear producing episode, that has given us fear beliefs, then unwittingly we may want the spirit to remain because we have the perception that it helps to protect us in some way.

4. Forgiveness

A common reason that people don't receive freedom is because they refuse to forgive others. Again, there may need to be healing of the hurts before the spirit loses its place, and consequently the will of the person becomes to no longer participate.

Matthew 6:14-15, "*¹⁴ For if you forgive men their trespasses, your heavenly Father will also forgive you. ¹⁵ But if you do not forgive men their trespasses, neither will your Father forgive your trespasses*" (NKJV).

5. The 'strongman's goods'

We have explained this already in detail and this is why most often deliverance is along with *Truth Encounters* where necessary, rather than the other way around. As we have said, many of these problems can exist without having demonic power on the inside that needs to be evicted.

6. A mouthpiece

Once we have covered these positioning issues, all that remains is commanding the spirits to leave in the name of Jesus. You are simply God's mouthpiece; it is the Holy Spirit's work to manifest the promise of deliverance. I have seen many spirits come out of people, and I am well aware that it is the goodness of God, faith in Jesus name, and the work of the Spirit that has accomplished this, and not because I am anyone special.

Spontaneous deliverance

I have experienced in different settings across the world, times when praying for people in a meeting that they manifest a spirit and it convulses them as it comes out, as they did in Jesus' time on the Earth.

Mark 9:26, "*Then the spirit cried out, convulsed him greatly, and came out of him. And he became as one dead, so that many said, "He is dead*" (NKJV).

I very often have no idea what the spirit is. It is the presence of the Holy Spirit on the person that causes the reaction as He comes in through us. Usually it is to do with the individual that I am praying for. If the Holy Spirit is operating in power, I have experienced times such as once when I was praying for a lady standing in the front row, four or five ladies standing in the rows behind went into deliverance. In these instances, it is simply what the Holy Spirit is doing, and for me it feels the same as when someone is healed or touched in some way as a result of the anointing. Making ourselves available simply makes us a door or gate that the Spirit can work through and do whatever He wants.

At times people receive some kind of deliverance along with baptism in water or in the Spirit. This does not necessarily mean that they are free of everything. Equally many times people have been set free of a spirit in a prayer line and we have seen nothing obvious, or they have felt nothing, but the resulting evidence is that they are free in that area.

I recall as a young believer having found out that my great grandfather had been high up in freemasonry. I prayed a simple prayer to disconnect with anything to do with it and suddenly something left me. It was as if someone put a vacuum cleaner over me and something rushed out of the top of me. I was left thinking, *that didn't just happen* but knowing that it did. What, if anything, it was actively doing in me at the time I could not say, but clearly it had found a home down the family line!

Fallen nature or demons?
So, is your sin problem or bad habit demon powered or just your fallen nature and lack of self-discipline? When I was a young believer wrestling with this question, I had a little vision. It was a sieve and in it were three little stones. What I understood from the picture was that our fallen nature goes through the sieve of the Word of God which, if attended to and cooperated with, should filter our ungodly activities. At times though, there are a few issues that need to be ministered to and removed manually.

If you press in, pray, build yourself up in the Holy Spirit and discipline yourself to study the word and avoid unhealthy exposure to the world, and;

- You take ground and improve over time, even though you might be taking two steps forward and one step back, then your problem is most likely external pressure, unresolved beliefs, or fallen nature tendencies that have not been dealt with.

- Your problem gets worse than before, then in that instance it is probably an evil spirit within you that you are dealing with. We are mainly talking habits and sin here as opposed to hurts. A spirit, if it is still armed with some unresolved possessions such as deliberate sin or emotional pain then it will immediately seek rise up, exert pressure, and bluff you that it is too strong for you, in order to get you or the minister to give up.

This could come in a form such as struggling with negative or lustful thoughts, confusion, discouragement, self-rejection, or a manifestation in the prayer setting. It is a *stronghold*.

There is personal responsibility that the person receiving ministry must be prepared to take.

1. Man is responsible for his choices and responses. Once you realize that you are participating with another will that is operating inside of you, then you must conclude that there is no substitute for repentance.
2. It has been well said that deliverance will not give a person self-discipline, as it must be learned, practiced and exercised. It brings order to a person's life. The devil does most of his work through disorder [8].

Proverbs 25:28, *"Like a city whose walls are broken down is a man who lacks self-control"* (NIV).

The best defence then, is restoring God's order to the life of the person. Remember that the demon can be cast out but the *place* or *topos* cannot be cast out. It must be brought under the authority of Christ or be healed. Unless the ground is dealt with, the deliverance may not be maintained which is why the main focus is *Truth Encounters*. Notably the word disciple is used around 300 times in the New Testament, and Christian only 2 or 3 times. From God's perspective which should we be? There are all kinds of things called Christian in our world, but *disciples* are a little harder to find.

The strength of the enemy will depend on the amount of submission and cooperation that he has received. So, the human will and desire

---

[8] Pastor Carroll Thompson 1977

is a very important factor in coming to freedom. Several years ago, I ministered to a man who suffered from sexual, alcohol, and other addictions. A strong motivator for seeking Gods freedom was the fact that he was about to lose his family. In the course of his *Truth Encounters* ministry time he had a glimpse of his own possibilities in Christ, which further encouraged him to seek a full healing. He was freed from all of his issues and later, along with his wife, they entered into this ministry and began setting others free as well. We need to overcome passivity and desire our freedom so that we can possess the land.

Fighting with a demon
In the event that, as a minister, you find yourself fighting with a demon for some reason, let me suggest a couple of possibilities as to why;

1. The person has unforgiveness, unhealed belief areas, deception, lack of repentance, a failure to confess something relevant, or doubt and unbelief.

2. You may actually be wrestling with your own doubt and unbelief that the battle is over. Or, that you are worthy to have been given complete authority over all of the works of the enemy.

If you are fighting, it may be because you have been taught that the enemy is not defeated and has not been totally disarmed, and that Jesus has triumphed (Colossians 2:15). In that case you believe that you have to fight which is not true. The only power that the demon actually has, is wilful or deceptive cooperation from the host.

Jesus never argued with demons because He knew that He was in the Father and that the Father was in Him. Now we are seated in Christ (Ephesians 2:6). Jesus never told us to fight with demons He instructed us to expel them and set the captives free.

John 14:10-14, " [10] *Do you not believe that I am in the Father, and the Father in Me? The words that I speak to you I do not speak on* **My own authority;** *but the Father* **who dwells in Me does the works.** [11] *"Believe Me that I am in the Father and the Father in Me, or else believe Me for the sake of the works themselves.* [12] *"Most assuredly, I say to you, he who believes in Me,* **the works that I do he will do also;**

and greater works than these he will do, because I go to My Father. ¹³ "And whatever you ask in My name, that I will do, that the Father may be glorified in the Son. ¹⁴ "If you ask anything in My name, I will do it" (NKJV, Emphasis mine).

Satan's position has changed?
Some people have suggested that Satan's position changed at the cross. Did his position change? He is still called the god of this age, the ruler of the World, and the prince of the power of the air in the Epistles, after the cross. I would suggest that he is still causing wars, disharmony, sickness and deception just as he always did.

Did Gods position change at the cross? No. He was always in authority over Satan and all of creation so His position didn't change either. Whose position did change then? The believers' position changed. We went from being under the devil to being over all of his power. We do not however have authority over human will. So, if for some reason they are submitting to the devil through deception or choice, they may be allowing the demon to remain.

Finally
Let me say that, although I have discussed the topic of demons or evil spirits at length, in ministry they are not our focus and I rarely think about them. The purpose of this section is simple awareness of their workings so that they can be discerned if present. Let me encourage you again to not make the ministry about looking for them. In practice you are working on the person's wholeness and you may simply, with the permission and cooperation of the person, cast one out here and there as you go along where applicable.

Do I throw away my Bible?
Will Truth encounters and deliverance solve all my problems and make the World perfect? No. The world is a hostile environment. Jesus said that the Kingdom of God will be within you. So, your inner world needs to be built on the foundation of Jesus, the Word made flesh. This foundation of the living word, God's truth, on the inside, is that which is needed for you to be at peace in the World just as Jesus was.

John 14:30, "I will no longer talk much with you, for the ruler of this world is coming, and he has nothing in Me" (NKJV).

Chapter 33: Final thoughts

From a quick study of the Greek language, as revealed in Strong's concordance, Jesus is saying in the preceding verse that there is no area of hold, no ability to affect Him, no wrong beliefs possessed by the evil one to manipulate Him. Further, there is no condition in Him such as not knowing who He is, what His purpose is, or how Father God sees Him, that gives the devil any influence over Him in this earthly environment. He stood complete and whole, and untouchable in truth. This is what we need to seek for ourselves as a part of the process of being conformed to the likeness of Christ.

SECTION 5

DISCIPLES AND THE WORKS OF JESUS

In these final chapters I want to summarize and or contextualize the previous sections to some extent in terms of how they relate to the whole healing and freedom picture.

Section 5: Disciples and the Works of Jesus

CHAPTER 34
The Church and the Holy Spirit

According to the Spirit
John 16: 7, *"Nevertheless I tell you the truth. It is to your advantage that I go away; for if I do not go away, the Helper will not come to you; but if I depart, I will send Him to you"* (NKJV).

Jesus considered that we would be in a better place if He returned to heaven and sent the Holy Spirit to us. In His flesh body, manifested as the son of man, He was limited by problems such as distance and exposure in terms of how many people He could help. He taught the disciples how to live according to the Spirit in regards to behaviour and attitudes. He also trained them in how to work with, and be led by, the Holy Spirit to allow Him to set people free. He did no recorded works that I am aware of prior to His baptism and the subsequent filling with the Holy Spirit. We can confirm then that He did no works as a man, but only began to fulfil His calling as the *word made flesh* when He allowed the Holy Spirit to work in and through Him.

Clearly, His ultimate intention was for many disciples to be trained to minister to the needs of a hurting and captive humanity just as He did. This working through many *sons and daughters*, meant that He would be able to reach the entire world with God's goodness, and the offer of salvation.

It is worthy of note that there are activities that only came with the beginning of the Holy Spirit dispensation and ministry through believers. Speaking in tongues and the gifts of the Spirit, for example, were not present until the beginning of the Holy Spirit era. Although Jesus demonstrated all of the gifts of the Holy Spirit, it appears that they only became available for all believers when the Spirit was poured out. We should not be surprised then if Holy Spirit ministries such as *Truth Encounters* are specific to this time. It is not an extra Biblical event or non-scriptural in that He is called the *Spirit of truth*. It is a thoroughly biblical concept that a major part of His ministry was and is to bring truth to whatever area of our being that it is needed. Perhaps we could even go so far as to take the liberty to comment that the outpouring of the Spirit of truth means that being filled with the Spirit is largely to be filled and permeated with God's truth.

John 16:13, *"However, when He, the Spirit of truth, has come, He will guide you into all truth"* (NKJV).

The Church that God is pleased to anoint
The criteria for us to be the church that God is pleased to anoint, is for us to be led by the Spirit as Jesus was.

Luke 3:22, *"And the Holy Spirit descended in bodily form like a dove upon Him, and a voice came from heaven which said, "You are My beloved Son; in You I am well pleased"* (NKJV).

Having received the Holy Spirit the next thing that happened was that He was led by the Spirit into the wilderness, *being filled with the Holy Spirit.*

Luke 4:1, *"Then Jesus, being **filled** with the Holy Spirit, returned from the Jordan and was **led** by the Spirit into the wilderness"* (NKJV Emphasis mine).

In the wilderness He dealt with that which we might describe the *self-life.* This is dealing with your *self-life,* in terms of putting what you could have or want for yourself aside, in favour of being where the Spirit led Him and the Father wanted Him to be. This meant denying physical wants and items that He was fully entitled to, such as the most basic thing for the body, food, all for the sake of the will of God. Later as we know the devil came and tempted Him, offering Him the same things that he had tempted Adam and Eve with in the beautiful Garden of Eden. In parallel, the devil tempted Him to turn the stones into bread. Eve saw that the food was good to eat. The devil let Jesus see the kingdoms of the world and their glory. Eve was impressed by what she saw.

Genesis 3:6, *"So when the woman saw that the tree was **good for food**, that it was **pleasant to the eyes**, and a tree desirable to **make one wise**, she took of its fruit and ate"* (NKJV, Emphasis mine).

As we know each time Jesus was tempted, He used the written word of God as His reference point for which spirit He was going to align with. So, it happened that the devils' final temptation was using the written word of God in order to get Jesus to bow down and submit to him. The written word is always true, but if it is initiated by the wrong spirit, and used out of context to manipulate, then it can bring you under the authority of the work of Satan.

Luke 4:9-12, " *⁹ Then he brought Him to Jerusalem, set Him on the pinnacle of the temple, and said to Him, "If You are the Son of God, throw Yourself down from here. ¹⁰ "For it is written: 'He shall give His angels charge over you, To keep you,' ¹¹ "and, 'In their hands they shall bear you up, Lest you dash your foot against a stone.'" ¹² And Jesus answered and said to him, "It has been said, 'You shall not tempt the LORD your God"* (NKJV).

The devils last effort found Eve tempted to be special, being made wise by eating the fruit. In this final temptation from the devil Jesus was tempted to prove that He was *someone special*. Had He not already known who He was, being already full of truth and complete in the Father's love, He may have been susceptible. This action would have been a promotion of the superiority of self, pride, which was Satan's own downfall. So, to follow the Spirit of God Jesus dealt with, and refused, all of the aspects of the fallen self-life which were instigated by the devil.

1 John 2:16, *"For all that is in the world; the lust of the flesh, the lust of the eyes, and the pride of life; is not of the Father but is of the world"* (NKJV).

Having dealt with what the World offered, the elements of the fallen self-life, and also the devil who works through the first two, Jesus returned in the *power of the Spirit*.

Luke 4:14, *"Then Jesus returned in the **power of the Spirit** to Galilee, and news of Him went out through all the surrounding region"* (NKJV, Emphasis mine).

This all happened immediately before Jesus announced the beginning of His ministry and the confirmation of the Prophetic word of Isaiah 61, that a person who came in the flesh would make the Word true, by the working of the Holy Spirit through Him.

Luke 4:18-19, " *[18] The Spirit of the LORD is upon Me, Because He has anointed Me To preach the gospel to the poor; He has sent Me to heal the brokenhearted, To proclaim liberty to the captives And recovery of sight to the blind, To set at liberty those who are oppressed; [19] To proclaim the acceptable year of the LORD"* (NKJV).

The preceding verse is only one of two places in the New Testament where the anointing of the Holy Spirit on Jesus was mentioned. Christ means the anointed one or in Hebrew, the *Messiah*, and so the fact that He was anointed was also evident in His name. On both occasions where it does directly mention His anointing, it clearly indicates that the purpose of the anointing of the Holy Spirit is to minister to humanity which are afflicted by the works of the devil.

Acts 10:38, *"how God anointed Jesus of Nazareth with the Holy Spirit and with power, who went about doing good and healing all who were oppressed by the devil, for God was with Him"* (NKJV).

What does all of this mean to us?
So, why is the anointing of the Holy Spirit on the Church today? Is it there to make us feel good, and it does, or is it to empower us to do the works of Jesus today, by the manifestation of the Holy Spirit working through us also?

John 20:21-22, " *[21] So Jesus said to them again, "Peace to you! As the Father has sent Me, I also send you." [22] And when He had said this, He breathed on them, and said to them, "Receive the Holy Spirit"* (NKJV).

We all have an anointing from the Holy One to continue this work of proving God's love, acceptance and grace to His hurting creation, and to set the captives free. When we read the scriptures or hear the word preached, we know if we are hearing the truth or not. Our renewed human spirit acknowledges the confirmation of the truth through the Spirit of Truth, even though our minds need renewing and our broken hearts need healing.

John 1:20, *"But you have an anointing from the Holy One, and all of you know the truth"* (NIV).

Walking in the 'anointing' on us
We know that the Holy Spirit uses people, working through them, and giving gifts as He decides is appropriate and commensurate to their sanctification, development and character. But how do we qualify to be used by Him in this way so that we can serve God's purposes in the World? Jesus showed us the way. He began, having received the Holy Spirit, to now be led by the Spirit. If we are going to be led by our own desires, priorities and self-realization, then we will probably not be too attentive to what the Holy Spirit may have for us.

When Jesus said to take up our own cross, deny *ourselves* and follow Him, He was saying that we need to lay aside our own *fallen self* tendencies to have what the world may offer. Jesus' cross meant doing something that He would prefer not to do for the sake of the Father's will, and laying aside things that He could have had, even life. Our *cross* may be laying aside a career or some other thing that we could have for our *selves*, and this represents our *lives* that we choose, in favour of fulfilling the will of God for us. When we lose this inferior natural life, we gain a super abundant life in the spirit.

Romans 8:14, *"For as many as are led by the Spirit of God, these are sons of God"* (NKJV).

In a very basic form, we note that the works of the *flesh, sin nature, or fallen self nature* as it could be called, listed in the book of Galatians chapter 5, and verse 19-21, all stem from some form of **self**-realization. If we go on to the fruit of the Spirit, we see that they are attributes such as goodness, kindness, patience, love which are characteristics directed outwardly and purposed towards dealing well with **others** rather than self-seeking. So, they are fruit or evidence that you are being led by the Spirit, walking with and cooperating with Him.

Galatians 5:18, *"But if you are led by the Spirit, you are not under the law"* (NKJV).

In order for the works of the flesh or sin nature to be dealt with, many times in addition to being led by the Holy Spirit, we need ministry from Him by some means to set us free. We may need to let go of our own ideas and our *right to our self* before we are prepared to entertain receiving help from others who *walk in the spirit*.

This leads us to another Biblical example regarding how we relate to working with the Holy Spirit as junior partners. Strong's concordance instructs us that the word translated *walk* is in the Greek language *peripateo* from which I imagine we derive words such as *patio* where we walk. Permit me to expand its meaning from the original language and underline a few key meanings that relate to our attitude towards our relationship to the Holy Spirit.

4043. Peripateo, to tread all around, i.e. walk at large (espec. as proof of ability); fig. to live, deport oneself, **follow (as a companion or votary)**:--go, **be occupied with**, walk (about).   (Emphasis mine)

So, in a very real sense our lives are to be spent walking around with and following our companion, and being occupied with His priorities for us. If our personal focus is on Him and His plans for an abundant life for us, then we will not be preoccupied with our inferior *fallen self* plans.

To put the following passage in context, our 'lusts' are our strong desires to meet our own perceived wants. It does not mean that all strong desires and enjoyment of life are evil, but rather that selfish desires that are forbidden such as immorality are lusts.

Galatians 5:16, "*I say then: "Walk in the Spirit, and you shall not fulfill the lust of the flesh*" (NKJV).

Galatians 5:16-17, " *[16] So I say, live by the Spirit, and you will not gratify the desires of the sinful nature. [17] For the sinful nature desires what is contrary to the Spirit, and the Spirit what is contrary to the sinful nature* (NIV).

Finally, let us look at what we may expect to see working in and through us, as the Spirit has increasing sway through our wilful cooperation. But first let us examine one more passage to put in context how a true disciple, usable by God, will regard the Holy Spirit.

Romans 8:1, *"There is therefore now no condemnation to those who are in Christ Jesus, who do not walk according to the flesh, but according to the Spirit"* (NKJV).

Aside from the obvious implication that those who walk according to the *flesh*, fallen self, or sin nature may well still potentially be subject to condemnation, I want to focus on this word *according*. What I am saying is not toward those who struggle with *self* issues so much, because they often require healing and release from captivity. But more those who do not give the Holy Spirit His rightful place. The dictionary definitions for *accord* and *according* to are; be in agreement and harmony with, consistent with; in a manner corresponding and conforming to; on the authority of the pattern of; and carries the sense of giving place to, and according position to. Although that is a lengthy description of the word, I think it is worth thinking over in the sense of how we qualify to be exempt from condemnation, and resultantly be promoted as being of use to the Holy Spirit.

God gives grace; we do not presume to take it. I was once talking with a Christian man who was living a carnal self-centred lifestyle with no indication of wanting to serve God whatsoever. He was explaining to me how he was under grace and could live how he wanted. I attempted to convey to him that God gives us grace so that we can learn to do His will, and not so that we can continue to live for our will and wants. If we are in genuine relationship with Him under His Lordship, then His wants will become our wants as we choose to bow down under His will. Then we know that all things that we need will be added to us, and everything we could need for our enjoyment will be given. (Matthew 6:33, 1 Timothy 6:17) Indeed, those things that are in His will, and that He wants for us, are far better than anything that we could try to provide for ourselves.

1 Corinthians 6:19-20, *"* [19] *Or do you not know that your body is the temple of the Holy Spirit who is in you, whom you have from God, and you are not your own?* [20] *For you were bought at a price; therefore glorify God in your body and in your spirit, which are God's"* (NKJV).

CHAPTER 35
The 'tools or equipment' of the Holy Spirit

Previously in Section 4 we discussed the workings and manifestations of unholy spirit. We would be remiss and it would be improper if we did not talk about the work and evidence of the presence of the Holy Spirit working in someone's life. In order to do this, we will mention the fruit of the Spirit, the ministry of the spirit, and the gifts of the Spirit.

The fruit of the Spirit
We have already described the fruit of the Spirit as being largely directed towards considering and preferring others. The works of the flesh or *fallen self* nature is all about self-gratification or meeting the perceived *self* needs coming from distorted identity or situations beliefs. We have also already described that often the fruit of the Spirit appears as a result of the Holy Spirit ministering to these *self conflicts*.

While the deceptive beliefs remain, then the corresponding behaviour will also be present. Whether it is dealing with deliberate self-centeredness stemming from the programming of the world system, which is resolved through the renewing of the mind, or if it is resolving heart beliefs that produce the behaviour, we could say that the fruit of the Spirit is the evidence of the influence and work of the Holy Spirit in our being. You do not therefore try harder to be joyful, peaceful or loving for example. Rather it is evidence that He has further influence and consequent cooperation from your being as you receive His truth.

Galatians 5:22-24, " [22] *But the fruit of the Spirit is love, joy, peace, longsuffering, kindness, goodness, faithfulness,* [23] *gentleness, self-control. Against such there is no law.* [24] *And those who are Christ's have crucified the flesh with its passions and desires*" (NKJV).

In saying this I believe that your human spirit is regenerated, born again and complete in Christ. It is a matter of participating with Him as He works through the healing of your heart that results in a soul and body that are in order. King David certainly understood that this was the root cause of his selfish and fallen sinful behaviour. He knew that his own spirit had to be committed to the process and that without the Holy Spirit's work that this would never be achieved.

Psalm 51:10-11, "¹⁰ *Create in me a clean heart, O God, And renew a steadfast spirit within me.* ¹¹ *Do not cast me away from Your presence, And do not take Your Holy Spirit from me"* (NKJV).

There are those who believe that we will achieve the fruit of the spirit simply by our own self effort. My daughter once gave me a key ring that was engraved with the instruction to *be joyful always,* and then after a semicolon, to *pray continually.* I am not sure when the semi colon was added, but to me it was like saying; *Be clean, break, shower daily,* as if they were two separate unconnected activities. The joy comes as a result of our communication with God, not because we simply decide to be happy.

1 Thessalonians 5:16-17, "¹⁶ *Be joyful always;* ¹⁷ *pray continually"* (NIV).

The ministry of the Spirit
The fruit of the Spirit is evidence of the nature of the Holy Spirit changing our attitudes and behaviour. There are also attributes of the Holy Spirit that equip us, or give us the tools to minister to others; hopefully we are able to minister in the right spirit and motivation. Having received healing and freedom ourselves it is a normal consequence to become aware of the needs of others and want to give out that which we have *freely received* ourselves. Most times if we are still wounded or in bondage we will be preoccupied with our own real or perceived *self needs.*

Matthew 10:8, "*Heal the sick, cleanse the lepers, raise the dead, cast out demons.* **Freely you have received, freely give**" (NKJV, Emphasis mine).

I am not suggesting that these attributes of the Spirit that I am about to list only appear when all of the fruit is fully established in us, more that they grow along with the fruit. So, what are these characteristics that empower us to fulfil the call and work out the anointing that is on us for our time? Isaiah prophesied that the Spirit of the Lord would be on Jesus to minister to the broken hearted, free the captives and so on in Isaiah 61. Jesus quoted from this passage in Luke 4:18 announcing that He was now going to fulfil that which the prophet had seen happening around 600 years earlier. Prior to this, in Isaiah chapter 11, before He announces that the Spirit of the Lord is upon me and so here are the things that I am going to do, is a list of the manifestations of the Spirit that explain by what means He will be able to do this once He has received the Holy Spirit.

Isaiah 11:2, *"The Spirit of the LORD will rest on him - the Spirit of wisdom and of understanding, the Spirit of counsel and of power, the Spirit of knowledge and of the fear of the LORD"* (NIV).

The preceding list reveals what is known as the seven spirits or sevenfold spirits of the Holy Spirit. There are other references to them, particularly in the book of Revelation where they are mentioned four times. This was a time when the Apostle John was writing to the believers in such a way as only they would understand, as they already had the scriptures.

Revelation 4:5, *"And from the throne proceeded lightnings, thunderings, and voices. Seven lamps of fire were burning before the throne, which are the **seven Spirits of God**"* (NKJV, Emphasis mine).

Revelation 5:6b, *"... stood a Lamb as though it had been slain, having seven horns and **seven eyes, which are the seven Spirits of God sent out into all the earth**"* (NKJV, Emphasis mine).

God gives us physical examples or types in the Old Testament that we understand to be representative of spiritual realities. We see what is known as the *Menora* standing in the Holy place in the temple as representative of the Holy Spirit. In type, the Holy of Holies was where the presence of God dwelt and the Ark of the Covenant containing the two stone tablets of the Ten Commandments, Aaron's rod, and a pot of manna were kept. This is considered to be representative of the human spirit. You may recall that he who is joined to the Lord is one spirit with Him. (1 Corinthians 6:19). Under this new relational Covenant, the Commandments were going to be written on our renewed, sensitive to God, hearts.

2 Corinthians 3:3 *" ...clearly you are an epistle of Christ, ministered by us, written not with ink but by the Spirit of the living God, not on tablets of stone but on tablets of flesh, that is, of the heart"* (NKJV).

Before you came to the curtain, which separated the Holy of Holies, was a room called the Holy place which we understand to be the soul. After that, the outer courts which interfaces with the world are representative of the body. In the Holy place amongst some other articles were the Menora and the table of showbread, representing the bread of the presence. You may recall Jesus described Himself as the bread of life in John chapter 6 that we must eat from, indicating that in a sense we consume His presence as our daily provision.

The Menora was a candle stand with seven arms which bore the candles which were representative of the seven spirits of the Holy Spirit. Perhaps it was placed in this area because of His working out from the Spirit and presence of God through the human faculties, mind and soul. It is common to find these spiritual manifestations in isolation or grouped together in places throughout the scriptures.

Deuteronomy 24:9, *"Now Joshua the son of Nun was full of the spirit of wisdom"* (NKJV).

In the following passage from Proverbs we see six of the seven spirits or attributes grouped together.

Proverbs 8:12-14, *"* [12] *I,* **wisdom**, *dwell together with prudence; I possess* **knowledge** *and discretion.* [13] *To* **fear the LORD** *is to hate evil; I hate pride and arrogance, evil behavior and perverse speech.* [14] **Counsel** *and sound judgment are mine; I have* **understanding** *and* **power**" (NIV, Emphasis mine).

This list of spiritual attributes or equipment should become increasingly evident in our lives. The Holy Spirit works through us in our work for others as revealed in Isaiah 11:2 in the following ways:

1. The Spirit of the LORD – we understand this to be the Revelatory Spirit, as seen in prophecy. It knows the mind of God for a particular situation. Let me propose that in the NT this manifestation of the Holy Spirit is revealed as the *mind of Christ*.

2. The Spirit of wisdom
3. The Spirit of understanding
4. The Spirit of counsel
5. The Spirit of power
6. The Spirit of knowledge
7. The Spirit of fear of the Lord

I think that sometimes the modern church is guilty of seeking the power, and neglecting the other works of the Spirit. In any case these are the manifestations of the Holy Spirit that we should expect to see operating. These are evidence of His activities and presence, rather than strange extra biblical events. As we scan the list it should become evident that most of the operations of the Spirit will then be most apparent through words. It is notable that at times the works of Jesus were attributed to wisdom and knowledge rather than power.

Mark 6:2, *"And when the Sabbath had come, He began to teach in the synagogue. And many hearing Him were astonished, saying, "Where did this Man get these things? And what wisdom is this which is given to Him, that such mighty works are performed by His hands!* (NKJV).

Personal testimony

In this and other sections of this publication I relate various things that God has done through us. I want to highlight that it may be read as though we or I am some sort of extraordinary person. On the contrary, I am extremely ordinary and no different to anyone else. We have simply tried to learn how to help other people, and as we have understood what to do, we have created a door for the Holy Spirit to move through. I could say that as I look back, the Seven Spirits have established a greater use of my faculties over the years. If I hold a correct perspective, whatever wisdom, understanding, power and so on that works through me are not my own. Check with my kids; minus the Holy Spirit and when I am not about God's business, I am still just a simple person who tells bad dad jokes. It is the extraordinary supernatural presence of the Holy Spirit who has joined with our spirit and made His home within us that does the works. Paul the Apostle knew this well.

2 Corinthians 4:7, *"But we have this treasure in earthen vessels, that the excellence of the power may be of God and not of us"* (NKJV).

In terms of ministry, a person comes to you with a problem; it is God who has the answers and power to resolve it. Our part is to be equipped to be the little piece of fuse wire that makes the connection between their need and God's promised provisions. In this sense we make His Word *flesh*. In other terms, it gives an expression in the natural realm, through being a door aligned with the Word of God that the Holy Spirit can confirm and make manifest.

It's truly a privilege that God allows us to co labour as His children in the family business in this way.

In terms of personal growth on our journey, we are becoming conformed to the likeness of Christ through our cooperation, decisions, attitudes and behaviour as we receive His Truth. This creates an increasingly open door for the Holy Spirit to continue the ministry of Christ through us. We measure our progress against the word of God in terms of our actions and deeds. If we are to be conformed to Christ, we will also be conformed to the Word of God as He was.

Romans 8:29, *"For those God foreknew he also predestined to be conformed to the likeness of his Son, that he might be the firstborn among many brothers"* (NIV).

We too, will become people full of grace and truth.

John 1:14, *"The Word became flesh and made his dwelling among us. We have seen his glory, the glory of the One and Only, who came from the Father, **full of grace and truth***" (NIV, Emphasis mine).

If Bill Gates approached me and invited me to be a partner in his business, and stated that whoever works for him now works for me, and whatever finances and resources he had I could now use to grow his business, I would consider that I had significant potential.

How much more potential when God comes to us, gives us the Holy Spirit, and then invites us to share in the work of the Kingdom. Bill Gates plus anyone has a lot of possibilities, but this is nothing compared to the Holy Spirit plus anybody at all, no matter how insignificant or foolish we may be in the eyes of the world!

The Gifts of the Spirit
We have just detailed the seven Spirits that represent and manifest the work of the Holy Spirit through us. As we now look to the New Testament gifts of the Spirit we would be surprised if they did not match up with the prophesied attributes that we have discussed. So, the gifts are the practical outworking of the seven Spirits. Let us list them here and make a comparison;

OT	NT
Spirit of wisdom	Word of wisdom
Spirit of Knowledge	Word of Knowledge
Spirit of power	Working of miracles (Greek 'power')
Spirit of counsel	Different types of healings
Spirit of understanding	Discerning of Spirits
Spirit of the Lord	Prophecy

1 Corinthians 12:4-7, " *⁴ There are diversities of gifts, but the same Spirit. ⁵ There are differences of ministries, but the same Lord. ⁶ And there are diversities of activities, but it is the same God who works all in all.⁷ But the manifestation of the Spirit is given to each one for the profit of all:*

We can observe here that all of the different activities of the Spirit are for our benefit. As we examine the next verses, we can all possibly identify with having given someone counsel, or heard wisdom, knowledge or understanding come out of our mouths that was much more than our personal cleverness or intellect. Perhaps we did not recognize or acknowledge it as being a gift or inspiration from the Spirit of Christ.

1 Corinthians 12:8 continues, " *⁸ for to one is given the word of wisdom through the Spirit, to another the word of knowledge through the same Spirit, ⁹ to another faith by the same Spirit, to another gifts of healings by the same Spirit, ¹⁰ to another the working of miracles, to another prophecy, to another discerning of spirits, to another different kinds of tongues, to another the interpretation of tongues".*

As we consider the following verse, can I suggest that the number of gifts that work through you emerge over time, and that you are released into them increasingly as your character is conformed to Christ Jesus as the Word of God. You may also find that you are drawn to some particular gifts or enabling that specifically help you facilitate and dispense your calling, which was the choice of God to begin with.

"*¹¹ But one and the same Spirit works all these things, distributing to each one individually as He wills"* (NKJV).

With the absence of the fear of the Lord in this preceding passage, and without doing a deep study, we can confirm that all spirits have an expression. Fear of the Lord, and consequent healthy self perspective, as we are in awe of Him, opens us up to being candidates for the gifts of the Spirit. Further it keeps us in cooperation with the leading of the Spirit as we avoid the consequences of walking after the sin nature. If Jesus required the Spirit of Fear of the Lord as a part of His equipping to achieve His purposes on Earth, then how much more should we cherish it as He did?

Isaiah 11:2-3, "*² The Spirit of the LORD shall rest upon Him, The Spirit of wisdom and understanding, The Spirit of counsel and might, The Spirit of knowledge and of the fear of the LORD. ³ His delight is in the fear of the LORD, And He shall not judge by the sight of His eyes, Nor decide by the hearing of His ears*" (NKJV).

It is noteworthy in verse 3 of the preceding passage that Jesus was going to live by knowledge coming from the Holy Spirit, through the Seven Spirits manifestation on Him, rather than through His senses.

CHAPTER 36
Healing Streams and the river of God

Seven Healing Streams

To recap, before moving into the healing streams, we have mentioned seven problems that afflict mankind (Section one, chapter 10). We have also covered the seven spirits that are the manifestation of the Holy Spirit given to work through believers to resolve these problems. Now I would like to propose seven healing streams that flow together to become the river of God that bring gladness to the inhabitants of the city of God.

Psalm 46:4, *"There is a river whose streams make glad the city of God, the holy place where the Most High dwells"* (NIV).

These streams, or ways that God heals, often work together just as the gifts do, constituting Gods healing river towards wholeness.

Stream 1 - Truth encounters

I will not spend a great deal of time on the first two streams as the bulk of these writings are centred on their importance as a basis to all kinds of healing and wholeness. From God's perspective, it appears that resolving areas of deception that lead to sin are more important than the condition of the temporal outer man.

I recall hearing a story from a minister whose group had been ministering to the hurting and lost. One day a prostitute came for prayer. She had lost an eye to a disease and now was suffering with the disease in her remaining eye. As the story went, not only did God heal the diseased eye as a response to prayer, but He also did a creative miracle and replaced the other eye. She was back in prostitution within a week! There was a profound miracle in her body, but no response or healing in her soul or spiritual condition.

I recall a man who one night had an amazing miracle healing in his leg. He then went home and proceeded to abuse his wife and children. In God's order I believe there is a high priority on mental, emotional and resultant relational healing.

Matthew 5:29-30, "²⁹ *If your right eye causes you to sin, pluck it out and cast it from you; for it is more profitable for you that one of your members perish, than for your whole body to be cast into hell".* ³⁰ *"And if your right hand causes you to sin, cut it off and cast it from you; for it is more profitable for you that one of your members perish, than for your whole body to be cast into hell"* (NKJV).

We have already described some of the many cases of physical healing that we have seen as a result of dealing with beliefs of the heart, in the process of having a soul that prospers.

Many people cannot receive healing by faith because they believe in their hearts that they are not worthy or important, or perhaps that God does not care about them. More often than people realize, these beliefs need to be resolved before they can accept healing for their bodies through the provisions of the cross. Anything is possible if you have faith, so it is reasonable that in a meeting where believing for a miracle is running high that if your body can be healed, then deliverance or some level of emotional release is of course possible.

Typically, in a really good meeting where many are receiving various kinds of healing by faith, there can be as many as 5 or 10% of people receive physical healing. Can I suggest then that the figures for emotional healing, if it is occurring, would not be expected to be greater than this percentage? In contrast, almost all of people who come for release through *Truth Encounters* and commit to the process predictably receive their freedom. So, God heals any way that you are able to receive.

If people cannot receive physical, emotional healing or deliverance in a faith meeting, that does not mean that God has given up on freeing them. We should not be saying; *Oh well, you didn't have enough faith, try again another time!* It may well be that God has a different pathway to healing, and He certainly never gives up on being committed to fulfilling the provisions of His word to us.

Another point is that if only 5 or 10% of people are able to receive healing in a faith meeting, what is happening with the other 90 - 95% of people. Normally they have wrong believing or doctrine in the mind which needs to be resolved through good teaching. They may also hold wrong believing in the heart which needs to be dealt with through healing by the Holy Spirit.

Remember that there are thoughts that you hear in your mind, and also thoughts that you may not necessarily hear or be aware of, that are automatized and are proceeding from your heart. We have already quoted Hebrews chapter ten and verse fourteen which states that those who are being sanctified are already perfected through Christ. God declares us as perfect and this means that to Him, we are both sinless and healed through Jesus who dealt with both of those needs for us on the cross. We receive this provision by believing it sufficiently that we come to Him in faith for His promise. Many don't receive because they do not seek Him or His gifts in this regard because of unbelief or wrong believing. So, we could say that most people have enough faith, a tiny mustard seed, to be changed, but hold incorrect beliefs at some level that nullifies the positive confession.

Some people say that we need to get our hearts right with God. More often than not I think we need to bring our hearts to God and He makes them right. King David certainly understood that it was God who would create a clean heart in him and not his own self effort. (Psalm 51:10)

Stream 2 - Spiritual release
As we have already described, often what we believe opens the door, and leads us towards giving a *place* to the devil. In the event that a spirit has come through a breach, via a weak mental or emotional moment, a demon may be present to hold onto this weakness. In the early part of these writings we proposed that our thinking and beliefs releases hormones and neurotransmitters in order to chemically elaborate the feelings or responses that we call emotions. When these hormones and belief-based emotions are imbalanced then our physical self will be prone to disease. Remembering that demons amplify, intensify and replay beliefs producing emotions, we see that they can greatly accelerate, worsen and promote an environment producing the likelihood of disease.

Often, we see physical healing come when a *spirit of infirmity* (weakness) is addressed. The *ground* or *terrain* that it has many times are the deceptive beliefs that are held, which eventually produce disease. Of course, disease can be present because of emotional imbalances without demonic interference, but it may not be as serious, or it may emerge more slowly as we age. Obviously spiritually influenced cultural environments such as high sugar and fat diets, alcoholism, drugs and so on contribute to the ability for the diseases to prosper as the body's defences are broken down.

The problem that we are often confronted with is that we may be aware of the spiritual element of an issue in a person, and as a result, we very much want to see them free. However, it is very difficult to get a demon out of a person who does not believe they have one. Or deliver those who are not prepared to deal with the ground that gives it place through healing or repentance. So, no matter how much you want to cast out spirits, you need to remember that you have authority over evil spirits and not the person's free will. Clearly if they have placed themselves in your prayer line, they have put themselves under provisions that might come through you to help them. Even the Gadarene demoniac with his legion of demons came to Jesus for help.

Mark 5:6, *"When he saw Jesus from afar, he ran and worshiped Him"* (NKJV).

Some Biblical exceptions to requiring the desire of a person to be free seems to be if a person is in a meeting or interfering with the business that God has you on. In those arenas you are under the authority of Christ and over the power of the enemy to achieve the outcome that God has purposed for the ministry time.

Some time ago we were ministering in Micronesia and a woman who was suffering from terminal cancer was set free in a prayer line from a spirit along with a great release of grief. Many people carry a great sadness relating to matters such as the loss of identity or lack of affirmation that they have suffered. This can be associated with bitterness towards others who have damaged their self-worth, as well as resentment towards self, for not being what is seemingly needed to be valued. In this case, we later heard that, the result of her deliverance was healing of her body, and so the spiritual power working within was implicated in her disease.

Stream 3 - Sanctification
As we are conformed to the likeness of Christ, as we have mentioned, we will also be conforming to the Word of God. This holds health benefits for us, for example, when we no longer respond by holding

bitterness, resentment or unforgiveness. Instead of releasing negative hormones, as we grow in love, grace, joy, acceptance and positive emotions we release healthy chemicals into our bodies.

I once read an article that stated that our bodies should be slightly alkaline and disease cannot prosper within us. Along with a long list of foods that it claimed were acidic was a list of negative emotions that also produced acidity. Dealing with these toxic responses through finding our way to line up with the Word of God therefore is a doorway to health.

Proverbs 3:6-8, "*⁶ In all your ways acknowledge Him, And He shall direct your paths. ⁷ Do not be wise in your own eyes; Fear the LORD and depart from evil. ⁸ It will be health to your flesh, And strength to your bones*" (NKJV).

The following passage encourages us to meditate deeply, deliberately and continually on the word of God. It carries a promise that as we are hearers and doers that these alignments with God's order will bring order into your physical being.

Proverbs 4:21-23, "*²¹ Don't lose sight of my words. Let them penetrate deep within your heart, ²² for they bring life and radiant health to anyone who discovers their meaning. ²³ Above all else, guard your heart, for it affects everything you do*" (NLT).

An area of the medical world known as Bio psychiatry proposes that if we could have everybody thinking properly then no one would get sick. As we have described already, this is because there would be chemical and electrical balance in the body and all of the 12 major systems would work together in perfect harmony.

In a sense when Christ is given the headship of His body then it works together in harmony because it outworks in the natural world all of His perfect thoughts and ways. When our head has perfect Biblical thoughts and deeds we can expect to be in perfect health as well. For the world this is simply an unrealistic ideal. For the body of Christ, as we conform to the word, and our thinking is sanctified by the Holy Spirit, and we have our hearts healed, we can expect the final outworking to be improved health and longevity.

Psalm 92:13-14, "*¹³ Those who are planted in the house of the LORD Shall flourish in the courts of our God. ¹⁴ They shall still bear fruit in old age; They shall be fresh and flourishing*" (NKJV).

Sin and sickness
Another element of sanctification, through receiving God's truth and conforming to His word, is knowing the truth about redemption and God's promise of healing. Sin and sickness are linked and so when we examine the scriptures, we see them both being dealt with at the same time.

Psalm 103:2-3, "*² Praise the LORD, I tell myself, and never forget the good things he does for me. ³ He forgives all my sins and heals all my diseases*" (NLT).

In the case of the paralytic man we see Jesus saying directly that forgiving sin and healing of the body are exactly the same thing.

Matthew 9:5-6, "*⁵ Is it easier to say, 'Your sins are forgiven' or 'Get up and walk'? ⁶ I will prove that I, the Son of Man, have the authority on earth to forgive sins." Then Jesus turned to the paralyzed man and said, "Stand up, take your mat, and go on home, because you are healed!*" (NLT).

Even with communion we see that Jesus paid for our sins with His blood as the Lamb of God and also provided for our healing with His broken body (1 Corinthians chapter 11). The book of James chapter 5 and verses 15 and 16 require that as a preface to the prayer of faith making us well that we confess our sins. There have been significant healing revivals that have occurred in previous eras as well as our own times that have been based around the confession of sin in this way. This is accepting that we are out of order and that sin is implicated in our problem. Confess simply means *say the same as*. So, we are taking responsibility for our actions and behaviour and saying the same about it as does the word of God. This agreement with God deals with the Lordship issue and nullifies our rebellion making us candidates for healing.

The final scripture that I am going to use to illustrate the connection between forgiveness of sins and healing, points us directly to our next stream. In the middle of the verse it relates to changing our thinking in regards to what we are living for. This is an important component of being positioned to receive the healing promised through redemption.

Peter is quoting from Isaiah 53:5 which says by His wounds *you are* healed pointing to the cross, whereas the New Testament passage says that *you have been* healed pointing back to the finished work of Jesus.

1 Peter 2:24, *"He himself bore our sins in his body on the tree, so that we might **die to sins and live for righteousness**; by his wounds you have been healed"* (NIV, Emphasis mine).

It is noteworthy that the message that we are instructed to preach is repentance and forgiveness of sins. In other words, change our thinking in regards to how we live and what or whom we are living for in terms of our choices and actions. (Luke 24:47). Sadly, this message no longer appears in some of the newer translations.

Stream 4 - Repentance

Many people do not want to *change their thinking or reconsider their ways*, which as we have stated is what repent essentially means. They are happy being in control of their own lives and doing what they want. And yet an unrepentant heart is often a large blockage to receiving healing of any kind.

Galatians 6:7-8, *"7 Do not be deceived, God is not mocked; for whatever a man sows, that he will also reap. 8 For he who sows to his flesh will of the flesh reap corruption, but he who sows to the Spirit will of the Spirit reap everlasting life"* (NKJV).

You can imagine somebody who reads in the Bible that drunkards will not inherit the kingdom of God, but they persist in drinking a bottle of whisky a night. Why would they be surprised if they end up with liver disease? Is that what God wants for them? No.

I have never seen God not be prepared to free someone from an emotional, physical or spiritual problem regardless of the condition of their lives. So, we are not confusing repentance with only being able to be healed if you do everything right, never sin, and are perfect. The fact that you come to God wanting His help to change is repentance. However, many do not come, being content in their own solutions and so do not receive their freedom .... or perhaps want healing so that they can get into more mischief.

Let us qualify the need for repentance through the eyes of grace and mercy. A man responded to a word of knowledge a number of years ago and was set free from a spirit of infirmity and healed. We discovered three years later that He was in an adulterous relationship at the time and yet God healed him and he remains healed to this day!

Would you have healed him? Perhaps not? When the relationship was exposed three years after the healing the man responded by coming to get help. He had been in denial, and had not let himself accept what he was doing just as King David had done with Bathsheba. He received emotional healing of the rejection that led him into the relationship, and deliverance from associated spiritual strongholds. His Christianity continues to bloom and increase today. Underneath he hated himself for what he was doing all of the time. God looks on the heart and knows the end from the beginning; just like Zacchaeus he knows who will repent.

Let me reiterate, repentance is the desire to follow God's ways not necessarily the ability within yourself to achieve it, or having already attained it. Very often we need God's help to accomplish repentance and the changing of our thinking and reconsidering our ways is an ongoing journey. It begins with accepting the fact that we are out of order with God's ways. We confess and agree with how He sees our issue and take responsibility for our part in it. Sadly, churches are largely unequipped to help repentant people to receive God's freedom through the ministry of the Holy Spirit.

I was at a healing meeting that an acquaintance was running at one time and a lady came out and received healing through his ministry. He asked if her husband was in the meeting and she reported that she didn't have a husband, she had a partner and he was present. Between meetings a Pastor friend was speaking of the lady and asked me if I would have drawn alongside her and let her know that she was living in sin? I responded that I would not; I would have a coffee with her and talk about how amazing God is and how awesome her healing was. Eventually, somewhere down the track at the right time no doubt her relationship would come up. Our mission is to connect people to God, not to make them perfect. He already did that through redemption, so we need to have grace and patience as they grow in their desire to respond to God's kindness with repentance.

Romans 2:4, "*Or do you despise the riches of His goodness, forbearance, and longsuffering, not knowing that the goodness of God leads you to repentance?*" (NKJV).

This lady did not have a problem with God, or the Evangelist who the healing came through. But she might well have had issues with a church that dealt with her in a way other than the revealed character of God. Later her *partner* came up for prayer and received healing as well.

We could suggest then that repentance is an attitude of the heart that God is looking for, as opposed to having no weaknesses or shortcomings. He is looking for us to choose Him as a response towards His goodness and the freedom that He brings to us. So, if we posture His warnings in that way as a matter of love, we see it all in a different light.

John 5:14, "*Afterward Jesus found him in the temple, and said to him, "See, you have been made well. Sin no more, lest a worse thing come upon you*" (NKJV).

His merciful dealings with our failings demand that we rethink how we are going to live. When the woman who had been found in adultery was brought to Jesus, He knew that ALL sinned and fell short of the glory of God without exception. The church is a group of ALLS who have received His grace. When the accusers put themselves under His authority for a decision, He challenged any without sin to cast the first stone, knowing full well that under the law if they claimed to be without sin, they would have to be stoned themselves. Jesus forgave and extended grace to the woman instructing her to rethink and change how she lived. As someone put it there are no special sins.

John 8:10-11, "[10] *When Jesus had raised Himself up and saw no one but the woman, He said to her, "Woman, where are those accusers of yours? Has no one condemned you?"* [11] *She said, "No one, Lord." And Jesus said to her, "Neither do I condemn you; go and sin no more"* (NKJV).

Repentance and expectation

Evangelists running healing meetings early last century would look for expectation of healing in the eyes of those coming for prayer and considered this to be visible faith. They were fairly certain in those days that those who had no intention of attending church or ever serving God need not to expect to get healed.

1 John 3:21-22 *"²¹ Beloved, if our heart does not condemn us, we have confidence toward God. ²² And whatever we ask we receive from Him, because we keep His commandments and do those things that are pleasing in His sight"* (NKJV).

Our hearts could condemn us because we have no intention of changing our ways or following God, or because we have a condemning belief that needs healing first. In our times I have even seen God heal even sceptics, as He knows where they will go from there. They may well prove to be the best at testifying to His power and willingness to heal. It is often unchurched people with no expectations of what should happen who are touched by God in healing meetings, as opposed to those who have had the experience of sitting in a Church with wrong beliefs, who for years and have never seen anyone healed.

Stream 5 - Faith
Positioning our minds

It doesn't matter what kind of receiving from God that we are discussing, there will always need to faith and believing involved somewhere and in someone. A number of years ago I received a fairly detailed word of knowledge regarding an older man who had, as the word went, played football some 20 years earlier and had an injured knee that still troubled him. I understood him to be sitting on the left-hand side four rows back in a congregation of reportedly around 450 people. This was more detail than normal but then the setting was a church that was not used to words of knowledge, so I am guessing that the Holy Spirit was raising faith. The man came forward with a lady whom I assumed was his wife. As I looked at the man, I could see that he had no faith whatsoever, not the slightest bit. As I looked at his *wife*, I could see that she was full of faith and trying to work out how I knew all of this as even the Pastors were not aware. Now we think of the case where Jesus healed a servant based on the faith of the centurion that he was serving, and how the Syrophoenician woman's daughter was healed based on her mother's faith. So, I went ahead and prayed and the man's leg was healed. I heard later that for the next several weeks leaders from the church kept on dropping in and checking on him to see if he was still healed.... he was. The point is that there needed to be faith somewhere before God could work.

In its most fundamental form faith and believing in God is; to be persuaded or convinced that you can trust in God. If He has said something then we expect that it will be so.

Believe: Greek *Pisteuo*; to have faith (in, upon, or with respect to, a person or thing), commit (to trust), put in trust with.

Faith: Greek *Pistis*; persuasion, i.e. conviction.

In the book of Romans, we see that Abraham was **fully** convinced or some translations say **fully** persuaded that God could and would do that which He said He would do. In this he is the Father of faith, in that he trusted in God and it was credited to him as righteousness. This was because he was right about God and His nature, rather than because he was perfect in actions within Himself.

It appears to be more important to God how we regard Him, and His integrity, rather than our efforts to be perfect ourselves. If we were able to be perfect in our own right, we would probably not consider that we require Him or His grace anyway. So, we could say that without trusting God it is impossible to please Him because we do not regard Him accurately. But if our picture of Him is correct then we are righteous, justified in our believing about the matters of God. So, it is Jesus taking our sin and sickness at the cross, as a perfect representation of the Father's goodness that we put our faith in. Many people don't receive their healing because they feel that they need to be perfect or good enough, rather than believing that Jesus paid for our provisions.

Romans 4:20-22, " [20] *He did not waver at the promise of God through unbelief, but was strengthened in faith, giving glory to God,* [21] *and being fully convinced that what He had promised He was also able to perform.* [22] *And therefore "it was accounted to him for righteousness"* (NKJV).

When we consider our walk and work with Jesus, we see that He lays this foundation of believing in God, and walking in faith and trust as our basic job description as disciples.

John 6:28-29, " ²⁸ *Then they said to Him, "What shall we do, that we may work the works of God?" ²⁹ Jesus answered and said to them, "This is the work of God, that you believe in Him whom He sent"* (NKJV).

Persevering faith and being 'fully convinced'
Being fully convinced, I believe is something in the heart rather than mental assent or wishful thinking. We can believe in theory for anything in our minds, but belief in our hearts comes largely from experience of God doing what He said that He would do. At times we have had no experience of God confirming His word because of our environment, or we have heart beliefs that prevent us from believing that God would want to prove His word in or through us. This could be because we believe in our hearts that we are not worthy, not really loved, not cared about, or good enough depending on what was programmed into us as children.

So, healing through *Truth Encounters* can open up new realms of faith as can attending meetings where God is proving His word through a person of faith. In any case Jesus said that we can have whatever we believe in our *hearts*, having dealt with doubt, as opposed to what we believe in our minds.

Mark 11:22-24, "²² *So Jesus answered and said to them, "Have faith in God."* ²³ *"For assuredly, I say to you, whoever says to this mountain, 'Be removed and be cast into the sea,' and does not **doubt in his heart**, but believes that those things he says will be done, he will have whatever he says.* ²⁴ *"Therefore I say to you, whatever things you ask when you pray, believe that you receive them, and you will have them"* (NKJV, Emphasis mine).

Once someone has experienced God healing people, it is very difficult to convince those people that He won't. This applies to emotional healing, deliverance, or physical healing. Some people have stronger faith in some areas than others because they mainly work in one stream and as a result have experienced God's provisions mostly in that setting.

A few years ago, we went directly from one nation to another where the faith dynamics were considerably different. Fortunately, we had been in the country that had been far more open to physical healing first. When we came to the second nation, we had to persevere for a little bit longer to get the breakthroughs. I recall going along the prayer line and some people were being instantly healed. Others beginning with some changes from the initial prayer, improving or receiving more healing on the second occasion, and then coming right through as we continued to pray.

There was one woman towards the end of the line with some kind of lung problem. As I prayed for her, she reported over and over again no change. The fact that I had just experienced God healing so many people in the previous country meant that I simply could not let go of trying to get her free. Eventually we ran out of time and she was still reporting no change. A few minutes after we began to hear testimonies from the front, she joined the line and testified that something had happened with her. She said that it was as if fresh wind had come into her lungs. She was a middle-aged woman, and had had the problem since she was a small child.

The point is that if we had not had fresh experience of that which God wants to do, I would not have pressed through. It is amazing how many people are healed when we persist in prayer rather than giving up when nothing or not much happens immediately.

Possibly my favourite healing story is from the American Apostle Che Ahn [9]. We get so hung up on instant miracles that people often give up on their healing before they reach the church door to head home. As his story goes a man came up to him in a prayer line and in an accident his finger had been cut off at the second knuckle. His teenage daughter had been helping him trim the hedges when she unintentionally cut of his finger with the hedge clippers. He demonstrated his faith saying; *Pastor, I believe God wants to grow my finger back, and I want you to stand with me in faith.* Che Ahn agreed with him, as he put it, hoping for the best.

A couple of months later the man was back in the prayer line. As he approached the apostle he was smiling and as the story goes

---

[9] Reference book. Say Goodbye to Powerless Christianity. Destiny Image publishers. Author: Che Ahn

held up his hand to show his brand-new finger complete with a new nail! Che humbly reported that at the time he may not have believed that the finger would grow back. It was the man's faith to receive that brought about the results. We modern Christians have to some extent been programmed by microwaves and fast food chains. We expect to go through the drive through requesting; *One physical healing, two deliverances, and complete emotional restoration to go thanks.*

In reality, healing and deliverance is a journey that has miraculous moments here and there. Sometimes patience and perseverance are developed as we contend for the faith. Jesus often asked questions such as; *do you believe that I can do this?* He also made comments such as; *your faith has healed you, according to your faith* and so on.

We learnt a similar lesson on one of our first times overseas preaching a healing gospel. We were in a developing nation in the Pacific and God was miraculously healing various physical problems. I recall preaching and praying for the sick in one church and then being raced off an hour away to do the same in another congregation. A couple of days later we were back at the original church and my wife and I were approached by the Pastors wife. She came up to us and enquired; *did you see that lady who you prayed for the other day who was carried in?* We responded that we did and she went on to explain what had happened. *Did you know that she had terminal cancer and notice that she walked out of the meeting by herself after prayer? The following day she was walking around the hospital by herself and the day after she was released to go home.* My wife incredulously proclaimed wide eyed; *really*. I gently elbowed her and whispered in her ear that this is what we have been telling these people that God wants to do for them. *Don't look too surprised or they may not expect it to keep happening.* As comical as this was, we learnt the lesson that their receiving faith was why God was touching them. Indeed, they had more faith in what God would do through us than we did at the time ourselves.

Another man that I know of had terminal liver cancer. He went to one healing meeting after another all over the country and finally received His healing. Having received the object of his faith he then proceeded to have his own healing ministry. Clearly it was the certainty of God's promise in his heart that made him persevere.

Some people spend years, *standing on the word*, and never receive because they are trying to make something happen by their own will and effort. If we come as *little* children, we are not trying to do anything, we are just presenting ourselves because Abba daddy said to. If we have received then we will know immediately or discover it in due course as the evidence of the healing appears.

Giving faith and receiving faith

Clearly there was never a problem with the faith of Jesus. But He was limited in what He could do by the faith of the people to receive. In His own home town, the people had experiences of Jesus growing up and attending the Synagogue with them; perhaps school, and maybe some of them had furniture in their homes made by his father or perhaps himself. Their experience of him as *the carpenter's son* shaped their expectations more than seeing Him as the miracle working Messiah.

Mark 6:3-6, " *[3] Is this not the carpenter, the Son of Mary, and brother of James, Joses, Judas, and Simon? And are not His sisters here with us?" And they were offended at Him. [4] But Jesus said to them, "A prophet is not without honor except in his own country, among his own relatives, and in his own house." [5] Now He could do no mighty work there, except that He laid His hands on a few sick people and healed them. [6] And He marveled because of their unbelief. Then He went about the villages in a circuit, teaching"* (NKJV).

Over the years we have learnt that miracle healing can be difficult in your own home church as people become familiar with you. A few years ago, we amalgamated our long-term church and took on another congregation who had lost their Pastor. We ministered there four years before finally transitioning it to a new leader in order to concentrate on other ministry demands.

For the first few months that we were there I was able to work in words of knowledge and people were healed, but as they became more familiar with us you could see the expectation gradually *drying up*. It was time to bring in other people that they did not know, who weren't from their hometown, as a contact point for their faith.

I did one of our two-week healing schools for a church some time ago, and in the course of the school God faithfully demonstrated every kind of healing that I taught on. At the end of the two weeks my personal faith was at an all-time high. I was brimming with faith and felt that anything would happen that I prayed for.

I went directly into another church the following weekend. They brought up a lady who was suffering from breast cancer. I prayed for her with great faith and expectation and the power and anointing of God was on her quite strongly. A few months later I heard that she had died. What had happened? I realized that I had not taught her the word, prepared her, or done anything to evoke her faith to receive.

Additionally, the environment that she was in was one of an expectation of a negative outcome because her husband and children had seen his first wife die a few years earlier. I learnt that my faith to give is not as important as is the ability of the person to receive. Our work then is to raise the faith of the people through teaching and testimony to position them to receive.

Let me briefly contrast this with times when I have taught all week and been very tired by the time it comes to the prayer line. I am too worn out to feel much personal faith and at times have prayed very feeble prayers indeed, and yet the subject has still been healed.

One such instance was in Asia some time back. At the end of a week of teaching and ministering we were heading back to our hotel. On the way some of the Pastors took us to the home of an old lady who needed prayer. When I prayed for her, she became quite irate and pointed to her eyes. She was apparently blind. I laid my hand over her eyes and prayed a tired prayer commanding them to open. Almost immediately she was counting the fingers of an excited young Pastor across the table. She certainly did not get healed by my energetic faith, and looking at her I don't think that she personally had either faith or unbelief. The Pastors however had seen people being healed on the school through the week and they had great expectations.

Reading the great healing Apostle Smith Wigglesworth, I noted that there were occasions where he would go to minister in a home and would not immediately pray for the sick person. He commented once that *there was not an atom of faith in the house.* He would proceed to minister the Word of God in order to deal with the environment, and then he would pray sometimes the next day and get his result.

In the case of the Apostle Paul in the book of Acts, we observe him *seeing* faith in a man who was responding to his teaching. Evidently others in the room had problems as well but were not moved by faith and convinced that God wanted to touch them at heart level. So, it is good for us to be aware of the effects of our sharing, testifying, teaching or preaching in terms of raising faith for people to understand and receive.

Acts 14:9-10, " [9] *This man heard Paul speaking. Paul, observing him intently and seeing that he had faith to be healed,* [10] *said with a loud voice, "Stand up straight on your feet!" And he leaped and walked* (NKJV).

Believing for yourself
Many times, it is more difficult to believe for yourself than it is for others. This is probably because you have experiential knowledge of your symptoms being present each day. Most times rather than try hard, we need to keep it simple, and seek out the healing gifts that God has placed in the body to meet these needs. In Australia a great many people are trying to resolve their problem themselves by some means. God has placed healing gifts in the body for a reason and they can help us to receive.

Even Smith Wigglesworth suffered from appendicitis and almost died [10]. It was a praying woman of faith and a young man who came and addressed the problem that brought about his healing. He was apparently unable to believe and come to faith for his own cure. In fact, as the story goes when they visited Wigglesworth's home the young man jumped up on the bed and commanded the spirit causing the appendicitis to go, and before Smith could tell him that he couldn't possibly have a demon, it left. So clearly, he had no faith for cure by those means at that time either.

We need to be convinced of God's goodness and power, and trust His character and willingness to set us free. This believing response is the basis of both our salvation and Him empowering us to overcome in the World.

10 Smith Wigglesworth on Healing. Publisher: Whitaker House

John 5:4, *"For whatever is born of God overcomes the world. And this is the victory that has overcome the world; our faith"* (NKJV).

How should healing look?
Many people don't receive their healing because they believe that it should look some particular way, or that they should feel this or that. I would estimate that with most of the people that we see healed physically through our ministry nothing obvious happens. This can be true also of deliverance or baptism in the Holy Spirit. One minute they are sick or have demonic power working in them and the next minute they don't. One minute they can't speak in other tongues, and the next moment they can.

Jesus actually admonished the man in John chapter 4, and I imagine all of those present, for needing to see something happen before they believed and would receive. The man had come to Jesus requesting healing for his son.

John 4:46-53, *" ⁴⁶ So Jesus came again to Cana of Galilee where He had made the water wine. And there was a certain nobleman whose son was sick at Capernaum. ⁴⁷ When he heard that Jesus had come out of Judea into Galilee, he went to Him and implored Him to come down and heal his son, for he was at the point of death. ⁴⁸ Then Jesus said to him, "**Unless you people see signs and wonders, you will by no means believe.**" ⁴⁹ The nobleman said to Him, "Sir, come down before my child dies!" ⁵⁰ Jesus said to him, "Go your way; your son lives." So the man **believed the word** that Jesus spoke to him, and he went his way. ⁵¹ And as he was now going down, his servants met him and told him, saying, "Your son lives!" ⁵² Then he inquired of them the hour when he got better. And they said to him, "Yesterday at the seventh hour the fever left him." ⁵³ So the father knew that it was at the same hour in which Jesus said to him, "Your son lives." And he himself believed, and his whole household"* (NKJV, Emphasis mine).

Nobody reported seeing anything happen; the boy was simply healed because his father believed the word that Jesus spoke. Some people have preconceived ideas in regards to perhaps something that they have seen in a meeting or on U tube and believe that all healings should look this way or it *didn't work*. When you consider that our thinking is the limiting factor, and when our minds get in the way, then our expectations block the work of God through faith. Remember the devil is forever defeated, the only power he has over you is the areas of deception that you hold. This could include receiving and accepting the thought that you cannot be healed or freed.

At times I have been in churches where there may be a cripple or the like who has been in the church for many years. As a result, the people are used to them being in that condition. So, you are dealing with mass expectation of how he should look and be. We could say that the mind in regards to what God can, or wants to do, is the limiting factor. Perhaps people have seen him prayed for many times before.

There is the well-known story of the lady who touched the hem of Jesus garment in Matthew Chapter 9 and received her healing. If you can picture the event with the crowd all around them, and the disciples urging Jesus to hurry or they will miss the last bus. The woman touches His hem and is healed. Who knew that something had happened? Most likely nobody other than Jesus who felt the power go out of him, and the lady who felt that she was healed. The others didn't see anything happen, and there is no evidence that she fell to the ground or shook for ten minutes, or any other event that some might expect should be present for healing. She simply touched His hem and was healed.

I have often seen people looking bored because they don't see much happening in healing meetings and assume that nothing is going on. Very often, but not always, the minister can feel the flow of the power going through Him, and the person receiving can feel themselves being touched. God does not need to be showy and comes as He pleases.

I think that we need to be bottom line Christians, and be all about caring about people and not putting on a show. The testimonies are how we know that God has been working.

I heard a story of two healing ministers in modern times. Reportedly one of them prayed in a very dignified gentle manner and people would be healed without anything obvious happening. When the other man would pray for people they would shake violently and fall to the ground.

On one occasion as the more dignified man went through a particular town, he went past a healing meeting being conducted by the other man. He commented to his driver that the way that this man prayed and that what happened when he did was unseemly. As they drove on, he began to get a headache. Inquiring of the Lord he was instructed to go back and get prayer from the other man. When he did apparently, he shook violently, fell to the ground, and got up healed. Regardless of the validity of the story it does raise the point that if we take a; *that's not how you do it* approach we may well miss our healing.

God will come through various ministers as He pleases. Whether this is to do with the personality of the minister that the Holy Spirit is working through or not, I could not say. We do however have to have our eyes fixed on Christ the healer and not the man that He is working through. In any case it is important to not get hung up on seeing something happen or particular methods. Simply pray with faith and leave the details to God.

Remember it is largely the person's ability to receive that matters, and your job is to position them with truth about God to release their faith. It is not somebody with a big name or ministry that has healed you. Seven times in the gospels according to Jesus it is; *Your faith has healed you.*

I have a friend who is a well-known minister from Uganda. At one time he was running a gospel crusade in Kenya, and at the end of the service he began to pray for the sick. He remembered a sick man who had been brought in on a stretcher and laid under the platform, so he went and prayed for him. After he had prayed, he began to walk away and the crowd erupted. It turned out that the man was not in fact sick, but actually dead. After prayer he had sat up on his stretcher to everyone's amazement. The point is we just pray for God to touch the subject, refuse to doubt His goodness, and you never know what might happen. Certainly, the dead man didn't have any unbelief to complicate the issue, which leads me to the next portion of this stream.

Faith verses unbelief
Faith puts us under God's provision and outcome. This is evidenced by Abraham who was fully convinced that God could do that which He said He would do. As we have said, once we have our convictions

about God's promises and intentions for us, we need to leave the details to Him in terms of how it will look and when it will take place. Doubt, unbelief and scepticism put us, or keep us under Satan's outcome, which will not be positive, changing or redemptive in nature.

One day I was praying for a lady who was booked in for an operation, and the power of God was on her heavily. We needed three or four people to hold her up through the ministry time. She had been the last person in the prayer line, and so after we had finished, I headed for the church cafe to get into the coffee queue. From where I was standing, I was not visible to the lady, and she had entered the kitchen to talk to some friends. From this position I could hear her explaining to another lady how pleased she was that God had provided somebody to look after her after her operation. I was thinking back to 5 minutes earlier when she could not stand up, as she was overwhelmed with the healing power of God. I later reflected on the situation and how her expectation was set on the outcome of the operation and not the power of God. She doubted that His power would heal her and did not believe that anything would change. In a sense she had switched off whatever God wanted to do immediately after the prayer.

I have seen many times when asked how people are feeling immediately after prayer, they may make statements such as; *at the moment I have no pain*. This can mean that they are struggling to get their minds around what has just happened. There is every chance that if challenged that they will accept and receive the return of their symptoms before they even get home. This is according to the faith and expectations that they hold, based on their knowledge of God and His word. I have seen a number of people who have had some symptoms beginning to come back who have stood on the word and refused to accept the sickness or injury again.

One time I prayed for three people who responded to a word of knowledge for the same back problem. When I prayed for them one of them fell to the ground, shook and stood up proclaiming that they were healed. The other two reported nothing. The following week I enquired of each of them as to their condition. The one who had manifested and reported healing had the back problem back again. The other two both independently said the same thing as each other, and that was that the day after prayer the problem was worse, but the following day that they were both healed, and reported remaining healed. So, what happened? I think that the two people just accepted it for whatever it was going to be, not having doubt or unbelief, and the other who was sensitive to the Holy Spirit was probably also sensitive to unholy spirit, and when some symptoms came, they received their problem back. We need to be fully convinced that if the son sets you free, then you are free indeed.

We have already quoted that Jesus said that we can have whatever we believe in our hearts if we do not doubt. The basis of the word translated as doubt holds the meaning of intellectual deciding, judging, wavering, hesitating or contending. In other words, the matter isn't settled, you are not fully convinced.

Matthew 21:21-22, " *²¹ So Jesus answered and said to them, "Assuredly, I say to you, if you have faith and do **not doubt**, you will not only do what was done to the fig tree, but also if you say to this mountain, 'Be removed and be cast into the sea,' it will be done. ²² "And whatever things you ask in prayer, believing, you will receive."* (NKJV, Emphasis mine).

Each of us has been given a measure of faith. So, having faith, however undeveloped, is not the problem as we only need a mustard seed of faith. The issue then is usually not how much faith we have, it is how much unbelief. Both can exist in us at the same time. I have ministered in churches that were not denominationally predisposed to healing and the working of the Holy Spirit. As Jesus did, I have sometimes spent a week ministering one on one behind closed doors healing the sick and hurting. As the testimonies have circulated through the church there has been expectation building, and we have been able to see people healed in a prayer line by the following Sunday.

So, the issue really is not about having a great amount of faith, it is more about dealing with unbelief or wrong beliefs. At times you hear of prayer chains where they try to get 500 people praying for a sick person. May I gently suggest that this is unbelief and fear that God will not hear, and that He needs many to persuade and pressure Him? My Bible says that healing was His idea and not ours; we don't have to talk Him into it! He already promised, paid for it, and commanded that we minister it. If we simply receive without doubting it is ours.

Dealing with doubt and unbelief

So how do we deal with our doubt and unbelief? In two Corinthians chapter ten and verse five we see that we are to demolish and destroy arguments that set themselves up against the knowledge of God. The Greek word here that is translated; as *arguments* is *logismus*, and it means; computation, i.e. (fig.) reasoning, imagination, thought. It is reasonably obvious that we get words such as logic from this root word. So, the passage is really saying to pull down and destroy all logical reasoning out, and trying to compute and understand the word of God.

There is no working out the word of God. Think about it. Jesus walks on water, talks to storms, drachmas appear in fish's mouths, He feeds five thousand with next to nothing, axe heads float, water becomes wine, seas part for the Israelites to cross, donkeys talk to their riders ... shall I go on.

2 Corinthians 10:5, *"We **demolish arguments** and every pretension that sets itself up **against the knowledge of God**, and we take captive every thought to make it obedient to Christ"* (NIV, Emphasis mine). The point is that you cannot reason out something that you will never be able to understand. The things that God does are not natural. So, then the word of God and His promises are technically not logical or possible. They cannot therefore be worked out. They can only be received.

We need to take control of our thought life and refuse to try to work it out, otherwise your reasoning is going to go into; *Maybe God doesn't heal today*, or *He only heals in Africa where they don't have many doctors*, or *He will only heal good people, but He won't heal me because I am not good enough!* Etc.

I have heard that if you buy a loaf of white bread today that by the time the grain has been broken down and processed by man that there is no nutritional value left in it for us. When we begin to process the word of God, and *manize* it, instead of taking it whole and untouched, we render it of no value to us either.

Smith Wigglesworth who very clinically dealt with his own unbelief, proclaimed his well-known default position. *God said it, I believe it, that settles it*. In other words, there is no more to think about, and nothing to work out; I trust His integrity, promises and ability without question. He also made the statement that; *carnal (worldly) reasoning will always land you in the bog of unbelief.*

I taught on these principles in Africa recently, and on the Sunday morning the young man leading worship that day gave in his own language a testimony, and received a round of applause. Although I did not know what had happened, I was told after the service that having heard these principles, he became inspired and decided to try it out and see if it was true. He stepped out boldly praying for a lady with a disease and she was healed.

Whether you want to receive your own healing or help in the ministry to others you need to take captive, and deal with your doubt and unbelief. Once you have decided to refuse to even think about the possibility of God not being true to His word, it can be helpful to meditate over and over on His nature. When you are receiving or praying for others you can be expecting something to happen based on your meditations regarding how God is towards us. There is an appendix of redemption scriptures in the back of the book to consider as a basis for your healing and freedom.

Psalm 103:2-4, *"2 Praise the LORD, O my soul, and forget not all his benefits, 3 who forgives all your sins and heals all your diseases, 4 who redeems your life from the pit and crowns you with love and compassion".* Also verse 8, *"8 The LORD is compassionate and gracious, slow to anger, abounding in love.* And verse 13, *"13 As a father has compassion on his children, so the LORD has compassion on those who fear him"* (NIV).

Let me make a final observation relating to doubt and unbelief. Some people think that if you don't pray a particular way, or for the right thing, or long enough, then healing won't happen. Laying on hands and a prayer such as; *be healed in the name of Jesus* really is all that you need. Let me reiterate, you do not have to talk God into it; this is His idea, and as we have said, He even commanded us to go out and heal the sick. You may need to work through the doubts of the people that you are ministering to though, before you see or sense enough expectation to pray for them.

I once prayed for a lady who wanted prayer to confirm a positive outcome to a cancer operation that she'd had. I heard a couple of days later that, at the same time, God had healed her back and she no longer needed her brace. I didn't even know that she had a bad back, and so I certainly didn't pray the right prayer, if there is such a thing, but God knew. We don't need to get everything right; we just have to believe that in His love and compassion that He will do whatever is needed.

I recall one well known American evangelist being addressed by a lady; *I know that you can heal headaches, but I have cancer!* His reply was something along the lines of; *Lady, I can't heal anything, but God can and it doesn't make much difference to Him what you've got!*

Famous people both from the past, and those in the present age, who have *faith healing ministries* are so convinced of God's willingness and ability to heal that they convince many other people in their meetings that this is so. Some expound powerfully the promises from the word; others share testimonies or demonstrate healing in their meetings, or a combination of all. The key is that they are so persuaded from their own experiences of God, that others are moved from their normal believing to the faith of the minister, and as a result they become open to God's power and ability as well.

Stream 6 - Gifts
Spiritual gifts raise faith. For someone to call out your details through a word of knowledge as you sit in a service shows that God knows you, and knows what your needs are. In the 1950s and 60s, William Branham from the U.S. was a famous healing evangelist. He used the word of knowledge to great affect calling out people with specific details such as where they were from, and street numbers, and this opened people up to the supernatural realm sparking off faith. He used to say that it was like lifting himself up to look over a fence, the higher he raised himself the more he could see. Very few of us will ever be gifted to this level but we can all work in the gifts if our motivation is right. If you want to look good or be someone it may not be for you. However, if your motivation is that a person may go home without some ailment or other if you step out, and you just want to help, then you can be reasonably sure that what comes into your mind will be from God.

Some time ago I was reading an article about fitness training and they mentioned the term; *hard gainers*. What this refers to is that some people are naturally athletic and only have to look at weights or do exercise and they put on muscle or get into shape. This seems to be true of spiritual gifts as well. Some are very gifted or *pre-wired* by God for spiritual gifts and it is easy for them, while others of us are *hard gainers*. The thing to know is that we can still get there and help people; it just might take some of us a little longer to learn how to position ourselves to hear from God. I think some of us who have to learn the process and work for it a little more, may at times be those who may be going to help others to get going as well.

King David learnt to trust that God was with him in the place of obscurity by killing lion and bear whilst tending his father's sheep. This was necessary before he was thrust into the limelight with Goliath. So it is that we often learn to trust that we are hearing God's voice whilst we are ministering to others in environments such as helping people through *Truth Encounters*. If we are attentive, we will also note whether or not those being ministered to are particularly sensitive to the Holy Spirit in how they receive truth for themselves.

I recall one morning, calling out in the service that there was a lady who had been having headaches since she was a child. A lady of around 50 years old responded. I prayed a simple prayer commanding the spirit of infirmity to go and nothing visible or obvious happened. A few weeks later she realized that she had not had a migraine. At the time of writing nearly 4 years on she still has never had the complaint again. Normally we would minister to the roots of the migraines with Truth Encounters. But the lesson is that we know that God does not call out a complaint so that everyone knows that they have the issue, but rather because He is intending to heal them.

Stepping out
I used to consider words of knowledge akin to loosening all of the wheel nuts off on your car, and speeding around a curvy road that ran along the edge of a cliff. In other words, there is an element of risk. After a while, you find that if your heart and motivation are right that God will always come through. Two or three years ago in Kenya I called out a man with a liver problem and described him. This was the first word of knowledge that I had done in the meeting with several hundred Pastors attending. No response. I think God just smiles. The next few words that I had the people responded and were healed. Phew!

The following morning there was a lot of noise at the back of the church and the Pastor that I described with the liver problem came in, and proceeded to testify that he had been healed when I called the word of knowledge, while he was still in Hospital. The lesson, God is faithful. If you will step out, He will step in!

People commonly come to you after the service and have not come out for fear or some other reason. A few years ago, again my first word of knowledge in a large church in Uganda, was a man with a head injury sitting in a particular area. No response. Between services he emerged, confirmed that this was where he was sitting and that he had the head injury. The important thing is to help them and not your reputation.

Some people like to make spiritual gifts a part of their identity and worth, and feel that if they operate in them that they are somehow superior to others. The truth is that anyone can be used if they make themselves available. We often work in some activation on our schools so that people learn how simple it is. I recall one such meeting where we had several hundred Pastors attending the School of Healing and Freedom that we run. I invited anyone who wanted to be guided into bringing a *word of knowledge* to come forward. Nobody moved. Who wants to be the Pastor who didn't have a *word*, I get it! After a minute or two, four or five guys from the band came out. With a little guidance each of them called someone out. All of the complaints were there, and when they prayed for the people, all of them were healed which is what usually happens. The point is that God will use anyone who is willing to help and is prepared to trust Him. Many of the people that we train, most likely go on to be much better at getting *words* than I am, and that is the point of discipling. Probably the reason that I expect that others will be able to get words is that I am so ordinary myself. As a result, I think that in all areas of ministry that we train people in, that if I can do it, then anyone can. If you don't reach out for a word you will never get one. If you have opportunity, ask God for a word that will help someone receive from Him and you may be surprised at what comes into your mind. But I recommend that if you aren't going to bring it don't ask for it.

In my early days with this I was sharing in a healing elective at a conference. I had asked God for a couple of words and had something come to mind. As I went along, I called out the first one and she responded and I prayed for her. I thought; *Phew, made it.*

And being relieved, I thought, *I will just leave it there*. The problem was that on the way home I was convicted that the other lady that I had had the *word* for may have gone home sick, and may have not had another opportunity for healing in her environment. I decided to not hold back if I had a word again in the future.

A couple of years ago one of our team was preaching in a large church in Africa, and in the course of the service I received a word regarding a man with trouble and pain in both his kidneys. The problem was that it was a very busy service and our team member had an altar call, so I had no opportunity to call him out for prayer. Through the week I was teaching afternoons and evenings at the church. On the Wednesday night service most of the church attended so I decided to see if he was there. I called out the complaint and where the man had been sitting in the Sunday service, and he responded and was healed.

The lesson is that God is faithful and His word will not return to Him void, but will accomplish all that He has purposed for it. In my experience I see the highest percentages of people are physically healed through a word of knowledge, and the greater the detail the greater the faith response.

How do you receive a word of knowledge or prophecy?
You begin by making yourself available to God and looking to Him to put something into your mind to help or encourage someone. We were doing a healing school in a camp environment at one time, and as we were drawing towards the end of the week it occurred to me that we had not reached out for a word of knowledge yet. So, I enquired of the Lord if there was a person that He wanted to touch. A throat problem came into my mind followed by the picture of the face of a person who had been attending the school. When I stood up a little later, I asked the lady if she had a throat problem and she confirmed that she did. The Pastor asked if we should pray for her. I commented that we were about to have communion which includes the healing provision of Jesus' broken body. After communion the lady reported that she was healed. The point is, would I have had something put in my mind if I had not reached out? No. So we begin by giving our mental faculties to God for His use.

This book is primarily about ministering *Truth Encounters*. But let me just say here that because some of the gifts are all about hearing what God is saying in a situation, ministering *Truth Encounters* has a double edge for learning how to work in gifts. Firstly, if you are receiving ministry, you know that you just heard from God in some way because you are now different, and hearing from yourself never could produce that result. Secondly, if you are the minister you are looking for the leading of the Holy Spirit for the questions to ask, and to see what you need to see, so you are learning to sense what He is saying to you.

He will use different things to train you in that environment, such as put the belief that the person holds in their hearts into your mind, often long before the person is ready to accept it. The old saying is that; *God talks how you listen*. If you look back into Section 2 of *Truth Encounters*, you will find an overview of how God may communicate to your mind. The gifts operate in much the same way.

There are books on how to operate in the gifts so I will not delve deeply into that area here. Most gifts raise faith. Once one person is healed their testimony will raise further faith in others. There is a gift of faith where the faith that God has developed in you is not sufficient for the situation, and now, you have a supernatural faith that is His, that refuses to accept an unresolved situation. So, gifts are a stream or channel that God uses for healing various maladies.

Stream 7 - The Anointing
The final healing stream that I am proposing is the *anointing*, which is the presence of God, and can be the tangible power of God. It can come as the result of faith that has risen through gifts, testimonies, teaching or an act of faith for example. Equally faith can come as a result of the anointing or presence of God in a meeting.

Luke 5:17, *"Now it happened on a certain day, as He was teaching, that there were Pharisees and teachers of the law sitting by, who had come out of every town of Galilee, Judea, and Jerusalem. And* **the power of the Lord was present to heal them**" (NKJV, Emphasis mine).

We have already pointed out that the *Spirit of power* is one of the seven Spirits that are a working of the Holy Spirit. The Greek word for literal power in the New Testament is *dunamis* which means literal or miraculous power, force or might. We get words such as dynamo or dynamite from this root. This is the power to heal that was described in the previous passage, and also in stories such as the power that healed the lady who touched the hem of Jesus' garment.

We have at times ministered in places where the people are so hungry for the touch of God that they receive easily. There can at times be a powerful presence of God come in as the prayer line begins and the Holy Spirit move. I remember one occasion where people were being touched, healed and delivered, and the presence of God was so strong that we became very bold. With His power so eminent you nearly felt like asking if they had any dead people. It is almost as if His nearness gives you confidence that anything is possible. In section 4, I have already detailed how people are often spontaneously delivered when the anointing of the Holy Spirit comes upon them. At times people are healed or set free by the Holy Spirit while teaching is in process.

It can be distressing as at times we hear of people doing strange things to get the *anointing*. The Holy Spirit seems to be particularly attracted to obedient people and humble people. We know that Jesus had the Spirit without measure so He is always our model in all things, and we can look to Him for the secret to the anointing. John 8:29, *"And He who sent Me is with Me. The Father has not left Me alone, for **I always do those things that please Him**"* (NKJV Emphasis mine)

Most of the great healing ministries of the past understood that the way to having God come increasingly through you, was a process of getting yourself out of the way. Self can block the flow and make you a dam rather than a river. If you are not about yourself, but rather others, then even if you imagine yourself as a funnel, and the funnel has a few cracks in it, most of what is tipped in will still go through. So it is with us. Although we are imperfect, if we hold our funnel up to God for Him to pour His Spirit through to minister to the people, there will be enough tipped in by Him to achieve the result.

In terms of enlarging your funnel, it will cost you something of losing your life to gain a more abundant life in the Spirit. The natural life is not necessarily sinful, it is simply inferior. You can have a life on Earth and have things that are not essentially bad, but if you want

God to use you, then this natural life may need to go on the altar in preference for being used by Him. Smith Wigglesworth explained this process of walking increasingly as a clear channel for God in this way; *All of me none of God - less of me more of God - none of me all of God.*

'Special' anointed people

Many years ago, I was at a church where they were talking about the amazing *anointing* on their leader, and how they all wanted prayer from him for the *anointing* as if it was something that could be randomly handed out and given from this man. My first thoughts were about when Samuel selected King David. He was ready to anoint his impressive older brothers, but God showed him, not this one, not this one, until David came in and it was clear that he was the one. What I take from this is that God is very selective about who He anoints, and for what purpose. Even the great Prophet Samuel could not make this call or select who was to receive the anointing. I think that we can cheapen the anointing with this type of thinking.

1 Samuel 16:6-13, "⁶ *So it was, when they came, that he looked at Eliab and said, "Surely the Lord's anointed is before Him."* ⁷ *But the LORD said to Samuel, "Do not look at his appearance or at the height of his stature, because I have refused him. For the Lord does not see as man sees; for man looks at the outward appearance, but the LORD looks at the heart."* ⁸ *So Jesse called Abinadab, and made him pass before Samuel. And he said, "Neither has the LORD chosen this one."* ⁹ *Then Jesse made Shammah pass by. And he said, "Neither has the LORD chosen this one."* ¹⁰ *Thus Jesse made seven of his sons pass before Samuel. And Samuel said to Jesse, "The LORD has not chosen these."* ¹¹ *And Samuel said to Jesse, "Are all the young men here?" Then he said, "There remains yet the youngest, and there he is, keeping the sheep." And Samuel said to Jesse, "Send and bring him. For we will not sit down till he comes here."* ¹² *So he sent and brought him in. Now he was ruddy, with bright eyes, and good-looking. And the LORD said, "Arise, anoint him; for this is the one!"* ¹³ *Then Samuel took the horn of oil and anointed him in the midst of his brothers; and the Spirit of the LORD came upon David from that day forward. So Samuel arose and went to Ramah" (NKJV).*

God has called you for what He has called you, and you need to grow in your own anointing as you make room for God to rule on the throne of your heart. If you look inside and He is not sitting on the throne there, and you are, then that is a very good place to start on coming into the *anointing*. These people were suggesting that this man had a special *anointing* that was causing healing to happen around his life. In the night I wrestled with this concept inquiring of the Lord as to how you get a special anointing such as this. The answer came in the form of a scripture from John's gospel:

John 14:12, *"I tell you the truth, **anyone** who has faith in me will do what I have been doing. He will do even greater things than these, because I am going to the Father"* (NIV Emphasis mine).

This resolved the issue of special anointing for me. It is a matter of simple faith in God, and this might well release anointing, but it is for *anyone* who chooses to believe!

Finally, laying on of hands is a channel for the power of God to flow through. Some people feel it and others don't. That is not the point. Why does the laying on of hands work? Because Jesus said to do it! I have been in meetings where the people were spiritually not very alive. So, there was virtually no tangible presence of God in the room beyond that which came through my hands when I prayed for people. They still received deliverance. It reminded me of Jesus in His own home town, He could not do mighty miracles because of the unbelief of the general population, but He could still see individuals healed through His hands.

Mark 6:5-6, *"* ⁵ *Now He could do no mighty work there, except that He laid His hands on a few sick people and healed them.* ⁶ *And He marveled because of their unbelief"* (NKJV).

The streams often overlap as they run into the same river. For example, someone may receive the truth that God loves them and cares about them in a *Truth Encounter* and as we see their faith rise because of that touch of God, we take opportunity to pray for any physical problems presenting.

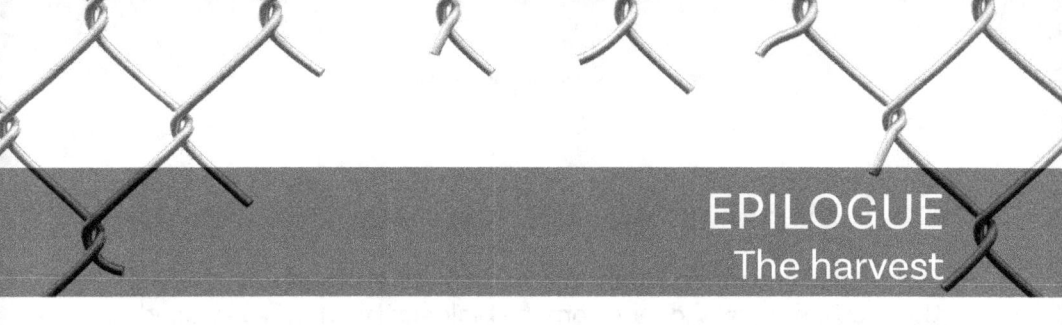

EPILOGUE
The harvest

I believe that we are in a time where God wants to revive and equip His church as never before. As believers are trained to bring the good news, the harvest of souls can proceed according to the desire of the Father that none should perish. For this to occur it will not be a matter of comparing religious philosophies that will bring in the souls, it needs to be a demonstration of the good news of the Kingdom as it was through Jesus. As I understand it, there are currently more people alive than have been previously born throughout all of History combined. At the time of writing there is an estimated 7.6 Billion people on the Earth. In the times that Jesus came to establish the Kingdom the entire world population was reportedly 200 Million people, less than the present population of Pakistan. The number of people on our planet has more than trebled since 1950 as the times have accelerated.

As Daniel prophesied knowledge has increased, and people do go here and there rushing about.

Daniel 12:4, *"But you, Daniel, keep this prophecy a secret; seal up the book until the time of the end. Many will rush here and there, and knowledge will increase"* (NLT).

Around 15 years ago the estimate was that knowledge doubled every 32 years. At the moment the general knowledge held by mankind doubles every 12 – 13 months. The forecast by some in the information world is that with the rapid acceleration of technology that the doubling of knowledge will soon be occurring every 12 hours. We have an information glut at our fingertips with an ever-decreasing supply of wisdom, understanding, and capacity to work out problems for ourselves as individuals. It has been suggested that we are heading for an intellectual dark age, with less than 3% of people ever thinking deeply about life. Indeed, our faculties are bogged down keeping up with media and being programmed how to think and act as a society. As the church I believe that it is critical that we are like the sons of Issachar, who understood the times, and knew what Israel should do. Jesus Himself pointed out that the people were good at interpreting the weather but they could not interpret the signs of the times that they were in. 1 Chronicles 12:32 and Matthew 16:2-3 .

Speaking of end times, an author I read a number of years ago posed this mathematical thought from the biological world. If you placed one bacterium in a glass which reproduced itself every minute, and the glass was to be full after one hour, at what time will it be half full, with a half a glass to go? The answer is 59 minutes. The point is that I believe that we need to be very busy and purposeful in regards to letting God revive us, create in us a clean heart, and use us for the harvest in this era. I heard someone very aptly use a term for our Christian youth today, calling them the *finishing generation*.

The two Harvests

In the book of Deuteronomy, we see a type or picture of a situation that Israel found itself in when God was moving them to the Promised Land. The picture is that they were going from a land where they were in control of growing their crops to a place where they were completely reliant on God for the harvest.

My wife and I used to own a vineyard and so I can comprehend the concept as we could flood irrigate our vines with water from the river, as the Israelites formerly could do from the Nile.

Deuteronomy 11:10, " *¹⁰ For the land which you go to possess is not like the land of Egypt from which you have come, where you sowed your seed and watered it by foot, as a vegetable garden.*"

But now He was taking them to the land of God where He was going to oversee the increase personally.

"*¹¹ but the land which you cross over to possess is a land of hills and valleys, which drinks water from the rain of heaven,*"*¹²* "*a land for which the LORD your God cares; the eyes of the LORD your God are always on it, from the beginning of the year to the very end of the year.*"

The success of the harvest in this new promised place was going to be contingent on doing things His way, humbly serving Him, and being mindful of His intentions and plans. This was going to involve lovingly working with Him in relationship as junior partners and co laborers.

"*¹³ And it shall be that if you earnestly obey My commandments which I command you today, to love the LORD your God and serve Him with all your heart and with all your soul,"*

The promise is that if we are prepared to serve Him in this way, then the early rain will be across the whole land in order for them to plant the seed, and then a latter rain to finish the crop will come to prepare for the harvest. Notably the grain, (bread of life), new wine, (The Holy Spirit poured out), and the oil, (symbol of the anointing), were the main resultant elements from the crop. There would no doubt be other rain here and there but not right across the nation to bring in the harvest.

"*¹⁴ then I will give you the rain for your land in its season, the early rain and the latter rain, that you may gather in your grain, your new wine, and your oil"* (NKJV).

As we consider the picture that God gave us of how He will work with His chosen people, we see in the New Testament the gospel seeded, widespread, and moving across the whole world through the outpouring on the early church. Then throughout history we see *showers* of rain and small outpourings of revival here and there in isolated places in the Earth as God typically raised up missionaries to go into different nations. Then at the beginning of last century revival simultaneously broke out in 20 nations at the same time. Some consider this as the beginning of a last days outpouring that continues to bring in the harvest in our times today.

Field by field
Around the year 2000, I attended a meeting where a well-known American evangelist was sharing the powerful happenings and signs and wonders that were occurring in various nations where they were ministering. Up until that time I had imagined the time of the end of the age that Jesus spoke of where the harvesters, the angels, reap the harvest would be a relatively short period of time right at the end of days.

Matthew 13:39b, *"The harvest is the end of the age, and the harvesters are angels"* (NIV).

I had a drive of some 4 hours home after the meeting, and as I travelled, I was considering what was happening in these nations.

A statement followed by a question came into my mind. *You used to harvest wheat when you were younger, how did you go about it?* It was true; when I was a young man, I did at times drive a harvester. I thought about it for a moment and responded that I would harvest a field at a time, as the farms were sectioned off into fields. The next question that came into my mind was; *... and what do you see in the Earth?* As I thought about all that I knew about the spread of Christianity around the World I became aware of a pattern.

There were the revivals in Argentina, and after many years of harvesting there in that field moving into Brazil and then other nations in South America. Then I began thinking of the underground church in China spreading across many regions. South Korea, with very few Christians in 1960 and then exploding to reportedly one in 3 South Koreans identifying as Christian. I considered Africa, and the move of God nation by nation, and how it is now considered to be the new Christian centre. We would have considered the Soviet Union to be an iron clad impossibility for the gospel, but when God says; *I am harvesting this field now...* then that is what happens.
As I looked across the earth, at least for me it settled matters. The harvest is not coming; we are somewhere in the middle of it as one field at a time is reaped. How long will this go on for? I do not know. But personally, I do not want to be a child of God who misses his part in the harvest.

Proverbs 10:5, "*He who gathers in summer is a wise son; He who sleeps in harvest is a son who causes shame*" (NKJV).

Having personally believed that this is how God is harvesting I was not too surprised in 2003 when I see situations such as the U.S., the UK and Australia agreeing to go into Iraq. These leaders are faced with not only a World that doesn't want them to invade, but also their own nations, and some pretty solid opposition within their own political parties. In spite of all of this if God says; *I am harvesting in the middle east now...!* then you can be sure that it is going to happen. Field by field, North Korea or any other nation for that matter, when it's time, it's time. Read the Bible, those who seem as though they cannot be removed often disappear in a way nobody could have predicted. If it's time the most powerful leader could choke on a pickle or something and be suddenly removed as an obstacle! We can be certain that the harvest will continue until the appointed time. Are we ready, are we involved?

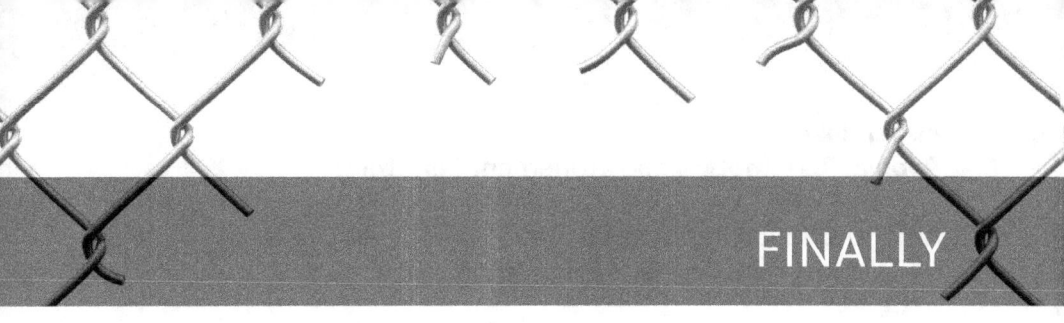

FINALLY

Finally

I write this book in the hope that the body of Christ will be further equipped to not only speak of the good news but to be the good news. There are many who need to be touched by God through believers walking in the Spirit who know how to help. In this, we, as did Jesus, prove God and His word to be true and uphold His integrity.

John 15:7-9, *"7 If you remain in me and my words remain in you, ask whatever you wish, and it will be given you. 8 This is to my Father's glory, that you bear much fruit, showing yourselves to be my disciples." 9 "As the Father has loved me, so have I loved you. Now remain in my love"* (NIV).

In all of our efforts we take comfort that our Lord will guide the whole process. I love Psalm 23 which details that we will walk through this hostile environment called Earth, but have the Lords guidance and the promise of restoration for our souls. Verse five encourages us that even in the presence of our enemies He has promised to take us out to lunch!

Psalm 23:1-6, *"1 The LORD is my shepherd; I shall not want. 2 He makes me to lie down in green pastures; He leads me beside the still waters. 3 He restores my soul; He leads me in the paths of righteousness For His name's sake 4 Yea, though I walk through the valley of the shadow of death, I will fear no evil; For You are with me; Your rod and Your staff, they comfort me. 5 **You prepare a table before me in the presence of my enemies**; You anoint my head with oil; My cup runs over. 6 Surely goodness and mercy shall follow me All the days of my life; And I will dwell in the house of the LORD Forever." (NKJV, Emphasis mine).*

Appendix 1
Popular Redemption and atonement Scriptures

All of the following passages are taken from the New Living Translation of the Bible and the emphasis is mine.

PSALM 103:2, *"Praise the LORD, I tell myself, and never forget the good things he does for me.* [3] *He forgives **all** my sins and heals **all** my diseases.* [4] *He ransoms me from death and surrounds me with love and tender mercies"*
and
"[8] *The LORD is merciful and gracious; he is slow to get angry and full of unfailing love.* [9] *He will not constantly accuse us, nor remain angry forever.* [10] ***He has not punished us for all our sins**, nor does he deal with us as we deserve.* [11] *For his unfailing love toward those who fear him is as great as the height of the heavens above the earth.* [12] *He has removed our rebellious acts as far away from us as the east is from the west.* [13] *The LORD is like a father to his children, tender and compassionate to those who fear him.* [14] *For he understands how weak we are; he knows we are only dust."*

ISAIAH 44:22, *"I have swept away your sins like the morning mists. I have scattered your offenses like the clouds. Oh, return to me, for I have paid the price to set you free."*

ISAIAH 53:4-6 and 10-11, *"* [4] *Yet it was our weaknesses he carried; it was our sorrows that weighed him down. And we thought his troubles were a punishment from God for his own sins!* [5] *But he was wounded and crushed for our sins. He was beaten that we might have peace. He was whipped, and we were healed!* [6] ***All of us** have strayed away like sheep. We have left God's paths to follow our own. Yet the LORD laid on him the guilt and sins **of us all**."*
and
[10] *But it was the Lord's good plan to crush him and fill him with grief. Yet when his life is made an offering for sin, he will have a multitude of children, many heirs. He will enjoy a long life, and the Lord's plan will prosper in his hands.* [11] *When he sees all that is accomplished by his anguish, he will be satisfied. And because of what he has experienced, my righteous servant will make it possible for many to be counted righteous, for he will bear **all** their sins.*

ROMANS 3:22-25, "²² **We are made right in God's sight when we trust in Jesus Christ to take away our sins**. And we all can be saved in this same way, no matter who we are or what we have done. ²³ For all have sinned; all fall short of God's glorious standard. ²⁴ Yet now God in his gracious kindness declares us not guilty. **He has done this through Christ Jesus, who has freed us by taking away our sins**. ²⁵ For God sent Jesus to take the punishment for our sins and to satisfy God's anger against us. **We are made right with God when we believe that Jesus shed his blood, sacrificing his life for us**."

1 CORINTHIANS 1:2, "We are writing to the church of God in Corinth, you who have been called by God to be his own holy people. **He made you holy by means of Christ Jesus**, just as he did all Christians everywhere--whoever calls upon the name of Jesus Christ, our Lord and theirs." **and**
"²⁸ God chose things despised by the world, things counted as nothing at all, and used them to bring to nothing what the world considers important, ²⁹ so that no one can ever boast in the presence of God. ³⁰ God alone made it possible for you to be in Christ Jesus. For our benefit God made Christ to be wisdom itself. **He is the one who made us acceptable to God. He made us pure and holy, and he gave himself to purchase our freedom**. ³¹ As the Scriptures say, "**The person who wishes to boast should boast only of what the Lord has done**."

2 CORINTHIANS 5:21, "For God made Christ, who never sinned, to be the offering for our sin, **so that we could be made right with God through Christ**."

EPHESIANS 1:4-7, " ⁴ Long ago, even before he made the world, God loved us and chose us **in Christ to be holy and without fault in his eyes**. ⁵ His unchanging plan has always been to adopt us into his own family by **bringing us to himself through Jesus Christ. And this gave him great pleasure**. ⁶ So we praise God for the wonderful kindness he has poured out on us **because we belong to his dearly loved Son**. ⁷ He is so rich in kindness that **he purchased our freedom through the blood of his Son, and our sins are forgiven**."

EPHESIANS 2:7-10, "⁷ And so God can always point to us as examples of the incredible wealth of his favor and kindness toward us, as shown in all he has done for us through Christ Jesus. ⁸ God saved you by his special favor when you believed.

And *you can't take credit for this; it is a gift from God.* ⁹ ***Salvation is not a reward for the good things we have done***, so none of us can boast about it. ¹⁰ *For we are God's masterpiece. He has created us anew in Christ Jesus, **so that we can do the good things he planned for us long ago.***"

COLOSSIANS 1:22, *"yet now he has brought you back as his friends. He has done this through his death on the cross in his own human body. **As a result**, he has brought you into the very presence of God, and **you are holy and blameless as you stand before him without a single fault**."*

HEBREWS 10:14, *"For by that one offering **he perfected forever** all those whom he is making holy."*
and
Then he adds, "¹⁷***I will never again remember their sins** and lawless deeds."* ¹⁸*Now when sins have been forgiven, there is no need to offer any more sacrifices.*

Appendix 2
Sample testimonies

Note: Following are testimonies from many of the people whose stories are used in this publication.

HEALED FROM A LIFETIME OF MIGRAINES
I have suffered for most of my life with Migraines beginning I think at around 7 years old. One morning in the Church that I attend Steve had a word of knowledge that there was somebody present, a lady, who had suffered with headaches since they were a child. I was prayed for and the spirit of infirmity left. That was towards the end of 2014 and I was healed from that moment on.

THYROID HEALED ALONG WITH EMOTIONAL HEALING
My thyroid counts were so high that my doctor was concerned and ready to start me on hormone replacement. After prayer all my tests are normal and the doctor can't believe that I was even sick!

It's so great to not be tired all the time. I am over the moon at being free from rejection, bitterness, anger and pride. Another big highlight is being released from fears and anxieties, one of which was being able to calmly have a blood test without having a panic attack.

PHYSICAL AND EMOTIONAL HEALING
I want to share with you the wonderful things the Lord has done in my life since I had the healing ministry with you. The following day I realized that I had no liver/pancreas pain that 1 had for 3 weeks. These episodes have been going on for years and I have been hospitalized because of it.

Pastor got his hugs and I was able to let him read my testimony before he left. I have been able to speak to and shake hands with male church members. I have been able to look them in the eyes when talking to them instead of eyes cast down.

Thank you for allowing the Lord to work through you reaching out to others like me. My prayer is that many others will come to know how wonderful He is too.

EMOTIONAL RELEASE AND BAPTISM IN THE HOLY SPIRIT
Steve and Em...hi there ....Wow you would not believe the changes in me!!!!!...but then of course you do believe!!! (Hehehe) Praise the Lord ...here we go....just overflowing with the Holy Spirit like the incredible hulk, just wants to burst out, the heaviness, anxiety, confusion, sadness, back pain, sleeplessness... all gone, zapped, now light, joyous, calm, strengthened. I'm loved and in love and am delighting in my spirit language, in praising God, in reading the bible just can't get into it fast enough.

…....so after the first night with you (Tuesday)...I haven't had to take Panadeine so that I could sleep, which always gave me a hangover, so consequently I'm waking early and clear headed...this morning I was communing with my Lord, planning what adventures to have today.... and have had a great day, when I was driving home I understood, that my time with you, that Jesus had been present, how easily he had changed the program, and because I had MY EYES OPENED I saw him thru you....what bliss. Thank you...God's blessings to you both. Your sister in Christ, I can now say that with conviction!

PHYSICAL HEALING THROUGH DELIVERANCE AND EMOTIONAL RELEASE
I got healed and delivered by God from my family's generational sin and my culture (Chinese). I got delivered from rejection and self-hatred. God healed me of my memories, of fear, anxiety and the fear of death. (Physical healing of lungs accompanied this) On the third day of Steve and Em's ministry, God healed me of a memory of fear of heights. Praise God. He is faithful. He restored my soul. (Wife)

Dear Steve and Em, thank you very much for your patient, anointed ministry to my wife. Many blessings (husband)

HEALED OF ASTHMA
I have had no Asthma for well over a year now. I am so glad to be free from the fear, and feel very peaceful. Praise God!

FREE FROM PANIC ATTACKS
No more panic attacks. It has now been months and I have not had a panic attack. I would have had several in a day. I am also able to go to bed and fall asleep almost straight away, instead of lying awake for hours. Bed is now a place of rest. Thank you for all your help.

REJECTION GONE
A life filled with never being good enough, not measuring up, feeling rejection and hurt was overcome by deliverance of the spirit of rejection.

DELIVERED FROM ARTHRITIS AND REJECTION
I had Arthritis in my ankles from as early as 30yrs old. My father was the same, and his mother before him. If I had been sitting for a while I would get up and limp around until I freed up. A few weeks after ministry into an emotional issue my husband and I noticed that I no longer hobble when I rose to walk. It has now been many years since my deliverance and healing and I have had no re occurrence. Thank God for His healing.

SET FREE FROM A MENTAL PROBLEM
For countless years I was plagued with another voice in my head, one that I would have conversations or even arguments with. It always seemed my head was cloudy or full. The real me sometimes struggled to surface. Then came deliverance by the mighty hand of God. Immediately after deliverance I had a clarity and singleness of mind, there was no longer anyone else in there but me.

TESTIMONY OF A MIRACLE HEALING
For around 2-3 months I was suffering from daily intermittent pain in my right jawline, going through into the inner right ear. This pain was very annoying and particularly disturbing to me first thing in the mornings, also during my meal times when I could hardly chew, and sometimes would also wake me through the night. I went to the Doctor twice about it over several weeks, and the realization came that the pain may have been due to a new mercury filling I had placed in my right back lower molar several months before the pain started. The Doctor advised that there was nothing she could do, that the inner ear looked good as there was no infection, but explained many nerves were along the jawline and she suggested the only remedy would be to get the Dentist to replace the mercury filling with some other type of filling.

So, I was booked into the SA Dental Health Clinic awaiting my call up date. When one Sunday, not long after my second visit to the Doctor, and during the Church service at Covenant Family Church, Port Elliot, Pastor Steve Pidd through a vision had a Word of Knowledge concerning somebody suffering with pain along the right jaw line, going up into the right ear. No doubt that was me, and I immediately went out for prayer regarding this. Praise the Lord the power of God came through prayer and I was completely and instantly healed of this complaint. Consequently, much gratitude to the Lord and a cancelled appointment to the SA Dental Clinic. He truly is our healer. And a wonderful gracious Lord that sees and is mindful of all our needs.

BACK PAIN HEALED
When the Lord delivered me from a spirit of suicide, I felt like I stood up on the inside. It was as if somebody put a piece of string through me and pulled me up straight. I felt tall on the inside. As well as becoming free in my spirit I was healed of constant severe back pain.

FREE FROM FEARS
God works amazingly when you spend time with the Pidd's! Most of my life I had struggled with a range of insecurities and I felt God nudging me to address these areas and allow His love and grace to replace my own coping mechanisms. Through healing with Steve and Em during a healing and teaching camp, I left feeling so healed that my only disappointment was that I hadn't met them sooner! I no longer fear night times or wake up feeling imaginary spiders are coming at me. Before ministry, one of my biggest personal frustrations was my inability to hand over the reins to God. I wanted to! I prayed to Him often enough to take over and show me the way, but I would offer Him my problem with arms, fists and teeth tightly clenched around it! Through God's grace, and Steve's patience, I dealt with the reason why I struggled. Once the understanding was there God really moved and healed me. From my first ministry session, my life has simply improved. I am calmer, happier, peaceful, and my relationship to God has deepened to depths that amaze me! Thanks to my wonderful Father who as Steve says, 'Loves me to bits!'

RELEASED INTO MINISTRY
I have been a Christian 30 years and my husband 40 years, but nothing has ever impacted us as much as doing the School of Healing and Freedom. Even though I have been around the mentality and teaching of that flow of ministry for years, it wasn't until I had partaken of the School that it was actually cemented in my spirit

the overwhelming and desperate need for Christians to get a handle on what God desires and is able to do for them in their innermost beings. I know many people who have been transformed by the renewing of their minds by going deep to reveal the enemies hold on their lives. As a result, they have received deep and lasting freedom and often physical healing as their bodies respond to that release. Deep calls to deep.

Also, I now find myself helping others through this ministry, because the teaching of the school has given me more knowledge and confidence to step out in faith as I sit beside God and witness time and time again in awe as He moves in grace upon people's lives.

TESTIMONY FROM AN AFRICAN PASTOR
I praise God for Brother Steve who came to visit our country. (Kenya) My uncle has been ill for 20yrs and he has been taken to many hospitals and spending a lot of money and leaving his children hungry. Surely when the servant of God laid hands on my uncle, while he was in danger of dying in a few hours (In hospital) as the doctors said, my uncle was totally healed through the power of God. I believe that the Lord who healed my uncle from danger of death, He is able to heal you today. (Matt 11:28) May God bless you all abundantly as you take a step to accept Jesus as your High doctor in your lives.

RADICAL TOUCH FROM GOD
The last three months since I came back to God (the day I met you) has been insane! He is so faithful. So much is happening as I continue to yield to Him. I want to tell you some of the things that have happened since we met:
The day I came back to church God delivered me immediately from drugs, cigarettes and alcoholism. I haven't even desired them since and I feel so much better. The very day I stepped into the church! I was very, very, heavily into Marijuana. And He has given me the victory over my diet and I lost 20 kilos in the 10 or so weeks between returning to church and Christmas.

LONG TERM KNEE PROBLEM HEALED THROUGH WORD OF KNOWLEDGE
Yesterday I spoke to the man you prayed for in the church service when you were here three weeks ago. He had a knee problem which caused knee pain and since that prayer he has had no pain at all, God has healed his knee. Amazing hey!

SAMPLE TESTIMONIES FROM LEADERS

Pastor Steve Pidd and his wife Em are international leaders who personify a transformative way of ministry known as 'Truth Encounters'. The purpose and process of a 'Truth Encounter' is in the name. The purpose of an 'Encounter' is the wholistic restoration of an individual's broken heart. The 'Encounter' is facilitated by Steve and Em in an intuitive manner that releases the Holy Spirit to engage with beliefs inherent in our memories and prayerfully restoring the 'Truth' of these moments from the Lord's perspective. I had no reservation in writing this commendation having experienced this ministry and its release first hand. In addition, I have observed the transformative impact within my wife and friends where broken hearts have been restored.

PROFESSOR DAVID GILES
Professor of Educational Leadership, Flinders University
Adelaide, South Australia

I have been a Christian for 32 years and over that time I would say that I have been steadily growing in the Lord. However, it wasn't until a few years ago, when I did the School of Healing that Steve Pidd runs, that I really started to move in the supernatural. I became more prophetic and discerning as I learned to hear the voice of God more clearly, and began working in the area of counselling those in need of emotional healing and deliverance. I have found much success and satisfaction in this work.

It is my sincere belief that Steve Pidd and his wife Em would probably be the most experienced, knowledgeable, and authoritative people in this area of ministry in this country. I say that without hesitation. When you mix that with their humility and generosity, they are a truly remarkable couple.

In the counselling room, people are set at ease by Steve's calm and gentle manner. I have been in sessions with him and clients and am in awe of his experience and ease in that setting. I consider his influence in my life a great privilege. Despite all I have said about him, he is an unassuming and kind man. I can be myself around him, without fear of judgment.

PASTOR LYNETTE SCHOLAR
CRC Churches International, Mildura, Victoria

We have known Steve and Em Pidd for approximately 5 years. In that time, we have had them minister to individuals in our church community, our community as a whole and they have run a school of Healing and Freedom. In June 2011 Steve and Em ran a week-long school at Log Cabin Camp. We have seen much fruit from these times. Some of the things that our community appreciates about Steve and Em is their down to earth ness and practical approach to ministry. Steve's giftedness in presenting truths of healing and spiritual realities enables people to hear afresh and to understand powerful truths of the gospel. There is always a heart in their training to see others raised up to do the same type of things. The healing ministry that has occurred in peoples' lives in our community has seen marriages saved and lives changed dramatically for the better. Many of these people now see healing as a normal part of their faith and have helped others with their healing. Steve and Em work well as a team with Em bringing a love of worship and a strong prophetic gift to the ministry. We have also witnessed their sacrificial love for their family and church community.

GRANT LAIDLAW
Organic Church, Creswick, Victoria, Director Log Cabin Camp

I have known Steve and Em Pidd for something approaching fifteen years and during that time have come to appreciate and value their unique emphasis and style of ministry. Steve has the ability to 'pick the eyes out' of various styles of ministry to the hurting, and then blend them together to provide a simple yet comprehensive approach to providing solutions for people in distress. We have been fortunate enough to avail ourselves of his ministry in a church we were leading when it encountered a very delicate series of events. His assistance proved invaluable to those people concerned who were willing to accept his counsel. I don't know what I would have done without his assistance.

PASTOR ROBERT BAILEY
Melbourne, Victoria

Steve Pidd visited our church for 10 days ministry in 2012. The teaching and ministry he brought on personal healing was both thoroughly biblical and effective in its content. It led to transformation in many lives as well as helping greatly in the establishment of a ministry centre that continues today.

PETER VINCENT
The Community Church, Bishops Stortford. UK

Appendix 3
418Centre details and statement of faith

418Centre is founded on Luke 4:18, and is a training ministry purposed to equip and resource the saints with practical help to present and administer the gospel. Materials will be uploaded as the site continues to develop. The **School of Freedom and Healing** is the main training outreach which is run across the world in different formats tailored to the environment.

You can reach us via the website through the contact page
www.418centre.org

Disclaimer
It is not my purpose to validate every statistic quoted in this publication. As with any studies conducted the results are varied. These references are merely to indicate or illustrate typical data centred around the topics covered.

Note: Truth Encounters Flow Charts on PowerPoint slides are available on the 418centre website.

Truth Encounters Faith Statements
Position of faith:
"We firmly believe that the Bible says what it means and means what it says. Consequently, we believe in, and experience miracles and physical healing, and understand them as being for today. We also believe in healing for the broken hearted, and freedom for captives from various kinds of bondages. We further believe that the gifts of the Spirit are for all of time. Indeed, according to Jesus' promise this is the Holy Spirits era or dispensation, and we are in a better place for His presence and ministry."
JN 14:16   14:26   16:7

Possible differences from other similar ministries:
1. We believe in and practice the gifts of the Holy Spirit in the ministry setting. We acknowledge His work, leading and participation in inspiring our questions and calling to remembrance things learnt from past sessions or training. At times, even showing us what the people coming for ministry may believe. As the Spirit of truth, He is the one who communicates God's truth to the person coming

for help. All of this is in a naturally supernatural manner as we are joined with Him and are one with Him in Spirit.

1 COR 6:17 *(Note: people may be being inspired by the Holy Spirit and not be aware that it is Him. They may consider it to be their own thoughts and knowledge...which obviously can also be the case.)*
2. We do not necessarily always wait for the person to discover what they believe. Our position is that they have come to us to help them identify what they believe, so if we can FastTrack the process by landing them on or close to what they believe, then we have no problem in doing so. For example, a person comes for ministry and they are obviously agitated and nervous about being able to do the ministry. We have no hesitation in floating one or more possibilities. E.G.s

"Are you by any chance afraid of not being able to do this ministry session?" If the answer is affirmative, this could be followed by questions such as:
"Would it make you a failure if you could not do it?"
"Are you anxious because I might disapprove of you if you can't do it?" Etc. Etc.

People know what they believe and are quick to say things like:
"No, it is more like.... this or that."

We do not hesitate to do this for a number of reasons.
A. It can turn a 50min or more session into a 5min session giving you time to do other things.
B. If you see something and don't present it, you may either miss dealing with that problem or take longer to do other things because their fear of failure or other belief may create a blockage.
C. Sometimes people don't understand what types of beliefs that you are looking for. Suggestions can greatly help them in this. Your own sense of what you are dealing with will increase with experience.

3. Our understanding, experience and theology of the nature and activity of demons may differ considerably from others doing this type of ministry.

4. We may pray for and believe for physical healing in a ministry session, or include Biblical advice in a ministry time flowing in with the truth encounters.

5. We **never** ask people to visualize anything or put 'Jesus,' 'Angels' or any other persons in the memories. In a small percentage of cases people may report seeing these things. We acknowledge that our job is simply to help them identify and connect with what they believe. How the Holy Spirit communicates truth or frees the person is His ministry alone.

Where did 'Truth Encounters' as a term come from?
We first heard the expression 'Truth Encounters' used by Pastor Mike Connell from New Zealand at a conference. His reference to it was relating to a way that God brings freedom through truth to captives. JN 8:32
It was such a good way to describe the ministry that we were doing, that we adopted it as an identifying term.

Note: Ps. Mike may be using an entirely different model to arrive at the same outcomes.

www.ingramcontent.com/pod-product-compliance
Lightning Source LLC
Chambersburg PA
CBHW071853290426
44110CB00013B/1132